Before Us Lies the Timber

Before Us Lies the Timber

THE SEGREGATED HIGH SCHOOL OF
MONTGOMERY COUNTY, MARYLAND · 1927-1960

Warrick S. Hill

Bartleby Press
Washington • Baltimore

Cover design by Ross Feldner

Published by:
Bartleby Press
PO Box 858
Savage, MD 20763 USA
800-953-9929

www.BartlebythePublisher.com

Library of Congress Cataloging-in-Publication Data

Hill, Warrick S.
Before us lies the timber : the segregated high school of Montgomery County, Maryland, 1927-1960 / Warrick S. Hill.
p. cm.
Includes index.
ISBN 978-0-935437-62-1 (paperback)

1. African Americans—Education (Secondary)—Maryland—Montgomery County—History—20th century. 2. African Americans—Segregation—Maryland—Montgomery County—History—20th century. 3. Segregation in education—Maryland—Montgomery County—History—20th century.
4. African American high school students—Maryland—Montgomery County. I. Title: Segregated high school of Montgomery County, Maryland, 1927-1960. II. Title.

LC2779.H55 2003
373.182996'073—dc21

2003000672

Printed in the United States of America

To Christine,
my devoted wife and companion,
to our sons,
Marlin, Arnold, and David,
and to our grandchildren,
Shannon, Adam, Jonathan, Alexis, Jaydin, and Liana.

CONTENTS

ACKNOWLEDGMENTS

I am deeply grateful to numerous individuals for helping to make the writing of this book possible. There were those who gave words of encouragement, as well as some who gave financial and moral support. There were those who shared their school annuals and yearbooks with me, others provided pictures and commencement programs, and still others gave oral historical facts.

I am greatly indebted to several sources of historical facts, namely: Central Records (Montgomery County Public Schools), Howard County Public Library, Montgomery County Historical Society, Prince George's County Public Library, Wheaton Public Library, and White Oak Public Library.

I am thankful for the skillful advice and editing of Jeremy Kay.

I gratefully acknowledge the assistance of the following persons: Alma Daye Alexander, Edith Stewart Banks, Geraldine Barbour, Delores McAbee Brown, Phyllis Waters Brown, Georgianna Hopkins Campbell, Dorothy Rhodes Carroll, Earl Claggett, Nina Honemond Clarke, Florence Coffield Coleman, William B. Cooke, Yvonne Thompson Copeland, Bessie Hill Corbin, Irene Snowden Curry, Vivian Dorsey Davis, Marcus Dorsey, William B. Duvall, Mary Bruce Ganges, Maurice C. Genies, Florence M. Graham, Doris Plummer Hackey, Ida Prather Hallman, Helen V. Hawkins, S. Margaret Hill, Harold W. Howard, Mabel Dorsey Jackson, Betty Hawkins Johnson, Jean Mason Johnson, Gloria Campbell Jones, Bernice Ricks Joppy, Margaret Adams Love, Esther Hallman Lyons, Betty Prather McKenzie, Alice Bishop Moore, Marie Stewart Neal, Gladys Thomas Nelson, James C. Offord, Edith Hill Owens, Virgie Stewart Prather, Leona Pendleton Ramey,

Annie Procton Rhodes, Alma King Ridgley, Eloise Levister Shelton, Phyllis Awkard Smith, Helen Bacon Snowden, Edward V. Taylor, Maude F. Taylor, Dr. George B. Thomas, Mable D. Thomas, Oliver E. Tyler, Ruize O. Tyler, Clarence R. Webster, Jr., Margaret Foreman Williams, and Harvey W. Zeigler.

Finally, with deepest appreciation, I acknowledge the encouragement and support of my wife, Christine, who has been my inspiration during the writing of this book.

PREFACE

The purpose of this historical book is to make the general public aware of what it was like to be an African-American high-school student in the segregated Montgomery County, Maryland, public school system, as well as to acknowledge those persons who helped to improve the students' predicament and those who made this book possible. This commemorative book chronicles a historical, biographical, and pictorial account of black high-school students' educational experience as they strove to earn their diplomas prior to September 1960.

This book contains an account of the trials, tribulations, struggles, and successes that these students experienced in their quest of a better way of life. For the alumni, it will refresh their memories of the way it was back then, lest they forget the sense of accomplishment and the kindly spirit of those who cared. For the reader, it will be an enlightenment as to how it was in Montgomery County (and, briefly, in four other Maryland counties—Anne Arundel, Calvert, Howard, and Prince George's). Keeping the past alive is an effective way of ensuring the future—for everyone.

Until 1960, Montgomery County, Maryland, maintained a dual public school system. In 1927, a single, two-room school (with a room designated as a library but was never used for that purpose because of the lack of classroom space) was constructed. This school was known as Rockville Colored High School. Because of inadequate space, Lincoln High School was built in 1935 to replace it, and in 1950, as Lincoln High became too small for its enrollment, George Washington

Carver High School was erected. Each school was built within about three-fourths of a mile of the previous one and offered the opportunity for African-American children within the county to receive a secondary education.

It would be inappropriate to make a study and to compile information regarding one part of a dual system without making references to and including related facts and information about the other. Consequently, in relating the story of educating African-American students, references are also made to the education of their white counterparts.

Over the centuries, individuals of African-American descent have been referred to as colored, Negroes, black, and African-Americans. These racial designations have been used throughout this book.

PART ONE

THE HISTORY

AN UPHILL BATTLE

Prior to the twentieth century, little or no attention was given to the education of American Negroes, especially in the seventeen southern states. Since these states advocated slavery, most of their inhabitants felt that blacks were second-class citizens with no need for education. Maryland, one of the seventeen slave states, housed no schools for black children. In the early years of this colony, only the children of wealthy families received an education. They were taught by church leaders and private tutors who set up the kind of schools they had known in Europe.

Public Schools in America

During the 17th century, education was a particular concern of the Puritans. Their action was directed by university-trained divines, and it was embraced by middle-class merchants and landowning farmers, who had enjoyed the benefits of education in Elizabethan England. In the New England colonies, parents were required to teach their children and servants to read, or to send them to a village school for that purpose. It was necessary that everyone learn to read the Bible.

Most of the Northern states had a semblance of a public school system. With the support of Quakers and other charitable groups, the children of poverty-stricken parents received a free education. Nevertheless, about one-half of New York City's children received no education around 1820, since their penniless parents did not want to be labeled paupers. Therefore, free schools became unpopular. Likewise, there was opposition to free schools from property owners and immigrants.

In Pennsylvania, landowners opposed free public education because they resented being taxed to maintain schools their children would never attend. Similarly, the Germans disapproved of free schools because they were concerned about the loss of their culture and their language. In spite of the objections, 42% of children in the Keystone State attended free schools by 1837.

Philadelphia opened the first school for black children in 1822 with an apology to the public for doing something for qwhat Samuel Eliot Morison called "this friendless and degraded portion of society."

Richard Allen was a chief leader in establishing schools for Negroes in the North. On April 12, 1787, he started a day school for children and a night school for adults in Bethel AME Church in Philadelphia. In the same decade, Prince Hall used his home as a school for black children. Hall, the son of an English leather merchant and a Frenchwoman of color, left Bridgetown, Barbados on a British ship in 1765 and worked his passage to Boston where he became a Methodist minister and an advocate of equality and education.

About 1804, in Washington, D.C., a system of free schools was established for white students, but no consideration was given to black students until 1856. White residents disapproved of the thought, because they believed that an educated black person would pose a threat to their political and economic supremacy.

The History of Public Schools in Maryland

The first effort in the Province of Maryland to furnish public education was made on April 13, 1671, with the reading of "an Act for the Founding and Erecting of a School or College within this province for the Education of Youth in Learning and Virtue." However, the Upper House of the General Assembly vetoed the proposal due to various provisions and amendments relating to the establishment of a school. Had it been approved, school attendance would have been difficult, because the scattered population was less than 25,000 and the plantations were separated either by wide waterways or rough roads.

As a result, the education of the children became a responsibility of ministers, parents, priests, or an occasional schoolmaster or private tutor. When Sir Francis Nicholson, appointed Lieutenant Governor of Maryland in 1691, arrived in Maryland in 1694, to succeed Governor Lionel Copley (who died in September 1693), he found the educational facilities inadequate. Early in his administration, under the instructions of Queen Mary, he introduced the issue of education. He proposed to build a free school. He offered to donate £50 toward the construction of such an edifice and to contribute £25 annually toward the support of a schoolmaster. His generous offer inspired other persons to make donations, and, in the following year, it inspired the General Assembly to give public support to education. Hence, the Free Schools Act was passed in October 1694 for the operation of free schools for white children. To raise educational funds, Maryland imposed certain specified duties upon furs, beef, bacon, and skins exported from the province. Over the next 30 years, these duties were placed in Maryland's school fund. The administration of Governor Nicholson has been recognized as the trailblazer for public education in Maryland.

In 1696, the colony's first free school, King William's school (now St. John's College) was founded in Annapolis. However, colonial free public schools did not succeed due to insufficient public financial support. Consequently, large landholders found it more convenient to maintain schoolhouses on their plantations, and the clergy conducted private classes in some parishes. This practice failed due to the lack of members of the Church of England who led pious and exemplary lives and were capable of teaching grammar, writing, and mathematics.

Thomas Bray, an Anglican clergyman, was sent to organize the Church of England in Maryland in 1699. He found it difficult to keep abreast of recent literature due to the lack of good books. To meet this need, he established parochial libraries for each of the thirty Anglican parishes of Maryland and he set up many more semi-public libraries for Anglican churches from Boston, Massachusetts, to Charleston, South Carolina, as well as a number of laymen's libraries.

In the 18th century, while the colonies were being exploited by the ruling classes in England, they also received generous donations for setting up libraries, schools, and colleges and for the education and conversion of Indians and blacks.

In 1744, an energetic Thomas Bacon arrived at Oxford on Maryland's Eastern Shore and became an assistant to rector Daniel Maynadier. At the death of the rector in 1745, Reverend Bacon assumed the full responsibility of the Parish of St. Peter, where he was deeply concerned about the souls of black and white people alike. Subsequently, he proposed a charity working school, that would feed, clothe, house, and instruct the children of the poverty-stricken. His proposal, which made special provisions for the training of Negro children, was fulfilled by an endowment fund, which was raised in America and England a few years hence. Thomas Bacon's manual training school was actually founded in 1755, when the first master was hired to teach in the newly constructed brick building.

An Uphill Battle For Public Education

The American Revolution altered individuals' minds and lives, and it gave momentum to organized education and stimulated learning generally.

By the time the colonies declared independence in 1776, twelve of Maryland's seventeen counties were maintaining schools or academies which, though poorly supported, were offering secondary education to a limited number of students. In Maryland, as in other states, the wealthy individuals sent their children to private schools or hired private tutors for them.

During the 1790s, education was a continuing issue between democrats, who desired support for a basic education on the county level, and their conservative opponents, who declared that provision had always been made for marginal scholars. The struggle continued until 1798 when Frederick Academy master and winner of a prize essay on education awarded by the American Philosophical Society, Samuel Knox, addressed the legislature. He stressed the necessity of disseminating knowledge throughout the state of Maryland, as well as advocated the founding of primary schools and academies. By the early 19th century, the legislature merely committed itself to financing the county schools that were already in existence and to subsidizing new ones upon the request of the people in a designated locality.

While Maryland public schools could hardly be classified collectively as a state system, they were more comprehensive than those farther South. Most Maryland academies were privately operated and received a considerable amount of attention from local social and political leaders as did their Southern counterparts. Caroline and Queen Anne counties were the only Maryland counties that failed to have at least one such academy. In contrast, Carroll County had 30 academies (with only 47 teachers instructing nearly 1,000 students). On the other hand, Carroll County had no public schools and just 3% of the academies' revenue came from public funds. Frederick County had 17 academies with an average of four teachers and 43 students each.

Public support for high-school education started by an Act of 1798 when Maryland appropriated a few hundred dollars of state funds each to eight county schools—Eastern Academy, Washington Academy, and Washington College on the Eastern Shore; the Frederick County School, the Allegany County School, Charlotte Hall, St. John's College, and a planned Baltimore Academy on the Western Shore.

The 19th century brought with it some hope and a few setbacks. In 1807, the Maryland General Assembly incorporated societies that were dedicated to the education of orphans and poor children. The first fund to establish free schools was commenced in 1812 as part of an act to incorporate a company to make a turnpike road leading to Cumberland and for extension of Charters of the several Banks in this State and for other purposes. Under this law, the banks were required to give $20,000 each year to be used to maintain the county schools.

In 1814, the legislature changed the tax to $.20 on every $100 of paid-in capital stock of each bank and provided for equal allotment of the Free School Fund among the counties. In 1817, the legislature appointed Commissioners of the School Fund for each county and, thereafter, distributed the money to the counties for the maintenance of the schools. Maryland made a similar arrangement for Baltimore City, and Baltimore City soon surpassed the Maryland counties in establishing and maintaining public schools that were largely supported by city taxes.

In 1881, Maryland assigned public funds to: Hillsborough School in Caroline County, West Nottingham Academy in Cecil County, a school then being constructed in Cambridge in Dorchester County, and Rockville Academy in Montgomery County. All of the Eastern Shore counties had schools, and all of them, except Worcester County, received state assistance. On the Western Shore, Charlotte Hall served the Southern Maryland counties: Calvert, Charles, Prince George's, and St. Mary's. Schools were supplied to all counties, except Baltimore, and all of them, except Harford County, received state support.

However, Reverend Libertus Van Bokkelen (Presbyterian minister, former president of St. John's College, and a native New Yorker who relocated to Catonsville, Maryland, in 1845, as rector of St. Timothy's Church, and established St. Timothy's Hall a private school) deserves much of the recognition for instituting Maryland's public school system. After his appointment as State Superintendent of Public Instruction on November 12, 1864, he immediately embarked upon establishing a complete system of public instruction.

Starting with primary school, advancing through grammar school to the county high school (where young men were prepared for the state colleges from which they proceeded to schools of medicine or law, or the practical duties of active business), Van Bokkelen formed a complete system of public education. When Van Bokkelen attended the 1864 Constitutional Convention as a lobbyist, he capitalized on prevailing democratic attitudes and crusaded for his long-cherished public school system. He also formulated plans for an institution for deaf-mutes, a facility for the sightless, an institution for the mentally ill, as well as houses of refuge and industrial homes (charitable and remedial facilities). Although Maryland gave attention to these areas through special funds prior to the United States Civil War, it was not until 1867 that the Maryland General Assembly made provisions for a school for the hearing-impaired (in Frederick), for the instruction of the visually-impaired, and for financial assistance in the construction of the Maryland Institution for the Instruction of the Blind, a private school.

In addition, the House of Refuge, as well as other private charitable establishments, received some state financial assistance. Even though these educational facilities existed in the state of Maryland, the Maryland State Board of Education had no supervisory power over them.

In the census of 1860, Maryland ranked 24th in total expenses for education and 23rd in expenses on public education, among 33 states of the Union. The wartime Constitution of 1864 paved the way for a thorough restructuring of Maryland's public education system. In 1865, Maryland passed an act for "A Uniform System of Public Instruction for the State of Maryland," of which Van Bokkelen was the author.

The act stated that a state board of education was to be created to oversee all state financially-assisted colleges and schools. Further, each county was required to maintain one high school that supplied ample instruction for both sexes in mathematics, in Latin and Greek, and in the higher levels of English and science, to prepare students for enrollment in any state college under the management of the Council of the University of Maryland.

In accordance with the Act of 1865, Maryland attempted to collect an annual $.15 tax on every $100 of real and personal property for educational intentions. The state divided the revenue among the counties and Baltimore City in proportion to their populations between the ages of five and twenty. By 1870, Maryland rose from an insignificant 24th to a more respectable 15th place, among the states, in expenditures for public education.

In the school year 1866-1867, there were 1,279 schools with 71,000 students being instructed by competent teachers. In spite of Van Bokkelen's vision and administrative talent, there was some resistance to the organization and supervision of the state school system and the exorbitant educational expenditures. Additionally, during that school year, the selection and the administration of the series of uniform textbooks was publicly condemned. Despite these objections to the new public school system, there were 97,761 white and 7,674 black pupils enrolled in 1870 (five years after the enactment of the Public Instruction Act which made funds available for counties that wished to use it for the training of black pupils).

In 1870, there were 1,266 ungraded common schools, 159 graded common schools (public elementary), 49 grammar schools (grades 5 - 8), 3 high schools, and 72 classical, technical, and professional schools.

In 1826, when the funds derived from the bank taxes were insufficient to maintain a system of free primary education in the Maryland counties, Maryland proposed a comprehensive and fairly centralized system of public education. In that proposal, the legislature empowered the founding of a number of Lancastrian, or monitorial, schools at the primary level. Provisions were made for a state superintendent (who was to be appointed by the governor and council), a county commissioner of primary schools, and a corps of inspectors of primary schools for the administration of that system. Since acceptance of that system was made optional, six of the 23 counties—most in need of a free system to provide education for the children of poor laborers or impoverished farmers—Allegany, Caroline, Dorchester, Somerset, Washington, and Worcester—rejected the offers of state aid.

Nevertheless, public education was short-lived because of a lack of financial support and the Lancastrian system's loss of favor. During the War of 1812, the Maryland public school system was financed by the interest earned on the reimbursement of Maryland's expenditures by the federal government. In 1837, Maryland discovered that the surplus revenue could be another source of financial support for the local schools. Maryland received $955,838.25, of which $681,387.25 was deposited in certain banks, and the interest derived was assigned to the public school system. For the most part, the Maryland public schools were supported by the local communities; however, those schools in Baltimore City (the wealthiest school district in the state) were generally superior to the county schools.

Eventually, the influx of immigrants, coupled with births, increased the population and thereby created an imbalance in school population and school capacities. Nationwide, in 1840, there were 500,000 uneducated adults, and 10 years later, there were nearly one million illiterate adults. According to the 1850 census, there were 45,025 students enrolled in the Maryland colleges, academies, and public schools, and their total educational expenses were in excess of half a million dollars. Nevertheless, Maryland reported 41,877 individuals, out of a total population of 208,043, who could neither read nor write.

Education of Blacks in Maryland

The average illiteracy rate among white adults in the state of Maryland was slightly more than 20% in 1850. St. Mary's County (with the highest illiteracy rate among white adults in Maryland) had the highest percentage of white students enrolled in school (98%). Prince George's County was foremost in white enrollment, among the Maryland counties, with a higher percentage of girls than boys enrolled in school. Somerset County (with 26% of the white school-age population in school) and Allegany County (with 30%) represented the most educationally lagging counties. Maryland's large free black population was paid restricted attention; as a result, about 60% of the adults were illiterate (approximately three times the illiteracy rate of the white population).

During Governor Charles Goldsborough's administration (1818-1819), a special act was enacted to furnish education for children of needy persons in Anne Arundel, Cecil, Kent, Montgomery, and Talbot counties. But, while the General Assemblies of 1817, 1818, and 1819 approved decrees for the improvement of Maryland Negroes, other decrees were passed simultaneously that limited their assemblages and movements. As blacks in the

North were actively engaging in activities to free slaves, they were felt to be a menace throughout the United States, so their activities were limited.

Many black churches opened schools where children and adults could learn. Although most of the church schools emphasized basic reading, writing, and arithmetic, at least one black school in Baltimore offered French and Latin in the early 1800s.

In consideration of the problem of public education, the 1850-1851 Constitutional Convention named a committee on education that recommended the establishment of a permanent and substantial school fund, as well as a uniform state system of public schools. But, that report was not acted upon by the convention, which concluded its work in mid-May of 1851. In addition, there was opposition to that report by Baltimore City and the larger counties, since they had already made ample provision for schools in their jurisdictions. Thus, it remained for Maryland's next Constitutional Convention of 1864 to provide a state system of public education along the lines recommended by the 1851 committee.

For the first time, the Constitution of 1864 provided for a state system of education that empowered the governor to name a State Superintendent of Public Instruction for a four-year term at a salary of $2,500. It created a State Board of Education that consisted of the governor, the Lieutenant Governor, the Speaker of the House of Delegates, and the Superintendent of Public Instruction, and it authorized them to appoint a school commissioner in each county. The Maryland General Assembly was empowered to establish a uniform system of schools by which a free school would be set up in each district for at least six months annually. To finance the schools, an annual tax of $.10 was to be levied on each $100 of real and personal property throughout the state. The revenue derived from the taxes was to be distributed among the Maryland counties in proportion to their population between the ages of five and twenty. Additionally, a further tax of 50 cents on each $100 was to be levied and invested until a School Fund of $6 million was amassed. The minority in the Convention of 1864 endeavored to prohibit the application of the School Fund to the education of Negroes, but it was overwhelmingly defeated.

The free black residents of Maryland had their own schools and religious organizations, but the 1860 census revealed that only 1,355 free black children in Maryland were attending school. According to Donald Dozer, black children were deprived of an education because of "the general two-fold assumption by the dominant white class that the Negro was inferior and that if taught to read and write, he would not be content to remain a docile member of the labor force." As a result, for the most part, the education of African-Americans was left to humanitarian and dedicated teachers, like Daniel Coker who escaped from slavery and set up a school for Negro children in Baltimore.

The reorganization of Maryland's system of public education had its inception with the adoption of the wartime constitution of 1864. This legal passage specified that the governor was to appoint a state superintendent, who was to present a plan for a uniform system of free public schools to the General Assembly in 1865. Despite the General Assembly's obligation to furnish this system, there was no provision in the system for education of blacks.

Maryland's Freedmen

In the meantime, there was a growing number of freedmen in the state of Maryland. By 1820, one-fourth of the total population of Negroes in Maryland were free, and ten years hence, one-third were free. At that time, Maryland had the largest number (52,938) of freedmen of any state in the Union. By 1840, two-fifths of the total Negro population was free and by 1860, approximately 84,000 were free (out of a total state population of 687,000).

Some of Maryland's freedmen accumulated large plots of land and acquired some measure of intellectual renown. Benjamin Banneker, born of a white mother and a slave father, attended a pay school near Ellicott's Mills, where he attracted the attention of George Ellicott (a Quaker), who allowed him the use of his personal library and tools. Banneker became a notable astronomer and mathematician, and he published one of the first United States Almanacs and assisted Pierre L'Enfant in surveying the District of Columbia.

Another free African American, Ira Frederick Aldridge (a Bel Air native born in the early part of the 19th century) was apprenticed to a ship carpenter. On his visit to the United States in 1826, the great English actor Edmund Kean was so impressed with the theatrical talent of Aldridge that he encouraged Aldridge to return to England with him. While abroad, his acting, especially in his portrayal of Lear, Macbeth, and Othello, was so superior that he became a celebrity. European governments and cultural organizations acknowledged his exceptional talent and awarded him high honors.

Civil War Threatens the Nation

The Emancipation Proclamation, issued by President Abraham Lincoln in September of 1862 (effective January 1, 1863), solved one problem (freed the slaves) but created another.

Not only was there a struggle in the political arena, but there was one in the field of education as well. To teach enslaved people to write was a crime in South Carolina and had been such since 1740. In 1862, more than 95 percent of former slaves were illiterate, although they were enrolling as fast as the schools could be built. By May, a Coffin Point plantation school had an enrollment of 138 students, nearly one-half of whom were adult field hands, and a Beaufort school had 100 pupils in attendance.

In September, a school was started at Frogmore on St. Helena Island, South Carolina, by Laura Towne and her friend, Ellen Murray. At the end of 1862, there were 30 schools in the Port Royal area (South Carolina) in which 2,500 former slaves, adults and children, were receiving instruction. The freedmen were very responsive to the new educational opportunities that were made available by emancipation. John Roy Lynch, a former Mississippi slave who became a leading politician after the Civil War, reaped the greatest educational benefits through his cleverness and good fortune. Several weeks after the Union army invaded Vicksburg, Mississippi, he fled his plantation, worked at several successive jobs, and managed to stay out of refugee camps and the Union army. While on the run, his thirst for knowledge inspired him to attend a Yankee night school, where he learned the beginning of reading and writing, prior to the school's closure upon persistence of Natchez white residents. Since his appetite for knowledge had been whetted, this turn of events did not curtail his craving. In fact, John Roy Lynch became more daring in his quest. He was further enlightened by eavesdropping on recitations in a whites-only school across the alley. Like most African-Americans, he realized the significance of an education after being liberated from the clutches of slavery.

Black leaders, regardless of their attitude or their background, considered education a top priority for advancement. To resist the opposition, schools and churches were their strongholds, and their weapons included the spelling book, the Bible, the press, and the implements of industry. Hundreds of schools were established, and, as a result, thousands of freedmen became literate.

The War's Effects on the Education of Blacks

At the conclusion of the Civil War, on April 9, 1865, millions of Southern slaves were liberated by the Union victory and the Thirteenth Amendment to the U.S. Constitution, but no provisions were made for their livelihood. Some wanted to leave their plantations, but many wanted to stay with their former masters, who hoped to maintain their labor. Those who chose to leave were homeless and economically blighted. Being shelterless, they were unprotected from the forces of nature. Consequently, many of them assembled in the woods or congregated on the army posts, where they lived on handouts and died of camp diseases.

Recognizing this new responsibility, Congress established the Bureau of Refugees, Freedmen, and Abandoned Lands (widely known as the Freedmen's Bureau) on March 3, 1865, to help the emancipated slaves make the transition from slavery. The Freedmen's Bureau administered medical aid to some one million freedmen, set up more than 40 hospitals and social agencies, distributed more than 21 million rations (many of them to poverty-stricken white persons), and set up courts to adjust disputes between employers and employees. Moreover, the agency established day schools, night schools, industrial schools, institutes, and colleges, as well as founded or supplied financial assistance for four major black colleges: Atlanta University, Fisk University, Hampton Institute and Howard University.

Perhaps the most noticeable example of the freedmen's pursuit of self-improvement was their desire for education. Prior to the Civil War, every southern state, except Tennessee, forbade the teaching of slaves to read and write. Even though many free blacks had attended school and a number of slaves became literate through the help of sympathetic masters and through their own efforts, more than 90 percent of the South's adult black population was illiterate in 1860.

In 1865, in Mississippi, a Freedmen's Bureau agent reported that when he informed an assemblage of 3,000 freedmen that they "were to have the advantages of schools and education, their joy knew no bounds. They fairly jumped and shouted in gladness."

Parents were motivated to relocate to areas in which schools existed, in pursuit of an education for their children. It inspired plantation workers to make the institution of a school a condition of signing labor contracts. In Louisiana, an 1867 contract stipulated that the planter pay a five percent tax to support the education of black children. Adults, as well as children, crowded the schools that were organized during and following the Civil War.

In Florida, a Northern teacher reported how a sixty-year-old lady, "just beginning to spell, seems as if she could not think of anything but her book, she spells her lesson all the evening, then she dreams about it and wakes up thinking about it."

Whereas some desired an education for economic advancement, many adults longed for an education so that they could read the Word of God. A Northern reporter revealed that an elderly freedman, who sat beside his grandchild in a school in Mobile, Alabama, was reluctant to seek the teacher's assistance, even though he had a craving to read the Bible.

The Freedmen's Bureau, Northern benevolent societies, and state governments supplied most of the money for educating the black population during the Reconstruction Period of 1863-1877. Frequently, however, blacks took the initiative to start their own schools, which was the standard practice in the early stages of the Civil War.

Prior to the arrival of Northern teachers in 1861, Mary Peaks, the daughter of a free black mother and an English father, founded the first school for blacks in Hampton, Virginia. In 1862, the Gideonites (an association of American Christian business and professional men, organized in 1899, who began placing Bibles in hotel rooms in 1908) found two schools already in operation upon their arrival in the Sea Islands. For many years, a black cabinetmaker taught slaves secretly at night at one of the schools.

Following the Civil War, urban Negroes promptly organized schools in Virginia. They used whatever unoccupied facilities they could find as temporary classrooms, among which were abandoned warehouses and billiards rooms, and former slave markets in New Orleans and Savannah. At the end of April 1865, less than a month after the Union troops' invasion of the City of Richmond, more than 1,000 black children and 75 adults were enrolled in schools instituted by Richmond's black churches and the American Missionary Association. In 1866, Charles Hopkins, a freedman and Methodist minister, acquired a room in a deserted hotel in Greenville, South Carolina, where he taught lessons in reading and spelling. When Freedmen's Bureau officials arrived in rural areas, they were amazed to find that blacks had already set up classes that were being conducted in churches, basements and private homes.

Throughout the South, between 1865 and 1866, enterprising blacks organized societies and raised money to purchase property to build schoolhouses and pay teachers' salaries. Some communities chose to impose taxes on themselves, while in other communities, the students paid tuition. When his salary was increased by a monthly tuition charge of $.20 in 1869, one humanitarian teacher, Robert G. Fitzgerald, donated much of the money to poverty-stricken families. His charitable spirit was further evidenced when he cancelled the fee to make his school available to the affluent as well as the poor, to white students as well as black students, and to the upper class as well as the lower class. To further help the cause, skilled black workers donated their labor to construct school edifices, and black families offered room and board to teachers to supplement their salaries. A largely poverty-stricken community bought a lot in Georgetown, South Carolina, for $800, and spent $2,000 to support 56 schools in Georgia, in November of 1865. These expenditures represented a tremendous sacrifice on the part of a community with such a low financial status.

By 1870, blacks had an educational expenditure in excess of one million dollars, a fact that was remembered as a point of self-satisfaction. One black resident of Selma, Alabama wrote, "Whoever may hereafter lay claim to the honor of establishing schools, I trust the fact will never be ignored that Miss Lucy Lee, one of the emancipated, was the pioneer teacher of the colored children without the aid of Northern states."

However, their efforts did not go uncontested. The scarcity of funds weakened their educational endeavors and dispelled their self-sufficiency, which compelled them to seek financial assistance from the Freedmen's Bureau and the Northern societies.

In April 1867, Florida freedman Emanuel Smith requested the assistance of the American Missionary Association in providing and helping to pay a female teacher. He specified female, because "they can be had on cheaper terms. We have plodded along this far, the best we could. This is the first application that has been made to any source for help since we have been free."

A South Carolina freedman realized their need of outside assistance, but with outside assistance came outside control. When General William T. Sherman's 600,000 troops invaded Savannah in December 1864, they dealt slavery a death blow. Immediately, local black ministers organized the Savannah Educational Association, which, by February, raised approximately $1,000, employed 15 black teachers, and enrolled 600 pupils in schools. The American Missionary Association was a Northern benevolent society led by Reverend S.W. Magill. The organization was intent on educating the freedmen, and it favored integrated schools, but not racial social equality.

When the Freedmen's Bureau officials arrived in 1865, they were of the same attitude as the American Missionary Association and withheld funds from the black school system. Due to the lack of funds, by 1866, the Savannah Education Association relinquished its management to the American Missionary Association, which replaced the black instructors with its own white employees. Only a few of the black teachers were retained, and then, as assistants. Those events brought about resentment of the management of the white man in the school system. One Northerner remarked, "What they desire is assistance without control," but some of the black teachers were acutely aware of their lack of academic preparation and acknowledged it.

The Northerners considered the first black teachers, with their limited education, to be hopelessly incompetent, and they felt that having such individuals instruct the students on a daily basis would be a disservice to the students. Some of the teachers were aware of, and acknowledged, their lack of preparation, and besides being involved in education, they assisted freedmen in contract disputes, engaged in church work, and drafted petitions to the Freedmen's Bureau, state officials and Congress. Teaching, like the ministry, became a springboard to political office in the Reconstruction period, during which at least 70 black teachers served in state legislatures.

Further, the Freedmen's Bureau supplied legal assistance for the freedmen, supervised contracts with their employers, and protected their rights. It stood as a buffer between the freedmen and the resentment of their former slavemasters. Congress widened the powers of the Freedmen's Bureau in 1866 to include Southern white refugees, so as to dispel any idea of preferential treatment for the former slaves.

The Freedmen's Bureau Commissioner was General Oliver Otis Howard, a graduate of Bowdoin College and a veteran of the Civil War, whose close relationship to the freedmen's aid societies earned him the nickname "Christian General." Because Congress initially failed to set aside any funds for the operation of the Freedmen's Bureau, Howard chose army personnel to help operate the Bureau.

Besides army personnel, the Freedmen's Bureau was composed of a few Negroes, as well as individuals with anti-slavery backgrounds. Among them were John M. Langston, who was an inspector of schools who worked out of General Howard's Washington office, and Martin R. Delany, who was an official at Hilton Head, South Carolina.

As the administrator of the Freedmen's Bureau, General Howard focused most of his efforts on the education of the former slaves' children. The local agents in the various districts spent a large amount of time encouraging the establishment of schools for the children. Although the Freedmen's Bureau coordinated the activities of Northern societies that were devoted to the education of black students, it failed to institute schools itself, because of its restricted resources. According to reports to the Freedmen's Bureau, by 1869 there were more than 150,000 children enrolled in nearly 3,000 schools, and these figures did not include the numerous evening and private schools that the missionary societies and the blacks themselves operated.

In many of the Southern states, local white residents were instructors in the freedmen's schools, but for the most part, the teachers were middle-class white women from New England who were sent by the Northern aid societies. Most of them had acquired some higher education, either in normal schools or in the few existing colleges. One teacher reported that "it is a precious privilege to be allowed to do something for these poor people."

On the other hand, the Freedmen's Bureau was unpopular among Southern white residents because its equal consideration of blacks weakened the plantation labor. As a result, their fear of equality caused such uneasiness that they crusaded for the Bureau's elimination.

Despite its unpopularity and its financial insecurity, the Freedmen's Bureau strove to fulfill its obligation. When the federal government passed this responsibility to the states, there was disparity in the funding of black and white schools. In Savannah, Georgia, the school board spent $64,000 on white schools and $3,000 on black schools, in 1873. However, most black Americans felt that separate schools were better than no schools at all. By the early 1870s, newly established black colleges - Alcorn College in Mississippi, Fisk University in Tennessee, Howard University in Washington, DC, and others - were graduating hundreds of black teachers and other professionals annually. In South Carolina, there was a dramatic increase in the number of black teachers—50 in 1869 to 1,000 in 1875— many of whom were products of new black colleges.

Nevertheless, the Freedmen's Bureau was not without problems, as inadequate manpower and insufficient funds plagued the agency. When the financial structure became unstable after 1868, Northern charitable societies started to lessen their involvement. In spite of its struggles, the Freedmen's Bureau continued its work until 1872, spending more than $16 million on the education of former slaves.

Perhaps the greatest failure of the Freedmen's Bureau was its lack of understanding of the intensity of racial hostility and class struggle in the post-war South. Be that as it may, the Freedmen's Bureau did have an appreciative audience in the liberated slaves.

Post-War Schools in America

In 1868, three years after the Civil War, the School Act was passed which demanded basic education for Negro youths. At that time, many whites came to realize that a black neighborhood school promoted economic and social improvement, while also keeping black farm hands in the communities in which they were needed. Despite this insight, few emancipationists fought for black children. A handful believed in and supported the idea, but they were too few to force the position. Many such efforts were met with strong Southern resistance, because the Southern Democrats resented the interference of the radical Northern Republican Party.

Initially, most teachers who taught in the freedmen's schools were from the North. Some 5,000 Yankee volunteers, who were paid modest salaries by Northern charitable organizations, relocated to the South to teach. The teaching environments were less than ideal because the instructors taught large classes in primitive schoolhouses with a scarcity of books and other instructional materials. Even though Northern publishers shipped 200,000 textbooks for the students, there was still a need for more.

During the 1870s, black and white children attended school together in New Orleans for several years. Elsewhere, following the Civil War, few of the new school systems were integrated.

These troubled years from 1865 to 1877 forced the American people to cope with issues that have not been settled even today. The political phase of Reconstruction terminated in 1877, when the defeated Southern states rejoined the United States. Yet there were long-lasting political results, as the Southern states united in a "Solid South" that tended to split, rather than unite, the nation.

Then, there was the touchy social problem of racial inequalities, particularly as it pertained to the treatment of the 4 million liberated slaves. Their needs—physical and educational—were partially met, and that inadequacy exists even today, as many of the Southern states have the poorest school systems in the United States. The effects of the Civil War on education in the South were little less than disastrous. School-houses had fallen into ruin; teachers were slain or scattered. The impoverished south, then less able to bear heavy taxes than at any time, faced the additional burden of providing a public education for white and black alike. Higher education was all but paralyzed. Many private institutions lost part of or all of their endowments. Southern education did not recover from the effects of the Civil War and Reconstruction until the 20th century.

Separate But Not Equal in Maryland

The 1860 federal census revealed that, out of 686,869 residents of Maryland, 83,942 were free blacks and 87,189 were black slaves. Maryland reportedly had more slaves than any other state. When the 1870 census revealed that more than one-seventh of the total state population above ten years of age were uneducated, the majority of whom were black, Governor Oden Bowie reminded the legislature that a portion of Maryland's population consisted of black freedmen, who might sometime gain the franchise. He suggested that they ought to be given the education that would prevent them from being misled by the crafts and clamors of designing and unscrupulous politicians. He recommended that taxes paid by African-Americans be used for the establishment and maintenance of public schools for black children. *The Baltimore Sun* observed, "It is evident we cannot afford to let the colored people among us go uneducated. There is a duty to them as well as ourselves in that matter."

It was not until the early 1870s that real legislative action was taken in the establishment of public education for Negro children. While the School Act of 1868 failed to provide for a Maryland State Superintendent of Schools and a Maryland State Board of Education, it did recognize the educational self-government of the counties, and it permitted them to exercise nearly complete control over the public schools in their respective districts. It also required each county to erect one secondary school and as many elementary schools as there were election districts. That requirement accelerated the transformation of some of the county academies into county public high schools but, by 1874, some of the counties still had not established high schools. The School Acts of 1870 and 1872 re-instituted the State Board of Education, but the position of State Superintendent of Public Education was not revived until 1900.

In the counties, black education varied from scanty to disappointing. This caused Governor Oden Bowie (1869-1872) to urge the Maryland General Assembly to enact the 1872 law compelling Maryland counties to maintain separate but supposedly equal schools for black and white students. In the latter part of the 19th century, depending upon income, Maryland furnished approximately $400,000 for white schools ($1.69 per student) and nearly $100,000 ($1.46 per student) for the black schools. The county commissioners supplemented the state money with a little more to educate these students. By 1873, black schools were available in all 23 Maryland counties, but by 1892, eleven counties, all of which had large African-American populations, were contributing nothing to their black schools and letting them operate entirely on state appropriations and private donations. Along with legislative separateness in schools came a difference in school terms, as well as in teacher salaries. In 1918, the lowest salary in Maryland was $300 per year for a white teacher and $280 for a black teacher. In 1895, seven counties—Anne Arundel, Charles, Prince George's, Queene Anne's, Somerset, St. Mary's and Worcester—made no contributions to black schools from county funds. Frequently, black school buildings were edifices that white residents had declared unfit for their own children.

During the years of racial injustice, black leaders in Anne Arundel, Calvert, Howard and Prince George's counties, like their Montgomery County counterparts, put forth an extraordinary effort to gain educational facilities and opportunities, and adequate instructional materials for their children, as well as equal salaries for the teachers. In the process, their continual struggle to provide a quality education for Negro students revealed the uncongenial, inflexible attitudes of the county school board members and residents. Nevertheless, to the community leaders, education was the ultimate means of keeping hope alive for a brighter future.

Anne Arundel County Public Schools

In Anne Arundel County, no public schools existed for black children prior to 1865. Although this southeastern Maryland county had a thriving tobacco-growing industry, the education of its Negro students was much less desirable. Resentment and discrimination against black churches, black schools, and black homes was sometimes evidenced by violence fanned by fear of endangerment of "white supremacy." In some instances blacks were forcibly forbidden from attending school and teachers were not permitted to teach. Churches which also housed schoolrooms were frequently burned, while teachers were intimidated, insulted and in a few instances even killed.

Although most white residents embraced slavery in theory and in practice, a few of them felt that it was their Christian duty to help African-Americans in their "predicament." As a result, house servants tended to be among the privileged slaves and were educated on their owners' plantations. One such instance in 1863 was of Miss Alice Childs, who, on the farm of her father Dr. Waters, taught a number of black children in the southern part of Anne Arundel County.

Immediately following the Civil War, Freedmen's Bureau funds were used to set up schools in various parts of Anne Arundel County. The first school for black children was established on Mill Swamp Road in Mill Swamp in the southern part of the county in 1865, using funds supplied by the Freedmen's Bureau. The Freedmen's Bureau continued to provide funds for the construction of schools until President Andrew Johnson vetoed a bill in 1872 that terminated its existence.

At the conclusion of the Civil War, there was the intervention of earnest and well-meaning people of the North who endeavored to improve the condition of the southern states. Jeremiah B. Swann, who had been born a slave on a plantation in Tennessee, was sent to the West River section of Anne Arundel County as a teacher and an instructor.

With the assistance of the Presbyterian Church, Mr. Swann started a school at Mt. Zion with an enrollment of approximately fifty students. Those parents who had the resources paid Mr. Swann twenty-five cents monthly; the children of other parents received their instruction free of charge. Many of the students walked four to five miles each way to the one-room school, which, at one time, accommodated 90 to 100 students. The school day was from 9:00 A.M. to 3:00 P.M., Monday through Friday during the nine-month school year. For the benefit of the students who worked and who were unable to attend classes during the day, Mr. Swann conducted night classes. Mr. Swann was an asset to the teaching profession.

In the 1880s, black schools of Anne Arundel County failed to reveal the same improvement they had exhibited in the 1870s. White schools continued to enjoy most of the funds derived from local taxes, while the colored schools only received tax money from the state. While Anne Arundel County received $6,814 from the state for colored education, the total amount spent on colored schools was $6,840.02.

Prior to 1896, all students were obligated to pay for their books. But in 1896, the Maryland legislature set aside funds, for the first time, to provide books for both races. This act brought about an increase in the enrollment in all of the county schools. The increase in colored schools was from 2,323 in 1896 to 2,966 in 1897.

Until 1917, black residents still had no high school to attend in Anne

Arundel County. After the students graduated from elementary school, some of the parents sent their children to public schools in Baltimore or Washington, or out of state to boarding schools. But this practice terminated in 1917, with the establishment of Stanton High School, which was housed in a part of the existing Stanton School building on Washington Street in Annapolis. Benjamin Price, principal of Stanton Elementary School (which was on the first floor) together with Madeline Williams, taught all of the high-school subjects to the first class—Mary Brown and Bishop Ridgley who graduated in 1920.

Calvert County Public Schools

Calvert County is a rural, isolated, tobacco growing county in southern Maryland, nestled between the Chesapeake Bay on the east and the Patuxent River on the west. This climate facilitates both tobacco-farming and oyster, crab, and fish industries.

Calvert was one of the last Maryland counties to provide schools for black students; in fact, as late as 1865, it had no black schools. Until the early 1870s, Calvert County had done nothing to educate their black residents. With this attitude exhibited by most white residents, the black residents started their own plans to set up schools in Mt. Hope, Plum Point, and St. Edmonds Methodist Episcopal churches in the fall of 1866.

Black churches were the center for educational development, and ministers and their wives played a major role in instruction of students. They were often the first teachers in established schools in Calvert County during the nineteenth-century. Since the early schools existed on church property, they were usually maintained out of money collected from church contributions or other interested donations that were additionally able to help pay $10 or $15 a month salaries to teachers. These teachers enjoyed free room and board. All black churches participated in this endeavor. Some of the expenses were paid with the net proceeds from a two-day fair that was organized in November 1867 and was held in Prince Frederick, the county seat of Calvert County.

Several of these early schools were burned down during the periods of Reconstruction by anti-abolitionists, many of whom had served in the Confederate Army. They resisted emancipation and opposed the building of Freedmen's schools in the county.

On the other hand, a few white residents exhibited a humanitarian spirit, even at some risk. Joseph Hall, a county merchant, reported in 1866 to the Baltimore Association for the Moral and Educational Improvement of the Colored People, that he needed "the strictest confidence as it would not be well for the writer if it was known here in this hot bed of treason."

In spite of overpowering barriers, seven schools existed by 1869 and received most of their financial support from the Freedmen's Bureau, the Baltimore Association, and the American Missionary Association. However, as early as 1867, there was a noticeable decrease in charitable donations, and in the school year 1869-1870, there was a complete shrinkage. Consequently, the Freedmen's Bureau agents sought financial assistance from the state and county boards of education, with the state responding in 1873, following the enactment of the Fifteenth Amendment to the United States Constitution.

When the Maryland legislature set aside funds for textbooks during the school year 1896-1897, there was a dramatic increase in the enrollment in all of the county schools. In prior years, both white and colored children were required to pay for their own supplies.

In Calvert County, as in other Maryland counties, the black students had several handicaps: a shorter school year, dilapidated schools, inadequate instructional materials, overcrowded classrooms, lack of bus transportation, and poorly paid teachers.

The length of the school year for the black students was seven months while that for the white students was nine months. Because many of the black residents were tenant farmers, the school year for their children was even shorter than the standard one, since they had to assist their parents on the farm.

Recognizing the plight of Afircan-Americans in the southern and southwestern states, benevolent foundations were formed from the funds of generous individuals, to encourage the education of black children and to improve their educational opportunities and living conditions. Julius Rosenwald established the Rosenwald Foundation in 1917, and in 1937, Anna T. Jennes, George Peabody, and John F. Slater contributed to the formation of the Southern Education Foundation, to which the Virginia Randolph Fund was added in 1938. Not only did these philanthropic organizations function to address the problems, but they helped to pay teachers' salaries in fourteen southern states.

Despite their lack of recognition in the past, the black schools became a part of the Calvert County public school system in 1921. Then and only then were their instructors allowed to sign teaching contracts. In the same year, the first multi-room school, Central Industrial School, (which had four classrooms and a basement) was built, with Houston Jackson as its principal.

As in other southern jurisdictions with no schools for their black students, parents sent their children to live with relatives or friends in Washington, D.C., or Baltimore, Maryland where they could attend high school. Meanwhile, parents, teachers, and trustees made continual appeals to the Calvert County School Board for a high school curriculum.

This became a reality in the school year 1929-1930, as J.P. Layne, a Hampton, VA Trade School graduate, was appointed principal of Central Colored High School. Interestingly, his wife, Nettie, was made principal of Central Elementary School. (The two schools were housed in the same building.)

Although Central High was initially planned and approved as a vocational/industrial training school, it didn't provide either specialized equipment or specialized training. Instead, the students who went there got English, mathematics, science, and history. The Class of 1934 was the first graduating class and consisted of four young ladies—Audrey Gray, Selma Mason, Mary Morsell, and Rosalie Morsell.

Once a high school was established, transportation became a problem, and the Great Depression magnified the problem. School bus service for African Americans in Calvert County during the 1930s was developed because of their sense of self-help, self-determination, and perseverance. Clyde Jones, Zellers and his son, Leroy Berry, Vanderbilt Brooks, Raymond

Smith, Allnut Reid, and Robert Wallace, Sr., were some of the earliest African American school bus drivers during the 30s and 40s.

Two decades after the establishment of the first high school in Calvert County, with its dual system of education, the author of this book was hired as a mathematics teacher in September 1950 at W. Sampson Brooks High School in Prince Frederick. His salary was $1800 compared to $2200 for 10-month employment for a beginning teacher in his home county (Montgomery). The salary for his second year was $2000.

In September 1969, he became a teaching-assistant principal, which made him a 12-month employee in Calvert County. When he resigned in June 1962, to teach in Montgomery County, his salary was $7620. It is ironic that his 10-month salary in Montgomery County exceeded that for his former 12-month employment, even after he lost three years on the salary scale because his teaching experience exceeded the maximum allowed to a transfer teacher coming to Montgomery County.

Montgomery County also had more schools for both black and white students than Calvert County. During the 1929-1930 school year in Calvert County, when Central High School (the first high school for black students) opened, there was one white high school (Calvert County High School) in existence; whereas in Montgomery County, when Rockville Colored High School opened in September 1927, there were 10 public high schools already in existence for the white students.

The teaching-learning environment at W. Sampson Brooks High School was unique in that two teachers were assigned to teach two unrelated classes in the same room during the same class period during the school years 1957-1958 and 1958-1959. The first year Barbara Burrell (Robbins) taught shorthand and typing in the same period; the next year she taught office practice and typing in the same period in the same room as two other classes. The author of this book taught elementary business training and ninth grade general mathematics in the same period the first year and solid geometry and elementary business training in the same period the following year.

This was a valuable and rewarding experience, because the opportunity enabled each teacher to become skilled in organization and in classroom management that proved to be very useful in subsequent years. This unprecedented procedure was practiced at W. Sampson Brooks High School because three employees were non-teachers: the principal, the guidance counselor, and the librarian. In some schools, these persons did teach in the classroom.

At the elementary-school level, especially during the segregative era, it was the rule rather than the exception to have three or four grades—and in some cases, seven grades—in the same room being taught by one teacher. In such an arrangement, the lower-grade average and above-average students tended to learn from their upper-grade classmates. When they entered the next grade, many things were learned already, especially those done by oral recitation.

Howard County Public Schools

Neighboring Howard County (which was created from Anne Arundel County by Chapter 22, Acts of 1838) was officially instituted as a county in 1851 and was named in honor of a Revolutionary War officer, Maryland governor, and statesman, John Eager Howard (1752-1827).

During the last decade of the nineteenth century, when the county school buildings had to be replaced, the state provided no additional financial support for this purpose.

In 1892, differences existed in all areas pertaining to black versus white education in Howard County. There were three times as many white schools (forty-three) as there were black schools (fourteen). The white teachers' salaries ($95 to $110 per term) were nearly twice those of their black counterparts, and the white schools were allotted $28 each for fuel for the year, whereas the black schools received $7 to $12.

Likewise, there was a disparity in the length of the school term as well. When there was a shortage of funds in 1893, the Howard County Board of Education ordered that the school year terminate in mid-April for the black students and the following month for the white students.

Eventually, in the 1920s, Cooksville High School was built as an industrial school for colored youths. However, black youths in the eastern part of the county had to attend high school outside of the county, if they wanted an education, since Cooksville High was small and so far away. Some students walked nearly three miles to meet a bus that went to Lincoln High School in Montgomery County.

Prince George's County Public Schools

An enactment passed on May 2, 1695 sub-divided a large, sparsely-settled section of Maryland into Frederick, Montgomery, Washington Allegany, and Garrett counties, in order to foster more effective government. Prince George's County was also set apart as a new county and was dedicated on St. George's Day—April 23, 1696.

In addition, the District of Columbia was created from Prince George's and Montgomery counties after the acceptance of Maryland's offer to donate a portion of its territory for the new Nation's Capital. No changes were made in Prince George's County's boundaries after 1791.

Prince George's County, like most Maryland counties, totally neglected the educational and developmental needs of black children until the latter half of the 19th century. "In 1865, the Maryland legislature passed the Public Instruction Act allowing part of taxes paid by Blacks to be used to construct schools designed exclusively for Black children. Baltimore City was the first jurisdiction to take advantage of the Act in 1867. In spite of the General Assembly's action, Prince George's County took minimal responsibility in 1872."

The first public school for blacks that was built exclusively with Freedmen's Bureau funds was "Colored School Number 1 in the town of Bladensburg, on February 2, 1867."

An Act of 1898 by the Maryland legislature established the first public high school, Laurel High School, in Prince George's County. Laurel High opened in 1899 with Roger I. Manning as principal and with three teachers. It was the sole Prince George's County secondary school prior to the 20th century.

The first secondary school for blacks, Marlboro High School (later named Frederick Douglass High School, opened in 1923. It had 11 classrooms, an office, and a library. It housed both the elementary and high school grades.

Due to the enormous size of Prince George's County, it was necessary to have another high school for black students. In 1928, Lakeland High School (a Rosenwald school) opened with an enrollment of 845 in grades 8 and 9 and with Edgar A. Smith, Sr., as principal. One teacher taught math and science and the other, English and history.

The case of Homer Adolph Plessy vs. Judge John H. Ferguson was presented in May 1896 to the United States Supreme Court. The decision declared that a Louisiana law requiring separate-but-equal facilities for whites and blacks on railroads was permissible and was not a violation of the Fourteenth Amendment to the U. S. Constitution. Although this case strictly involved transportation, this racial separation was gradually carried over into public school systems as well as into other public spheres. The United States Supreme Court decision of 1896, which laid a legal foundation for the separation of the races in public facilities, stood for fifty-eight years in the school systems of the seventeen Southern states and the District of Columbia.

The 1916 Maryland legislature, in the Minimum Program of Education for all Maryland public schools, stated that public schools for white youths remain in session at least 180 days each year, public schools for black youths, at least 140 days each year. By ordaining separate minimum requirements and standards for the two races, the state suggested and encouraged continued bias against the education of blacks. These prejudicial practices were evident in all seventeen southern states.

Although the position of the state toward public education blacks had become institutionalized on the elementary level by 1900, there were still no county high schools as late as 1916. It was not until after 1919 that the Eastern Shore had any African-American public high schools. (At that time, the general status of education on the Eastern Shore was lower than that provided elsewhere in the state.)

The Montgomery County Story

In Maryland's Montgomery County, black residents were given a breath of fresh air. The Society of Friends (Quakers), who were zealous abolitionists, liberated their slaves by the early 1800s. They then helped them establish the Sharp Street Church in Sandy Spring—the first Black church in Montgomery County—while supporting them, educationally, in this edifice. By 1864 the Quakers had already begun to educate their former slaves in Sandy Spring. In 1866, they established the Sandy Spring Industrial School with the help of the Freedmen's Bureau. The school trained teachers as well as students. Its first teachers were white. Mary Coffin Brooke arrived in 1854 to teach at Fair Hill Female Academy. She was one of the most dedicated instructors, teaching former slaves at night after teaching at Fair Hill during the day. In her book, *Memories of Eighty Years*, she wrote: "Before I went to Maryland, I had never seen a slave. My knowledge of the institution had been obtained from books. Of course, the Friends employed, at that time, only the free colored people, and they were paid wages and were generally taught to read, there being no public schools for either white or colored children in Maryland at that time." The Sharp Street Industrial School was the first public school for blacks in Montgomery County. The Maryland General Assembly appropriated $50,000 of black real estate and state funds for public schools for black people in 1872, and Montgomery County received $532.24 of this allocation per quarter.

There were several restrictions when public schools for black students arrived in Montgomery County in 1872. Money from white taxpayers could

The Sharp Street School in Sandy Spring (1910)

not be used for the education of black children. At least 15 children, between the ages of six and twenty, had to attend daily classes and, again, the school term for the black students was of a shorter duration than that of the white students.

From November 1882 through January 1883, teachers received $75 quarterly. But by April of 1885, the funds were depleted at Sharp Street Industrial School. The school was closed until more money became available.

By 1908, Sharp Street Industrial School was renamed Maryland Normal and Agricultural Institute and had an enrollment of seven students. Its commercial and industrial departments each received $1,500 from the State that year. The school's reputation grew under the leadership of Principal George Williams and one teacher.

At the turn of the century, in Tuskegee, Alabama, Booker T. Washington, a leader in educating black people and founder of the Tuskegee Institute (president from 1881-1915), was an advocate of manual training. Since he and George Williams were both Hampton Institute alumni and had received training to that effect, they corresponded with each other pertaining to agricultural matters.

Principal Williams and his wife, Cora, who acted as Assistant Principal, had a combined annual salary of $800. During their administration, the school became a model school with departments in teacher training, manual training, elementary agriculture, nature study, domestic science, drawing and music. In addition, there were courses in carpentry, blacksmithing, sewing, dressmaking, cooking and shoemaking. A correspondence course in agriculture was a major accomplishment realized under the leadership of Principal Williams. Because agriculture was a required course in state schools, teachers of the first through the third grades required a knowledge of that subject. The institute, under Mr. Williams's leadership also benefitted from the allocation of $600 a year in state funds.

Williams resigned in January of 1910, when his health began to fail, and George Bell was appointed to be the new principal. Mr. Bell was paid $40 per month, whereas Mr. Williams was paid $75 per quarter.

A 1912 survey by the Presbyterian Church revealed some of the differences between the white and the black schools. The report spoke favorably of the Maryland Normal and Agricultural Institute's program, whereas most of the other black schools were described as "inadequate and in a dilapidated condition."

The Rosenwald Fund

When the Maryland Normal and Agricultural Institute burned down in 1922, the Odd Fellows Hall in Sandy Spring housed the school for $18 a month, until the Sandy Spring Elementary School was built with money from the Rosenwald Fund. Sandy Spring Elementary School was one of fifteen schools that were created between 1926 and 1928. In 1917, Julius Rosenwald(1862-1932), a Sears and Roebuck philanthropist, set up a fund from his personal assets to help finance better public educational facilities for black students in the South.

Born and educated in Springfield, Illinois, Julius Rosenwald entered the clothing business at age seventeen. He went to work for Sears in 1895, and by 1909 he was serving as the president of Sears, a post he held until 1924. He once said that it was easier to make a million dollars honestly than to give it away wisely.

Established in 1917, the Rosenwald Fund set aside money to improve the opportunities and living conditions of African-Americans. Rosenwald donated money, through the fund, to aid groups, rather than individuals. The fund contributed to the building of more than 500 rural Negro schools. It also contributed $63 million to black education, Jewish philanthropies, and a wide range of educational, religious, scientific, and community organizations.

Rosenwald made his donations in such a way that it stimulated others to contribute. In 1928, he reorganized and enlarged the fund's program to include the formation of clinics and other organized medical services to improve the health of African-Americans in low income brackets.

Rosenwald disliked perpetual endowments and felt that social conditions changed too rapidly to store large sums of money for the future. He expressed the wish that his funds be spent within twenty-five years of his death. He died at age seventy, in 1932, and the Fund was terminated in 1948, only 16 years thereafter. During that time, $22.5 million had been donated to various causes.

Five thousand Rosenwald schools were established by 1948; the Montgomery County school system, like other racially segregated school systems in southern states, benefitted from this fund in the building of schools for the black population.

Montgomery County School Pioneers

Historian Nina H. Clarke reported that the Quakers were not alone in founding schools. Enoch George Howard (1814-1895), the first of eight children born to Jack and Polly Howard near Unity, MD, was born into slavery. As a slave, he was appointed field foreman and was permitted to make a profit on the first crop of all the land that he cleared.

After he was freed in 1859 by his owner, Sarah Griffith, he purchased the freedom of his wife, Harriet Ann Lee Howard (1808-1882), in 1853, with his accumulated savings. But it was not until 1860 that they were able to buy the freedom for their children—John Henry, Mary Alice, Martha Elizabeth, and Greenberry.

Nearly twelve years after he gained his freedom, Howard bought 289 acres of the land on which he had labored as a slave. In 1869, he made another purchase of land from the Griffith estate—this time 300 acres. Currently, much of the land that he bought is incorporated into the Patuxent River State Park on the Montgomery-Howard County border.

Howard, although reportedly illiterate, believed in education and steered a committee of free blacks who petitioned the County Commissioners for the right to build their own schools. The petition was accepted, and black leaders provided land and hired teachers for the children. According to family historian Harold W. Howard, Enoch Howard and his wife donated land for the Howard School that opened in 1880 and remained functional until the black public school system became a part of the Maryland State Board of Education in 1939.

Prior to his death in 1895, Howard had acquired nearly 900 acres of land and was instrumental in establishing one of the earliest schools to educate black children in the county.

Through his lineage came a family of journalists, educators, and magistrates. His daughter, Martha Elizabeth, married John Henry Murphy and moved to Baltimore, where they founded the Afro-American Newspapers in 1892. From this marriage was born a son, George, who became a public school principal and who became the father of Judge William Murphy. Eventually, William Murphy, Jr. became judge of the Baltimore Circuit Court.

According to Mrs. Clarke, each community had to raise one-half of the cost of a new building, since the Montgomery County School Board did not use its money to build schools for black students.

Because there were no high schools for blacks in the county, some black teachers continued instructing their more advanced students at a higher academic level. In 1904, however, the school commissioners prohibited the teaching of blacks above the fifth grade level.

Graduates Ready for High School

So what was the future of those students who graduated from elementary school? Since there were no secondary schools for them, other options were sought by some fortunate parents. Of course, such cases were rare, since many of the parents were farmers and needed their children for labor.

One student, Elizabeth Awkward, relocated to Raleigh, North Carolina, where she attended a public high school and graduated in the Class of 1932. The following school year, she enrolled at Bowie Normal Institute (now Bowie State University) where she joined four of her native Montgomery County peers from Rockville Colored High School's Class of 1932. After the completion of her two-year teacher certification program, she was hired as an elementary school teacher in Calvert County. Her four classmates were employed in their native Montgomery County.

After receiving her elementary school education, another student, Mary Nugent, left Montgomery County to attend school in Baltimore City, which had the only black high school in the state of Maryland. Subsequently, she earned her doctorate in home economics and taught at Morgan State College (now Morgan State University) and Princess Anne College (now University of Maryland Eastern Shore). A third student, Alice C. Thomas, departed from Sandy Spring to receive her high school education in New York. After completing his elementary education, T. Edgar Thomas enrolled at New Jersey Manual Training and Industrial School in Bordentown, New Jersey, where he received a trade certificate in June 1927.

Students like these, who wanted to earn their high school diploma and whose parents were financially capable, migrated to other localities where there were established public high schools. In order to obtain her diploma, Mattie Williams Claggett recalled that they "went to stay with relatives, friends, or persons who opted to keep them." To help pay for room and board, some parents sent fruit and vegetables to the guardians. Most students, however, settled in Washington, D.C., to attend public high school.

Children were faced with a choice between leaving their families behind, or staying at home to eke out a living as a domestic or laborer. Most students who were forced to leave Montgomery County to attend school in D.C. came upon problems of transportation and accommodation. Yet for the select few who were fortunate enough to attend high school, those were the best of times, in spite of the hardships they faced. Eventually, they were able to obtain satisfactory employment. For the many students who did not have the opportunity to further their education, it was the worst of times, since they were left with no marketable skills. In their quest for a better quality of life, black students endured many hardships and inconveniences. They had to leave their families and friends behind to live in a strange city, they had to disprove the stigma that country students were intellectually inferior to city students, and they had to cope with the practice of the preferential treatment of their upper middle-class peers. Despite these drawbacks, the students were determined to follow through with their dream to earn a high school diploma—the key to a successful future. They had the strength of purpose and hope that even the odds against them could not shake, while their parents awaited the arrival of a high school closer to home. For the next sixteen years, those who could not afford to relocate elsewhere were prevented from furthering their education in Montgomery County.

ROCKVILLE COLORED HIGH SCHOOL: 1927-1935

T he lack of a high school for black students created quite a stir among the black trustees of several elementary schools; so much so that they organized themselves into the United Trustees of Montgomery County, Maryland. They made their voices heard, and the communities were responsive to their requests. Noah E. Clarke, chairman of this group of trailblazers sensed the urgency of the crisis before them and took the initiative to discuss, with the elementary school teachers at a field day, the idea of having a county high school. According to historian Nina H. Clarke, daughter-in-law of Noah E. Clarke, he then presented the positive results of their discussion to the trustees for implementation. Once the plans for a county high school were formulated, the trustees' voices could not be silenced in their meetings with the Montgomery County School Board.

Prior to the Montgomery County School Board's approval of building a high school, the board members had to be convinced that there were forty students to attend the school. This herculean task fell upon the shoulders of Edward U. Taylor, the future school supervisor, who visited the various communities to recruit children from the countryside. Trying to recruit 40 students to enroll in high school, at that time, was not an easy task. Even though many of them wanted to attend high school, they were unable to do so because their parents desperately needed them at home to assist with the farm and domestic chores. The land had to be plowed, seeds had to be planted, crops had to be cared for and harvested, and livestock had to be

Noah Edward Clarke, chairman of the United Trustees of Montgomery County

fed and cared for. Since the farmers were financially unable to hire adults to assist them, they kept their children home to help with the labor.

Mr. Taylor obtained the magic number of students, and through aggressive determination, tireless persistence, and effective teamwork, the construction of Rockville Colored High School resulted. It opened in September 1927 with Mr. Taylor, the lone teacher-principal, and forty eighth-graders.

Throughout the fight for a high school, the United Trustees endured many struggles, but these trials produced impressive results. They knew that with the construction of a high school in Rockville would come a time of change, a time of opportunity, and a time of hope. These pioneers envisioned Rockville Colored High School as a gateway to a comfortable standard of living for young black men and women.

To build a treasury, each trustee contributed five dollars. With their donations, contributions from the communities, and the Rosenwald Fund they obtained a two-room building on North Washington Street, opposite Beale Street, in Rockville.

Edward U. Taylor

In the meantime, a product of Montgomery County's dual educational system was soon to become a prominent leader in that system. When Edward U. Taylor graduated from Emory Grove Elementary School and enrolled at Dunbar High School in Washington, D.C., no one realized that that he would be a pioneer in the education of black high school students or a supervisor of black elementary school teachers. Upon his graduation from Dunbar High School, Mr. Taylor went on to Howard University where he earned a bachelor's degree in secondary education.

Later, when the supervisor of Montgomery County Colored Schools, Andrew D. Owens, resigned because of health problems during the latter part of 1923, Mr. Taylor became his replacement. "In 1924, he was officially appointed to fill the position," recounted Mrs. Taylor. With a bachelor's degree in secondary education, he was certified to teach only on the high school level. Therefore, having been appointed Supervisor to Montgomery County Colored Schools, Mr. Taylor attended night school courses in administration and supervision on the elementary level to become fully qualified for that position. Recalls Mrs. Taylor, he then went to summer school at Hampton Institute (now Hampton University) in Virginia for two summers and finally to Columbia and New York universities for four summers.

Mr. Taylor's initial experience with his new position involved several inconveniences. His only means of transportation was a horse and buggy which was driven by a neighbor. Also, there was no provision made for secretarial service, no office, and no monetary assistance. However, he was

Edward U. Taylor: Trailblazer and versatile administrator of Rockville Colored High School

undaunted by these trials and disadvantages. With the assistance and encouragement of his very supportive wife, he remained unshakably loyal to his commitment.

Mr. Taylor was quietly efficient in the discharge of his duties, in spite of obstacles. In 1924, Mr. Taylor bought a new car on the $75-per-month salary, eliminating his transportation problems. He paid for everything that pertained to his supervisory duties, as well.

Because of his role as the supervisor of the black elementary schools, he was in a key position to keep his fingers on the pulse of each community. Fortunately, Mr. Taylor worked with reliable individuals who would be supportive of the schools—some of whom would be involved in an even greater undertaking. Since he was a product of Montgomery County, he had a dream which would change the course of history for high school aged black youths, and he would not allow adversity to extinguish this dream.

Rockville Colored High School

The construction of Rockville Colored High School was a major breakthrough for several reasons. It afforded the opportunity for more high school-aged children to get a secondary school education in their home county, it provided an opportunity for the students to live at home, it allowed for students to work during the evenings in order to pay their bus fare, and it gave an opportunity for more students to improve their standard of living. Generally speaking, it revolutionized the futures of thousands of young black people.

By the time that Rockville Colored High School opened its doors in September 1927, there were ten public high schools in Montgomery County already in existence for white students. Rockville High (1891; name changed to Montgomery County High, 1904; now Richard Montgomery High, June 10, 1935), Gaithersburg High (1903), Sherwood High (1906), Poolesville High (1917), Damascus High (1920), Fairland High (1922), Dickerson High (1922), Germantown High (1923), Takoma-Silver Spring High (1924), Bethesda-Chevy Chase (1925). At this time, there were at least three black high schools in Maryland: Stanton High School (1917, Anne Arundel County), Cooksville High School (1920, Howard County), and Marlboro High School (1923, Prince George's County). The Department of Education defined a high school as any school that had at least two grades above the sixth grade. Rockville Colored High School was the first and only high school for black students in Montgomery County.

However, along with progress came confusion. According to Central Records (Montgomery County Public Schools), Montgomery County High School was erected in 1904, and it burned in 1940. The name Montgomery County High School was official, but commonly it had been called Rockville High School. With the opening of Rockville Colored High School, this became confusing. The student bodies of the two schools appealed separately to the Board of Education for name changes. So on June 11, 1935, the unofficial Rockville High School was officially named Richard Montgomery High School.

RCHS's First Year of Operation: Edward Taylor's Duties

The burdens of operating Rockville Colored High were carried mostly

Rockville Elementary School: Housed the high school's chemistry room and shared its toilet facilities with the high school

by Edward Taylor. Consequently, as principal-teacher of Rockville High, "He taught forty eighth graders in the morning and performed his supervisory duties in the afternoon," recalled Mrs. Taylor. This young Howard University graduate had to wear many hats, making this a tremendous challenge; he was supervisor, custodian, maintenance worker, school delivery man, teacher, husband, chauffeur and father. His experience, strong faith in God, a supportive wife, Maude, and resolute trustees enabled him to succeed in spite of obstacles.

Since there were no funds allocated for the employment of a janitor, Taylor performed the custodial duties. During the winter months, he arrived early to make a fire in an old pot-belly stove and to perform many other custodial chores prior to the arrival of the students. According to Mrs. Taylor, besides the numerous tasks involved in running his own school, he was occasionally given supplies to deliver to some of the white schools.

Even though a school was built, the students were still faced with problems. Initially, they received only a half-day of instruction, which placed a restriction on the number of subjects that could be taught during the time frame. In addition, the students did not receive new textbooks. In spite of being handicapped by inadequate instructional materials, the teachers endeavored to provide the best education possible for their students. To further magnify the problem, many of the students were kept at home to plant and harvest crops. As far as educational opportunities for the two races, in the South there was no equality.

In 1900, the ratio of the per capita expenses for white students to black students was 3 to 2; in 1930, it was 7 to 2, and in ten southern states during the school year 1935-1936, it was nearly 3 to 1. Moreover, there was still the problem of poor transportation. In his endeavor to advance secondary school education for Montgomery County black students, Taylor transported six students about nine miles daily from Emory Grove. These students (Henry Braxton, George Carroll, Alfred Duvall, Beatrice Taylor, Alise V. Tyler, Ruize O. Tyler) only enjoyed this privilege during the first year of school (1927-1928); thereafter, they rode the train. During Rockville High's first year in operation, another car was also used to transport students. Mrs. Bertha J. Bishop, a parent, transported four students (Lillian Awkard, William E. Bishop - her son, Richard W. Hall, & Lucy V. Scott) about 10 miles from Sandy Spring to Rockville.

The first students to attend Rockville Colored High School (twenty-two girls and eighteen boys) were from the westernmost parts of Montgomery County: Rockville, Sandy Spring, and the Spencerville area. Except those who lived in Rockville, many of the students lived on farms.

Only nine students were in the graduating Class of 1931: William E. Bishop, Beulah M. Clarke, Sarah Curtis, Richard W. Hall, K. Solomon Hart, Celestine M. Prather, Beatrice S. Taylor, Ruize O. Tyler, and Margaret Wood. At the time of this writing, Lucy V. Scott is the only charter member alive, and Celestine M. Prather (who passed away on December 10, 1997) and Ruize O. Tyler (on August 7, 1994) were the two next longest survivors.

RCHS's Second Year: Transportation and Space Problems

In Rockville High's second year of operation (1928-1929) several changes took place. The ninth grade was added which meant that ninth grade English, mathematics, history, science, and physical education had to be added to the curriculum. Edward Taylor, the first principal-teacher, was also employed as a Supervisor of Montgomery County Colored Elementary Schools and was obligated to spend more time in the supervision of them. When a full-time principal-teacher—Theodore Watkins— was obtained, Mr. Taylor became a part-time teacher of two social studies classes. This distribution of teaching duties finally allowed the students to have a full day of instruction. In addition to his administrative duties, Mr. Watkins instructed the eighth and ninth graders in English and mathematics. Queene E. McNeill, a former substitute in Washington, D.C., taught English. Each of them supervised physical activities.

With an increase in enrollment, there was a need to transport students from the Sandy Spring-Spencerville area. The United Trustees and the community members pooled their resources to purchase two buses and the Montgomery County School Board gave them a third bus. According to Edith Hill Owens, "Solomon K. Hart, a student, was paid five dollars per month to drive the bus, which was parked daily at the Spencerville residence of Trustee Peyton Campbell for proper maintenance, and the students paid $6.50 monthly for bus fare." The students amusingly claimed that when the bus approached an incline, the boys would alight from the bus to push it since it traveled so slowly up the hills.

Due to the transfer of some students from the District of Columbia public schools, there was a small increase in the number of ninth graders. Solomon K. Hart was one of the transferees who wanted to stay home with his family and attend school with his Montgomery County peers. Some of the students were elated that they did not have to leave their native Montgomery County to get their high school education; others were not so enthusiastic and remained at their chosen school in the District of Columbia. Some students "stayed because of the transportation problem," recounted Alberta Withers French, a former student. To some individuals, making the change was tantamount to sailing in uncharted seas. Transferring from an established high school to a fledgling one caused anxiety on the part of some students. There existed the possibility of inexperienced or incompetent teachers and an inferior academic program. On the other hand, a change to a new environment can be a breath of fresh air.

An increase in the enrollment also brought about a space problem. The small room situated between the two classrooms, which was designated as a library, had to be used as a classroom itself. Consequently, the United Trustees, together with community representatives, appealed to the Montgomery County School Board on February 12, 1929, and a second time on December 9, 1929. They requested a large brick building with a steam-heating system to replace the yellow two-room frame building with no indoor plumbing, but their efforts were fruitless for the time being. Temporary relief finally came three months later with the rental of a nearby community facility, Fisherman's Hall.

RCHS's Third Year: The Great Depression

Seven months after Herbert Hoover took office as president, education received a terrific blow, as the stock market crashed in October 1929 to usher in the Great Depression. By the end of 1929, the crash had caused losses estimated at $40 billion. Thousands of workers had lost their jobs. When Franklin Delano Roosevelt took office as President during the deepest part of the Great Depression, about one of every four people eligible to work in the United States did not have a job. Many families had no money to buy food. Others had lost their homes because they could not pay what they owed to the bank.

While the Great Depression hurt education all over the country, it was especially devestating to Southern black schools. In Montgomery County, individuals, both black and white, had to appeal to the Montgomery County Welfare Board for living expenses. Funds set up by humanitarians Anna T. Jeanes, George Peabody, and John F. Slater, to assist in the jurisdictions with dual systems of education, never were given to Montgomery County black schools during the Depression years. Without an income, black families could not meet their financial obligations and thereby produced no revenue for the maintenance of the school buses or for the payment of the bus operators. As a result, on March 4, 1933, the Montgomery County School Board undertook the responsibility of transporting the students and relieved the United Trustees of the debt accrued ($803.07) for the bus repairs.

RCHS's Third Year: Real Progress

During the third year of operation (1929-1930), more progress was made. The curricular offerings were upgraded with the addition of French and chemistry; the tenth grade was added; and there was an increase in enrollment. There was also a change in leadership and increase in faculty, with Thomas Kemp as the new principal and Namon Allen, Ethel Mae McDowell (former Randall Junior High School assistant principal in D.C.), and Robert Chase as teachers. (Mr. Kemp resigned the same year he took over as principal and Mr. Chase was his replacement.)

Along with a larger number of students came a need for added transportation. To meet this need, the United Trustees purchased a second bus from the Baltimore Inner-City Motor Coach Company, Inc., for $175. Millard E. Clarke, a student, was paid $25 a month to drive this bus, which was parked daily at the residence of Trustee Noah E. Clarke (his father). Since the United Trustees purchased the buses, it was their responsibility to oversee their maintenance when they had student drivers.

To fulfill the students' need for physical activity, intramural sports—dodge ball, soccer, touch football, volleyball, and track and field events—were added. In the spring, annual field days, which had begun in elementary schools on April 14, 1921, were held on the campus of Rockville Colored High School. White officials came from Baltimore to judge both the elementary and high school events.

During this school year, "some students, who remained in Washington schools the first two years that Rockville High was in operation, eventually made the decision to transfer. However, there were still others, for unknown reasons, who chose to remain in D.C. to obtain their high school diploma," remembered Edith Hill-Owens, a former student. Some students transferred from Washington public schools to Rockville High because it allowed them to stay at home with their families, which would be a financial savings—no room and board to pay.

RCHS's Fourth Year: Transportation Problems Solved

During the fourth year of operation (1930-1931), the eleventh grade was added, and the transportation problem was alleviated. To shorten the unusually long routes of the other two buses, the Montgomery County Board of Education gave the United Trustees a Chevrolet bus. The United Trustees paid Chester Hall, a Sandy Spring resident, $25 a month to drive this bus.

Maggie Prather, a former student, reported that her cousin "Thomas Prather, a student, was employed to drive a bus from the Laytonsville area during the school year (1930-1931). Some of the female riders took live-in jobs, and others worked as domestics in the afternoon to pay for their monthly bus fares." The males worked at home.

Like taxicab passengers, the students paid according to the number of miles they lived from the school. "The Spencerville-area students paid $6 a month; the Sandy Spring, Barnesville, and Poolesville-area students paid $5; the Norbeck-area students $4; and the Darnestown and Quince Orchard-areas, $3 a month. Some relief did come on January 14, 1930, when the Montgomery County Board of Education provided a $2-monthly allowance for each student who rode a school bus." These student fares were used to help defray the costs of purchase, operation, and maintenance of the buses.

First Graduating Class

Rockville Colored High School's fourth year was history-making, since that was the year it produced its first graduates. When 40 eighth graders

Members of the First Graduating Class (1931) of Rockville Colored High School. Front (l to r): Celestine Minerva Prather, Beatrice Sophia Taylor, Beulah Mae Clarke, Margaret Wood; Rear (l to r): Robert Chase (principal), Sara Curtis, King Solomon Hart (son of pastor of Round Oak Baptist Church, Rev. Neil Hart); Absent: William Ernest Bishop, Richard Wesley Hall, Ruize O. Tyler (courtesy Nina H. Clarke)

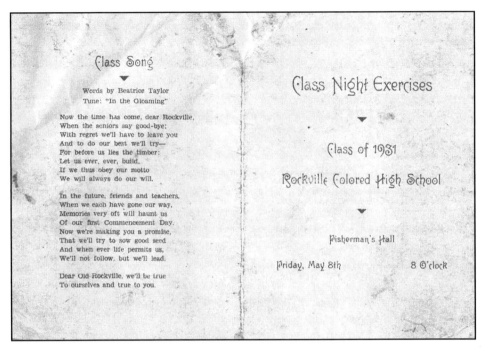

Program from Rockville Colored High School's first graduation ceremony, 1931

enrolled in September 1927, no one thought that the Class of 1931 would have just nine graduates. This small number, for the most part, can be attributed to the parents' need of the children's assistance on the farm and in the home.

Eventually, parents and teachers organized the Federation of Parent-Teacher Association to improve the educational climate of the students. They elected Noah E. Clarke as their president. Under his leadership, the association made numerous requests to the Montgomery County Board of Education for a new brick building with steam heat; all of which were rejected.

The next school year, 1931-1932, was a greater challenge than the previous four years because of a larger enrollment despite the same amount of classroom space. Yet, temporary relief came on September 8, 1931, when the Montgomery County School Board rented Fisherman's Hall, a facility owned by the Fisherman, for classroom usage, as well as for other assemblages, at a monthly fee of $18. The Fisherman was a fraternal association

Class Motto

"*Before us lies the timber—let us build*"

Class Colors

Orange and Blue

Class Flower

White Carnation

Class Roll

William Ernest Bishop

Beulah Mae Clarke

Sara Curtis

Richard Wesley Hall

King Solomon Hart

Celestine Minerva Prather

Beatrice Sophia Taylor

Ruize Osborne Tyler

Margaret Wood

Program

▼

Processional

Negro National Hymn .... High School Chorus

Invocation

Salutatory .... Celestine Prather

Class Roll .... Margaret Wood

History .... Ruize Tyler

Duet .... Dorothy Turner, Clara Luckett

Prophecy .... Beatrice Taylor

Will .... Solomon Hart

Gifts .... William Bishop

Valedictory .... Beulah Clarke

Class Song .... Class

Music .... High School Chorus

Recessional

of Rockville residents, and Fisherman's Hall was located one block from the school.

However, rental of the community facility failed to satisfy the entire need for additional classroom space, for there was the absence of a chemistry lab and equipment. To compensate for this inadequacy, the basement of the elementary school next to Rockville High School was divided into two sections—a furnace room and a chemistry room. The students had to pass through the furnace room in order to get to the chemistry room. The furnace room had a dirt floor and a pile of coal in one corner. The chemistry room did have a wooden floor, but there was little else—one Bunsen burner, one test tube, one beaker, and one clamp. In spite of the astonishing lack of supplies, the teachers and students had a good working relationship. To maintain such a relationship, the teachers had to frequently draw upon their inventive powers to compensate for the lack of instructional materials. For instance, the teachers used discarded magazines and newspapers in social studies classes.

They attended the annual November Maryland State Teachers Conventions in Baltimore and obtained meaningful free materials that were used as visual aids or to make visual aids for classroom use.

Again, the persistent Noah E. Clarke and his reliable United Trustees crusaded for a larger high school building, with a steam-heating system, on another site. On October 8, 1931, the Board of Education agreed that there should be a new high school for about $22,000 for black children, and this agreement was approved on November 2, 1932. After the approval of the agreement, there were two changes, and ultimately both of them were rejected.

There were noticeable gains not only in the field of education, but in the field of sports as well. Since there was no physical education teacher, funeral director Robert L. "Mike" Snowden coached the school baseball team. Their opponents were high school teams in Washington, D.C., Frederick, Maryland, and Prince George's County.

One family that benefitted from these athletic opportunities was the Israel family. Clarence "Pint" Isreal (Rockville High School Class of 1935) played professional baseball in the Negro National league for the Newark Eagles and the Homestead Grays. His younger brother, Elbert (Lincoln High School Class of 1946), played for the semi-pro American

Rockville High School Class of '32

Legion Post 151 team prior to being drafted by the American League's Philadelphia Athletics—a team that later became the Kansas City Athletics. In the minor league, Elbert advanced through the ranks to the top—AAA.

The Isreal brothers had both varying and similar experiences. "Pint," as he was widely known, played professionally on all-black teams, whereas Elbert played on an all-black team and then on integrated teams. At one point in time, "Pint" and Elbert even had the privilege of playing on the same team (the Homestead Grays) at the same time.

Moreover, both brothers demonstrated their surpassing talents on the playing field, at the plate, and on the base path. These exceptional skills and the opportunities afforded them by colored high schools enabled them to earn positions on prestigious professional baseball teams.

1932 Graduates

In the meantime, Mr. Taylor, as supervisor, asked the members of the Class of 1932 to attend Bowie Normal School (now Bowie State University), a two-year training institution for elementary school teachers. Four of the graduates honored his request. At that time, Bowie Normal Institute was the only Maryland black institution that tailored its instruction exclusively to the training of elementary-school teachers. Upon the completion of their two-year program, Mr. Taylor placed Alda Campbell and Edith Hill at two-room Stewarttown Elementary School, Zachariah Hart at one-room Brighton Elementary School, and Mary E. Johnson at two-room Poolesville Elementary School. "Veteran teachers failed to see wisdom in the placement of two teen-aged first-year teachers—Alda Campbell, principal-teacher grades 4-7, and Edith Hill, teacher grades 1-3—at the same school," remembered Mrs. Owens. Besides teaching, some of their responsibilities included house chores, feeding chickens, gathering eggs, and picking vegetables and fruits.

As a result of that placement, there were raised eyebrows among experienced teachers, because they knew the challenge of teaching three and four grades in the same room. They knew that it would require discipline, good organizational skills, and maturity on the part of the teachers. What they did not realize was the strong work ethic that these young ladies had acquired from their training and responsibilities at home.

Because of his decision to place two first-year teachers in the school without the visible presence of a veteran teacher, "Mr. Taylor submitted a weekly progress report to the Montgomery County Board of Education. These reports, along with the reports of other freshman teachers, at the end of the year showed their ability to operate an effective program. These reports also conveyed a message to the parents of other students that Rockville High School was worthy of educating their children," stated Mrs. Owens.

Mr. Taylor's determination not to be swayed by the mild objections of the experienced teachers reveals much about the character of this individual. The true character of an individual is not shown during one's times of advantage and ease, but it is revealed during one's periods of struggle. The success of these young ladies made Mr. Taylor appear ten feet tall and gave him a reputation of being a wise leader.

Public Attitude

Soon, there was a dramatic change in attitude toward Rockville High when its graduates were accepted at Bowie State Normal School. Things were even better when they successfully completed their academic program and were employed immediately in their home county. This change in attitude brought about an increase in Rockville High's enrollment, as well as an increased enrollment at Bowie State Normal School. The students held education as their highest priority because it would not only affect their intellectual development but would result in desirable employment. Many of the students who graduated from the black high schools in Maryland enrolled at Bowie Normal rather than at (Maryland) black institutions Morgan State College and Princess Anne College. That is because there were more opportunities for employment in their respective counties in the elementary field than in the high school area (there was only one in each county, for the most part).

Rockville High School, in its sixth year of operation, 1932-1933, experienced more growing pains —an increase in enrollment and extracurricular activities. The students were very competitive outside of the classroom, as well as in the classroom. They participated in lively debates in various churches, as well as in oratorical contests and other student-oriented activities. In fact, the studious efforts of some members of the Class of 1933 were quite remarkable, as far as debating was concerned. Also, a newspaper staff was organized for the first time.

The Class of 1933 was small in number, but what they lacked in size they made up in talent and wisdom. Mabel Dorsey and William B. Duvall were two academically talented students who enjoyed keen competition. During their high school career, they participated in many activities. One of the most memorable activities was debating in the churches. Dorsey would lead the affirmative team and Duvall would captain the negative team. At the next debate, they would switch roles.

Probably the most notable student activity of the Rockville High School era was the insightful debate in which the teams argued the need for a bridge across the Chesapeake Bay to connect the eastern and western shores. These young people had foresight; the Chesapeake Bay Bridge was started on October 1, 1949, and it was opened for traffic on July 30, 1952. A 4.4-mile structure, which brought the two shores closer together, was completed 19 years after that debate. The construction of that bridge paved the way for a quicker and more convenient trip to the Eastern Shore beaches, colleges, and industries.

In 1933, Namon Allen became principal of Rockville High School a second time, and the teachers included Henry Joyce, Queene E. McNeill, and Agnes Watson.

Although the curricular offerings for the school year 1933-1934 remained the same as those previously offered, there was a growing need for home economics classes to teach the girls how to make their own dresses and prepare nutritious, balanced meals. Nevertheless, a full-time home economics teacher was not employed until the school year 1935-1936, as for the first time in seven years, there was no change in the 1933-1934 principalship or teaching staff.

The Class of 1935, the last class to graduate from Rockville High School, had 15 graduates, three of whom attended institutions of higher learning.

LINCOLN HIGH SCHOOL: 1935-1951

Even with the rental of a community facility and with the partitioning of the elementary-school basement next door, Rockville High School had insufficient classroom space to accommodate the enrollment.

Finally, on October 13, 1931, the Montgomery County Board agreed to have a new high school built for black children. The bond was issued at $22,000; however, by this time, the enrollment was so large that the association saw a need for a new building on a different site. Nearly three years later, on August 14, 1934, with the crusading of Noah E. Clarke and his trustees, eight acres of England Tract were purchased for $2,800 at the intersection of Lincoln and Biltmore avenues (now Lincoln and North Stonestreet Avenues) in Rockville's Lincoln Park.

On September 11, 1934, the Montgomery County Board of Education consented to continue to rent Fisherman's Hall (for the increased price of $25 a month) to alleviate the space problem of Rockville Colored High School until the new high school was built. Subsequently, the Board of Education approved the United Trustees' request for a larger, more modern edifice to be built at the new site.

Soon thereafter, an abandoned building was transported from Takoma Park, was brick-veneered, and became Lincoln High School. Lincoln High School (named in honor of Abraham Lincoln, the Great Emancipator), the second historically segregated high school, was a replacement for the inadequate Rockville Colored High School. The building opened its doors in September 1935 with six classrooms, a principal's office, a boy's and girl's lavatory, and a water fountain in the hallway midway between the east and west entrances. The faculty included Namon Allen (Principal), Neil Cooper, Queene E. McNeill, Alberta Mebane, Caleb Rhoe, and Agnes Watson. The building provided adequate space for the time being.

Rooms 2, 4, and 6 were separated by sliding doors so they could be used for classrooms, assemblies, movies, plays, commencements, and any large gathering of individuals. Room 6 was equipped with a piano and a stage with sliding curtains. During the 1940's, the area was increased to 14 acres, on which sat the main building, a home economics building, a shop, and a two-room science building (erected in 1943). In 1944, room 3 in the main building was partitioned into rooms 3A and 3B to create more classroom space.

When Rockville Colored High School faded into history in June 1935, Lincoln High School flourished in September 1935 with an enrollment of 236 students (grades 8-11) and six faculty members, two more than its predecessor. For the first time, the girls had the privilege of daily instruction by a full-time home economics teacher. In prior years, the girls had the services of a part-time home economics teacher, who was assigned to all of the Prince George's County schools and who came to Rockville High only one day per week to teach sewing.

Lincoln High offered three curricula—academic, general, and vocational courses—for the preparation of its students for the real world. To broaden the students' horizons, the teachers took the students on field trips to sites of historical importance. The academic course was designed for college-bound students. It consisted of English 9-11 (English 12 after 1942-1943), civics, world history, United States history, biology, chemistry, physics, French (Spanish was added in 1942), algebra, plane geometry, trigonometry, and physical education, in addition to electives.

The general course was designed primarily for those students who planned to enter the work force; however, a few students entered college

*Lincoln High School: The school
where student-teacher relation-
ships were above average*

after graduation. The general course consisted of the same English and social studies classes and electives as the college-preparatory course, exclud-
ing the foreign language and the other academic courses. Instead, general
mathematics courses were offered, and home economics was offered for
the girls, and agriculture and shop for the boys.

The vocational course was designed for prospective homemakers and
farmers. It consisted of the same subjects and electives as the general course,
except vocational agriculture, offered for the boys.

Besides their academic work at Lincoln High School, the students were
involved in a wide variety of extracurricular activities. Standing committees included Attendance, Building, Culinary, Grounds, Health-Welfare-
Safety, Program-Coordinating, Social-Recreation, and Transportation. The
students particated in groups such as the Boy's and Girl's Clubs, the Dramatic Club, and the Home Economics Club. Other organizations included
Girl's Octette, Hi-Y, band, National Honor Society, New Farmers of America,
New Homemakers of America, newspaper staff, School Safety Patrol Force,
Student Council, and Victory Corps. Students also played a variety of sports,
like basketball, baseball (championship in 1937), volleyball, track, softball,
soccer, and touch football.

There was interscholastic competition between Lincoln High School
(Rockville, MD), Lincoln High School (Frederick, MD), Dunbar High School

Mr. Herbert H. Norton, Lincoln High principal, 1936

(Washington, DC), and Douglass High School (Upper Marlboro, MD). Other opponents included high school teams from New Jersey, Pennsylvania, Virginia, and Baltimore. Lincoln High teams competed annually against other Western Shore county high school teams, on the spring field day at Bowie State Teachers College (previously Bowie Normal Institute),

An increase in the number of course offerings and the number of students necessitated additional buildings, and six additional acres were bought on May 14, 1946, for $1,000, increasing the original site to 14 acres.

During inclement weather, physical education classes were nonfunctional. This problem was solved on November 12, 1946, when the Montgomery County Board of Education rented Fisherman's Hall to use for physical education classes when the weather did not permit outside participation.

In the spring of Lincoln High School's second year (1936-1937), the first issue of the school newspaper, *Rockville News*, was published. It contained news-worthy articles of school events, original poems, and student advice. The school newspaper was started to keep the parents and other interested community residents abreast of what was going on at Lincoln High School.

That year, Herbert H. Norton was appointed principal and also taught agriculture. New faculty members were C. H. Johnson, who replaced Neil Cooper, and Genevieve V. Swann (taught all subjects except music, home economics, foreign language; a graduate of Miner Teachers College in D.C.), who replaced Agnes Watson at the start of the school year.

That year, the baseball team also set a school record. The senior-dominated baseball team of 1936-1937 went undefeated against their opponents from Washington, Baltimore, New Jersey, Pennsylvania, and Virginia with 12 wins and no losses.

Because of their academic success in the classroom, the students were able to improve their quality of life. Some became elementary, secondary, and college teachers, some became federal government employees, others were self-employed, and still others were gainfully employed in surrounding communities. Just as religious discipline sustained their ancestors during the years of slavery, strong family values enabled the students to succeed in spite of poverty and segregation.

Lincoln High School and Science Building in the rear

These values, a significant part of their heritage, strengthened them from within.

Throughout the years, it had been instilled in black students to reject mediocrity and to prepare, perform, and persevere to attain individual excellence. The family, being the basic building block of both society and the church, provided stability, guidance, and love, so that children could cope with the nearly insurmountable obstacles that they faced. In school, the students practiced what they learned at home and in the church, especially during the school morning devotion.

The family—with its compassion, love, strength, and support —was the unshakeable base on which its members stood. It is believed that daily devotions, on the elementary and high school levels, set the moral tone (regardless of religious persuasion) for learning life lessons, patriotism, personal behavior, and respect for others and their property. This made for a somewhat smooth transition and a cooperative spirit because the parents had assumed their full responsibility at home by training their children to obey and respect those individuals in authority, as well as all adults.

Lincoln High School: The school where a caring and nurturing atmosphere existed

Lincoln High School: A building in which a cooperative spirit and a positive attitude toward learning existed

Prayer, once one of the principal forms of worship, had been exercised in public schools for years. The recitation of Scriptural texts, the Lord's Prayer, or one's own spontaneous prayer was a daily practice during devotional periods, along with the flag salute, and religious and patriotic songs. With students of several different religious persuasions—Baptists, Catholics, Methodists, and Seventh-day Adventists—there was whole-hearted participation on the part of all students during devotions, as well as support from the community.

Many students used opposition as fuel to strengthen their firm determination to get an education to keep their hopes alive for a brighter future. They had a thirst for knowledge because they realized that along with knowledge came power to express oneself effectively, to discern right from wrong, to change the circumstances that one can change, to cope with the situations that one cannot change, to make intelligent decisions, and to provide influential leadership.

The Class of 1937 had 13 more graduates than the Class of 1936, but just two more graduates went on to an institution of higher learning.

Teacher Equality

Not only were black students discriminated against, but black teachers experienced injustice, as well—in employment and salary. In December 1936, William B. Gibbs, Jr., volunteered to be plaintiff in a joint case of the NAACP and the Maryland State Colored Teachers Association (MSCTA), aided by NAACP attorney at the time, Thurgood Marshall. In 1937, Mr. Gibbs lost his job as principal and teacher at Rockville Colored Elementary School after he sued Superintendent of Schools Edwin W. Broome and the Montgomery County School Board in an effort to eliminate the existing salary inequities between black and white educators. In anticipation of a job loss, the members of the MSCTA agreed to donate a portion of their monthly salary to the association that, in turn, would submit a check to Gibbs to compensate him for a year of unemployment.

Prior to the suit, a black teacher with nearly four years of experience was paid $612 per year while a freshman white teacher received $1175. At that time, Mr. Gibbs was paid $577 per year. Nineteen states maintained dual salary scales for teachers. The struggle for equal salaries for black teachers was so widespread that the NAACP decided that they would intervene to alleviate that grievance.

Philip L. Brown reported in his book, *A Century of 'Separate But Equal' Education in Anne Arundel County*, that the NAACP's first endeavor to assist the Maryland teachers in their efforts to equalize salaries was in Montgomery County. The case of Gibbs vs. Montgomery County was settled out of court. The petitioner and the School Board agreed to increase the black teachers' salaries annually by 50 per cent of the differential, until 1938, at which time all teachers would be on the same salary schedule. The case, however, had no impact on the salaries of black teachers in the other Maryland counties.

Mr. Gibbs remained in the county another year, but he departed when he lost his principalship. Many individuals believed that he lost his job as a result of his having taken court action against the county. He was given the money donated by the MSCTA. He placed principle before self-interest and replaced fear with strength.

In 1936, William B. Gibbs, Jr. was in the spotlight as a dogged crusader against diversity in salary. He was undaunted by the magnitude of the problem and the influence of white residents and officials. In his courageous battle for salary equalization, he did not allow adversity to derail his dream.

Forty-three years later, Mr. Gibbs was in the limelight again, this time in appreciation for his leadership in the fight against separate and unequal salaries for black teachers in 1936. The Progressive Citizens' Association honored the Montgomery County trailblazer of civil rights at an awards ceremony at the Lincoln Park Community Center in Rockville, on Sunday, July 29, 1979. At that time, Mr. Gibbs was a pastor at his Westchester County, Pennsylvania church. In addition, he was active in public affairs, serving as minister of social service.

In Calvert County, H. Elizabeth Brown, principal of Mt. Hope Elementary School in Sunderland and the second Maryland teacher to challenge the salary inequity, filed a petition against the Calvert County Board of Education through the NAACP. In 1937, that suit was resolved out of court, as Calvert County agreed to reduce the difference in pay by one-third immediately and to put all teachers onto one salary scale in 1939. Unlike her Montgomery counterpart, Miss Brown retained her job for the next four decades.

Moreover, waves generated by the fallout from the salary disputes in Montgomery and Calvert counties swelled in Anne Arundel County. They not only drew a lot of attention, but much opposition, as well. Philip L. Brown, principal of Skidmore Elementary School, was spokesman for the disenchanted teachers when they met with the Board of Education on January 5, October 4, November 2, and November 23, 1938. Even with the threat of a lawsuit against them, the board members demonstrated little uneasiness, which prompted the teachers to enter a suit.

Walter Mills, principal of Parole Elementary School, acted as the plaintiff in the suit. The teachers association requested the services of Thurgood

Marshall, special counsel for the NAACP, in New York and apprised him of their plans. After his arrival in Annapolis, Mr. Marshall listened to an account of what the teachers had done already. Then, he advised them that a lawsuit was in order. While the *Gibbs v. Montgomery County* and the *Brown v. Calvert County* cases were settled out of court and had no consequence on salaries of teachers in other Maryland counties, this time they decided to sue the State of Maryland.

Thurgood Marshall, aided by Leon Ransom of the Howard University Law School, drew up the petition and named the State Board of Education, the State Superintendent of Schools, the State Comptroller, and the State Treasurer as the defendants. Civil Action No. 56 was filed in the District Court of the United States for the District of Maryland in Baltimore on December 16, 1938, with Judge W. Calvin Chesnut presiding. But Judge Chesnut dismissed the case with the condition that the plaintiff might amend the complaint within 10 days from March 1, 1939, if he so desired. Judge Chesnut observed that there was a uniqueness in the Maryland law pertaining to teachers' salaries: "… while there is prevailing inequality of pay between white and colored teachers in 19 states, Maryland is the only state which has a statute containing a minimum salary scale for white teachers, with a lower minimum for teachers in colored schools. On the face of the statute, the discrimination is based not on the race or color of the teacher but on the color of the scholars." Judge Chesnut interpreted the law to mean that if a white teacher was assigned to teach black students, that teacher would be paid on the lower scale, whereas if a black teacher was assigned to a white school, that teacher would be paid on the higher scale. The grievance was not revised, because the School Board members could not reach a consensus. One member stated that there were no funds available to make increases at that time. Another member strongly opposed raising the salaries of black teachers if it meant increasing the tax rate.

However, Mr. Marshall assured the teachers that it was not their last recourse, as they had sued the wrong party. The Anne Arundel County Board of Education was named as the new defendant. The re-entered case went before the Maryland District Court as Civil Docket No. 170, *Walter Mills versus the Anne Arundel County Board of Education.*

Upon being sued, Superintendent George Fox called a special meeting of the School Board on April 19, 1939. That session resulted in little more than a rehashing of the different salary schedules. Wide gaps still remained between the salaries, both on the elementary and high school levels.

For example, Mills, the plaintiff and principal of Parole Elementary School, was paid $1,058 and a white principal in a similar position was paid $1,800. On the high school level, Bates High School Principal Frank P. Butler, with 29 years of experience, received a yearly salary of $1,600, while a white principal with comparable high school experience received a minimum of $2,600.

Whenever the black teachers appealed to the school board about the salary question, they were never informed that the difference was based on lack of professional preparation or level of certification. In fact, that issue was always avoided, as the black teachers were usually more highly qualified than their white counterparts.

That fact was confirmed in the 1916 Flexner-Buckman Survey Commission Report on Preparation of White and Colored Teachers. Accordingly, elementary and special teachers had reached the indicated highest level of education: elementary school - white, 12.7% and black, 15.4%; part high school - white, 20.7% and black, 19.6%; standard high school - white, 33.7% and black, 21.8% (in view of the fact that there was not a single black high school in the State of Maryland outside of Baltimore); part normal course - white, 2.7% and black, 4.9%; nonstandard normal course - white, 20.0% and black, 22.5%; standard normal course - white, 4.8% and black, 7.9%; part college - white, 3.2% and black, 3.6%; college - white, 2.1% and black, 4.2 %.

At that time, there were two Maryland facilities for the training of white teachers—Baltimore Normal School (later Towson University), established in 1865, and the Normal School at Frostburg, founded in 1897. On the other hand, there was just a single institution available for training black elementary teachers—the Maryland Normal and Industrial School at Bowie, founded in 1911.

Training for black high school teachers was available at Morgan Academy (a Methodist Church school in Baltimore) and Princess Anne Academy (its branch on the Eastern Shore). Other institutions included Hampton Institute in Virginia, Dover College in Delaware, Cheyney Normal School in Pennsylvania, and Tuskegee Institute in Alabama.

A report compiled in 1940 revealed that, on the elementary school level, one black teacher held a Bachelor of Science degree, fifteen possessed advanced first grade college degrees (or equivalent degrees), and sixty-two had first grade college degrees and elementary principal certification. On the secondary school level, thirteen black teachers had college degrees. In reference to that report, all ninety-one black teachers in Anne Arundel County met the academic requirements of the Maryland State Department of Education and, therefore, were fully certified as teachers. Of the 243 white teachers that were employed in Anne Arundel County at that time, there was no mention of how many were fully certified as teachers.

Contrary to the aforementioned finding and in response to Judge W. Calvin Chesnut's questions, Anne Arundel County Superintendent George Fox related that "his poorest white teacher was a better teacher than his best colored teacher." Since "the white children were usually higher than or ahead of the colored children on various achievement tests and in any other [comparison]," he concluded that the white children must have better teachers. That was the rationale by which Superintendent Fox justified paying white teachers more than black teachers.

On November 22, 1939, Judge W. Calvin Chesnut declared the discontinuance of the discrimination in teacher salaries on the basis of race or color. On January 11, 1940, Judge Chesnut signed a final judgment and decree, and eventually the counsel for both sides formulated plans for the edict's implementation. After the Board of Education's acceptance of the equalization of teacher salaries on September 1, 1940, all Anne Arundel County teachers were put on the same salary schedule for the first time.

Likewise, the black children had legislation passed in their favor. For the first time, the two races had identical school years after the legislature, passed a bill in 1937that would equalize the school term.

Philip L. Brown

In spite of the School Board's approval of salary parity, Superintendent Fox continued to embrace the idea that the white teachers were superior instructors and informed the teachers that there would be two classifications - First Class and Second Class. Most black teachers were categorized as Second Class. Teachers with that rating did not receive raises for teaching experience until they were classified as First Class. The annual difference in salary between First Class and Second Class teachers was $250. At that rate, it required a considerable amount of time for black teachers classified as Second Class to catch up with their white counterparts, who had been classified as First Class from the beginning.

Lincoln High School 1938-1940: Faculty & Transportation

At the start of the 1938-1939 school year, the first school yearbook staff was organized. *Le Memoir* was chosen as the title of the yearbook, since all of its staff members took French.

The 1938-1939 school year was significant in the history of Lincoln High School because it marked the beginning of the eighteen-year Moore dynasty. With the appointment of Parlett L. Moore (Mathematics, Howard University graduate, Master's Degree recipient from Columbia University, native of the Eastern Shore) as principal, an end was put to the frequent changes in principalship that had taken place in the previous 11 years. Six principals preceeded Dr. Moore, who left St. Clair High School in Cambridge to be principal of Lincoln. A man of remarkable widsom and high intellect, Dr. Moore was a driving force behind the education of his students. He simultaneously served as an instructor of education at Morgan State College in Baltimore, and in 1950 established George Washington Carver Junior College in 1950. Dr. Moore served as principal of Lincoln until June 1956, when he accepted the presidency of Coppin State Teachers College in Baltimore.

The 1938-1939 school year was the first time since the year 1935-1936 that there was an increase in Lincoln's faculty members (from six to seven). As already stated, Dr. Moore succeeded Herbert H. Norton (who remained as an agriculture teacher). C. H. Johnson and Caleb Rhoe did not resume their teaching assignments and were replaced by Milton Turner and Allen T. Brown.

At the outset of the 1939-1940 school year, one teacher (Milton Turner) failed to return, and he was replaced by first-year teacher Maso P. Ryan, a June 1939 graduate of Morgan State College in Baltimore and a native of Newark, New Jersey. Mr. Ryan taught mathematics, science, and physical education for two years prior to relocating to his home city to teach.

In the early 1940s, transportation was still a problem, especially for students who attended school outside of their home counties. At least one family had this problem. It is known that a family of three girls braved the wintry weather as they walked approximately three miles from their home in Howard County to meet a school bus which went to Lincoln High School in Montgomery County. They chose to tolerate this ordeal because there was no school bus or other mode of transportation to carry them from their community to Cooksville High School in Howard County. During those cold, wind-swept days, these sisters came home crying many evenings, because their hands and feet were aching from the bitter cold weather. They continued this dreaded walk until they obtained live-in jobs in Montgomery County. These three sisters endured this hardship to fulfill their cherished dream—a better quality of life.

There was at least one other family of girls who had to decide whether to attend a high school outside of their home county. Two sisters lived in Montgomery County close to the Frederick County line. One of the sisters chose to attend Lincoln High School in Frederick, which was closer to their home, whereas the other sister opted to enroll at Lincoln High in Rockville, which, although it was in their home county, was a much longer ride.

Lincoln High School 1940-1941: Extracurriculars

At the start of Lincoln High's sixth year (1940-1941), the faculty was increased by one: S. Eloise Levister, a native of Rye, New York, and a graduate of West Virginia State College. Miss Levister brought a wealth of expertise to the faculty. She taught English and music, and she was instrumental in organizing the Lincoln Chapter of the National Honor Society in the fall of that year. She became interested in NHS because she was the first black student to be inducted into the Rye High School National Honor Society.

The Lincoln High School Chapter of the National Honor Society was organized in 1940. Its purpose was to recognize those students in the ninth grade and above who were above average scholastically. Miss S. Eloise Levister and Mr. Parlett L. Moore were the faculty advisers. The chapter was established by the Dunbar High School Chapter of Washington, DC.

The charter members of the Lincoln High School National Honor Society were Kathline Johnson, Betty Prather, Norman B. Ridgley, Maude Smith, Mable D. Thomas and Roland Wims.

This elite organization was instituted to inspire the academically talented students and to stimulate the development of their leadership skills as they served the school morally. It was built on four cardinal principles—scholarship, leadership, character, and service. Any student, above the eighth grade, who showed an impressive attainment of these principles was eligible to be inducted into this prominent society at a candlelight service.

During her second year at Lincoln High, Miss Levister organized a girl's singing group that performed at assemblies and other school programs. Not only was she a competent teacher, she was also a very skilled pianist.

In January 1941, Allen T. Brown, teacher of French, history, and guidance, sought employment elsewhere and was replaced by Martha A. Settle.

Some of the extracurricular activities that took place during the 1930s, prior to World War II, included debates (held in community churches), annual field days, exhibits, oratorical contests, junior-senior prom, senior class night, and commencement. Students who joined the school's Dramatic Club participated in plays that were presented twice a year in the school's auditorium.

Field Day was a day, set aside in April by the Montgomery County Board of Education, when Lincoln High School teams (boys & girls) competed in track and field events as well as ball games (volleyball & softball). The winners in each event were awarded medals - gold, silver, and bronze. The following Saturday, the first-place winners of all Western Shore county schools competed at Bowie Normal (now Bowie State University), while the Eastern Shore first-place winners competed at Princess Anne College (now University of Maryland Eastern Shore). The next Saturday, the Western Shore first-place winners competed against the Eastern Shore first-place winners for the championship in each event.

The members of the Lincoln High School newstaff worked diligently to publicize the news of school activities and current events. They used this opportunity to express their opinions and ideals, to report noteworthy events, and to exhibit their creativity. Their motto was "Truth and Loyalty."

The school paper, *Lincoln High School News*, was published biannually and was sold at ten cents per copy. It enabled individuals who were not involved with Lincoln High School to discover what was taking place in the lives of high school students there.

The program-coordinating committee was a new committee formed in the 1941-1942 school year with eight students and a faculty member. It coordinated the presentation of suitable programs to celebrate the holidays that occurred during the school year. It also chose monthly movies, that had an instructional value, to be shown to the student body.

Lincoln High School During World War II: The Victory Corps

During the early 1940s, schools across the nation unanimously wanted to help bring about a victorious close to the war in Europe. Groups began to form throughout the U.S. under the name, Victory Corps. By 1942, representative professors and instructors from such rallying communities met together in Washington, D.C. to formalize their efforts within a national program. Here, too, they decided upon a common method by which children could contribute—collecting needed scrap and selling war stamps and bonds.

At Lincoln High School, the Victory Corps program organized the students and faculty into six different groups. An instructor was assigned to lead each group and a community representative served as a counselor. Within the six divisions, student officers directed the Victory Corps activities.

Throughout the year, the Victory Corps organized projects such as scrap drives, in which tin cans, silk stockings, coat hangers, books, old rubber, and iron were collected. Many of the girls in the Corps looked after community children, while mothers were called on to perform special duties. Other members worked with the American Red Cross, while still others offered to fill positions abandoned by men drafted to the war—tending farms, for instance. Students also volunteered in areas such as the school's lunchroom, library, and School Patrol, and they joined efforts to recycle envelopes needed for rationing registration. Alternative jobs included providing messenger service for the community's civilian defense groups, as well as maintaining correspondence with the Lincoln graduates enlisted in the military. Lincoln's Victory Corps also raised enough money to purchase a service flag to honor former classmates who had been drafted to fight in the war. Most of the students and faculty involved in the Victory Corps efforts also planted their own "victory gardens."

The student officers of the Victory Corps established and distributed a bulletin that outlined these projects. The publication also included a roster of members and a list of faculty and student officers.

In 1942-43, for example, sophomore Maxine Claggett stood as president, while sophomore Doris Plummer acted as secretary. In turn, faculty advisors, like Mary C. Moore in 1942, supervised the activities of the student officers. The following year, Warrick S. Hill represented the same class, as Victory Corps vice president, under the guidance of faculty advisor, Thelma L. Gray-Barnum. It was under Barnum's instruction that, for the first time since the program began, student aid for the war was limited to selling bonds and raising money for relief. By 1944-45, Hill was the only remaining Victory Corps officer from the class of 1945.

The dedicated volunteerism of these Victory Corps members in aiding the war effort exemplified their spirited motto: "Victory is won by hard work."

Faculty and Graduation

The 1941-42 school year commenced with four new teachers, making a faculty of nine. Elsie Dorsey (home economics, a graduate of Hampton Institute in Virginia, and a native of Montgomery County) succeeded Alberta Mebane; Ruby E. Morris (Spanish, English, French) replaced Martha A. Settle; James T. Robinson (mathematics, physical education) replaced Maso P. Ryan, and Mary C. Moore was the new girls physical education teacher.

With 51 students, the Class of 1942 was the largest class to graduate from Lincoln High School until the Class of 1947, which graduated 58 students.

The 1942 -1943 school year was distinct in the sense that there was no formal commencement in June, and a science building (with two classrooms) was added in 1943.

Up until this time, eleventh graders graduated and enrolled in a college or joined the work force. That year, two of the eleventh graders—Gladys Owens and Betty Prather—fulfilled all the Maryland State Department of Education requirements for graduation and were merely handed their diplomas in June without pomp and circumstance. Because the twelfth grade was added that academic year, there was no graduation. The rest of the class waited another year prior to reaching that milestone. In compliance with an order from the state during the 1943-1944 school year, Lincoln High School received its 12-year program (nearly twelve years) after the Montgomery County white high schools.

The faculty continued to grow; the year was started with a total of 12 faculty members, four of whom were new. Doris M. Greene (home economics, a graduate of Princess Anne College in Maryland) replaced Elsie

Dorsey; Armentris P. Hooks (history, a graduate of Johnson C. Smith University in N.C., a native of Philadelphia) replaced Josephine Gordon, Maynard E. McPherson (acetylene welding), and Elizabeth Slade (home economics, a graduate of Hampton Institute) were additional teachers. Midway through the first half of the year, Lemuel A. Thomas (mathematics, physical education) replaced James T. Robinson, who resigned to seek employment elsewhere. To respond to the girls' musical needs, S. Eloise Levister organized the Lincoln High School Girls Octette in October 1942. The girls sang in two-part harmony in many school programs, including annual Thanksgiving, Christmas, Easter, and commencement programs.

The Lincoln High School Class of 1945 advisor, Genevieve Swann Brown, was peerless as a classroom teacher. Wearing many hats, Mrs. Brown skillfully taught every subject in the curriculum except foreign language, shop, home economics, and music, as well as coaching girl's sportsteams and a United States history team that won over big city-school teams in Washington, DC. Mrs. Brown's students were grateful for her exceptional instruction, her wise counsel, and her competent leadership. During the school year 1949-1950, she was apppointed vice principal of Lincoln High School, and she retired as vice principal of Carver Senior High School in February, 1952. Subsequent to her retirement from Montgomery County Public Schools, she relocated to Charles County and became a Charles County Supervisor of Education.

Wartime Precautions

Since the United States was involved in World War II, it was necessary to learn safety precautions. As a result, the Welfare and Safety Committee was instituted in September of 1942 to formulate rules and procedures to be followed during air raid and fire drills. Monthly air raid and fire drills were held at Lincoln High School, during World War II, to familiarize the student body with the emergency procedures. In case of an air raid, the students in the main building were instructed to proceed to the hall, face the wall, and shield their heads with their hands. The students in the shop and home economics building, and later the science building, were directed to move to the wall farthest from the windows (to be as far away as possible from flying glass) and follow the same procedure. Dark curtains were pulled down over the windows to shut out the light and restrain flying glass.

In the case of a fire, all students were instructed to evacuate the building and proceed, in a quiet and orderly fashion, to a designated area 200 feet from each building. Once outside the building, the students stood quietly in a single-file line and awaited their teacher, who was instructed to call the roll. After all students had been accounted for, the principal or his designee rang the all-clear bell as a signal for the students and teachers to return to their respective classrooms.

The School Safety Patrol, sponsored by agriculture teacher Herbert H. Norton, was on duty to assist in these drills when and where needed. It was also responsible for helping the Transportation Committee solve problems involving safety and protection on the school buses.

Attendance Policies

The Lincoln High School Committee, a standing committee, was instituted in the 1943–1944 academic year to encourage students to attend school regularly, to assist the teachers in reporting irregular attendants as well as unlawful absentees, and to help the teachers in the preparation of reports. Frequently, many boys and girls stayed at home to assist their parents with the farm and home chores. Only illness of the student or death in the family was considered a legal absence.

The 1943-1944 school year was history-making because, for the first time, Lincoln High School students had the opportunity to get twelve years of education. Before becoming a junior-senior high school with grades eight through twelve, Lincoln High had operated with grades eight through eleven for eight years.

Lincoln High School also had two more teachers, making a total of fourteen. In the fall of 1943, Thelma L. Gray (physical education, a graduate of Hampton Institute, a native of Americus, GA) replaced Mary C. Moore. The additional teachers included Jessie M. Drummond (mathematics and science, a graduate of Hampton Institute, a native of Newport News, VA) and Clarence L. Bond (shop and agriculture, a native of Lewistown, NC).

It is surprising that Montgomery County, a jurisdiction so close to the District of Columbia, which offered educational opportunities to blacks, was so slow in registering real progress to that end. Even deep south localities were ahead of the Montgomery County Public School System with regard to the education of black students. Lee County, Arkansas (a state dominated by a "cotton culture" and long labeled as "educationally backward"), began offering blacks twelve years of education in 1926, nearly a decade prior to Montgomery County.

Americana Quiz Broadcast

Not only did Lincoln High School athletic teams play the big-city teams, but the academic teams contended as well.

On Sunday, March 26, 1944, five Lincoln High School students— Helen Baker, Lillian Hayes, Violet Isreal, Mae Mitchell, and Mable D. Thomas—competed against five Armstrong High School students on radio station WMAL in Washington, D.C., in a history quiz. The Armstrong High School students, in jest, remarked about being in competition with a little country-school team. After leading the Lincoln High School team for two rounds, the Armstrong crowd rejoiced. However, they failed to realize that the race is not always won by the swiftest runner. The determined Lincoln High School team came from behind to tie the score at the end of regulation, and Mable D. Thomas correctly answered a ten-point bonus question to lead her team to an upset victory over a then-humbled Armstrong team. Helen, Lillian, Violet, Mae, and Mable each received five silver dollars as prizes for their unexpected victory.

The Draft

After the United States entered World War II, Uncle Sam made a rule that every male, 18-37 years of age, had a military obligation and would be eligible for the draft. They could serve in one of the four branches of the United States armed forces. Since Charles Frazier, Carlton Garrison, and Paul Fayne would reach their eighteenth birthdays almost a year before graduation, Principal Parlett L. Moore designed an accelerated course which would permit them to take their required junior and senior year subjects simultaneously, to fulfill their Maryland State requirements. Thereby, they could earn their high school diplomas with the Class of 1944.

During that school year (1943-1944), the student body felt the effects of World War II. Without taking the accelerated courses, some of the boys reached their eighteenth birthday before they had fulfilled the Maryland State Department of Education requirements for graduation and were drafted into one of the four branches of the armed forces. Others volunteered to serve in the armed forces.

Two members of the Class of 1945—Clifton N. Burgess and Charles E. Wood—had their education at Lincoln High School interrupted by a call to perform military duty, and after their honorable discharges, they returned to Lincoln High and obtained their high-school diploma.

Some of the white eighteen-year-olds were allowed to complete their high school education by occupational deferment, which local draft boards were entitled to bestow. The Selective Service, popularly known as the draft, was the agency which recruited young men for military service. In September 1940, Congress enacted the peacetime draft—the Burke-Wadsworth Act—by surprisingly large margins in both the House of Representatives and the Senate. The Selective Service Act originally called for the drafting of men between the ages of twenty-one and thirty-six (October 16, 1940). Later, by an act of Congress, induction was limited to men twenty-one through twenty-seven years of age.

At the end of that academic year, for various reasons (drop-outs, draftees, transferees, volunteers), there were 97 fewer students than there were at the end of the previous year. Fortunately, no male teach-

ers were drafted during World War II and our education was not interrupted.

When the United States declared war, the draft law was changed so
that the President had the power to defer men by age group. In November
1942, the conscription of eighteen and nineteen-year-old men began, and
the upper age limit was extended to thirty-seven. This remained the age
span for the duration of the war.

Segregation in the Military

Until 1943, many eligible black men were passed over for the draft
because of doubts about their physical and mental ability to serve, as well
as racist fears about the mingling of black and white soldiers. Regardless,
blacks were drafted in large numbers when uniformed manpower was in
short supply, and they served mostly in labor units. However, this practice
changed in the later stages of the war.

Segregation was the official policy that kept black and white servicemen
and servicewomen in separate military units. In 1940, the United States
Army had 12 black officers and 5,000 black soldiers. The Army Corps and
the Marine Corps did not accept blacks, and until 1942, the Navy admitted
them only as messboys. Even when blacks were later given other positions,
ninety percent of the Navy's blacks were still messboys. Black paratroop-
ers fought forest fires in the United States.

Under pressure from black leaders, President Franklin Delano
Roosevelt established the Fair Employment Practices Commission, which
would cancel government contracts of defense-industry employers who
practiced discrimination. But this partial breakdown in the segregation
practices in civilian life did not carry over to military service.

As the war progressed, the armed forces and affiliates relaxed their
policies with regards to black soldiers. The Army, Air Force and Marine
Corps finally began to accept them. The black marines were placed in a
non-combat segregated infantry battalion, and the Navy commissioned a
handful of black officers. Initially, the Red Cross blood banks refused blood
from blacks. They later accepted it, but isolated it from the other blood.

Prior to the war, the NAACP had campaigned vigorously for the integration of the armed services. Early in 1942, then Brigadier General Dwight D. Eisenhower, as liaison between the Army and the State Department, noted that the War Plans Division (later Operations Division) decided to send white and black troops overseas as American troops. Official bans on black troops were made by Greenland, Iceland, Labrador, Panama, and even Alaska, where black engineer units would help to build the Alcan Highway. Most of the men in the Engineers force that built the 271-mile Ledo Road (a road completed in January 1945 in the China-Burma-India Theater that connected the railway in northeast India with the Chinese end of the old Burma Road) were black. Chinese officials requested that black units not be used near Kunming because western Chinese had never seen blacks.

Additionally, in an April 1943 memo, Army Chief of Staff General George C. Marshall stated that the Negro troops should be placed where they will best serve the war effort. Whereas it had been Army policy to disregard blacks' desire for a proportionate share of combat units.

By December 1944, heavy casualties in European combat units created a sudden demand for more men and forced the Army into involuntary integration. Within two months, 4,562 black soldiers showed their patriotic spirit when they volunteered for combat. Many of them were noncommissioned officers who opted for demotion to transfer from supply-handling tasks to infantry units. They went into combat in platoons or companies, and sometimes as individuals. An Army study revealed that about two-thirds of the men in the average white company disliked the

Physical Education class, Lincoln High School (1943-44)

idea of mixed-race companies prior to the entrance of a black platoon into the company. The white servicemen and civilians frequently clashed with the black and Mexican-American servicemen. But following the test of combat, the percentage dropped dramatically to seven percent.

By the war's end, according to United States Army historian Ulysses Lee: "The services had learned that segregation hurt the war effort, because it wasted black man-power, lowered unit effectiveness, and created unnecessary racial tension. In the end, the war prompted the first small steps toward integrated military units and laid the foundation for the armed forces postwar desegregation."

The Effects of the War on Schooling

During World War II, the students at Montgomery Blair High School (all-white) and those at Lincoln High School (all-black), in some cases, had different experiences and, in other cases, were in similar situations.

The Blair High School students had the privilege of graduating from the twelfth grade, but the Lincoln High School students did not until the school year 1943-1944, when twenty-two students graduated grade twelve. The Blair student body was about twice the size of Lincoln's student population. The Blair Class of 1945 had slightly more than four times the number of graduates (165) as Lincoln's Class of 1945 (39).

At Blair High School, the teacher shortage became so critical that by 1943, Blair students were sometimes teaching younger schoolmates. John Benedict (Class of 1943) remembers that his wife taught geometry during her senior year, and when the baseball coach departed for the war, a University of Maryland football player coached the football team and taught the physical education classes.

Although World War II brought about a reduction in the Lincoln School enrollment, it had little impact on the number of Lincoln High School alumni. Norman Briscoe Ridgely (Class of 1942), a member of the United States Navy, was the only known casualty during World War II.

When the United States declared war on Japan, an added responsibility was placed on the citizens' shoulders. To help meet this challenge, Lincoln High School added three pre-induction courses—pre-flight aeronautics, electricity, and acetylene welding—to its offerings.

The pre-flight aeronautics class began on October 5, 1942, with 16 pupils enrolled and Herbert H. Norton as the teacher. After two boys and one girl withdrew, the others continued and qualified to take the theoretical examination given by the Civil Aeronautics Administration.

Mr. Norton taught the course in electricity, as well. It was a beneficial course because it involved a number of projects that served to prepare students for war-related technology, some of which included minor electrical repairs and wiring a hot-point electric stove.

Maynard E. McPherson, a part-time welding teacher employed by the Federal Government, taught acetylene welding at Lincoln High School, in the morning, and at Montgomery Blair High School (Silver Spring), in the afternoon. It was only open to boys and girls who were seventeen years and nine months of age and who were planning to seek employment at the close of the school year. The class gained valuable experience in welding broken parts of school buses and making tables and stools for shops in the county.

Wartime Extracurricular Activities

Realizing the seriousness of the crisis which enveloped the country, the Dramatic Club selected three comedies that impressed Americans with the problems they faced. On December 11, 1942, the Garnet Masque Club presented "Wildcat Willie Buys a Bond," "Paul Faces the Tire Shortage,"and "Pig of My Dreams." The plays were enjoyable, interesting, and financially successful. Two Class of 1945 classmates held offices in the Dramatic Club—Annie Procton (President) and Doris Plummer (Assistant Secretary).

Realizing the need for relief from the cares of the war-torn world, the club sponsors and members selected three light comedies —"Be Home by Midnight," "Swept Clear off Her Feet," and "Paul Loses the Ration Book"—that were presented in the high school auditorium on Thursday, February 24, 1944.

Basketball

A new sport, basketball, was introduced to boys in Lincoln High in November of 1944. None of the boys had ever played basketball before, so second-year teacher, Thelma Gray, had taken on a monumental task as coach. She taught the boys the basic skills of dribbling, passing, and shooting a basketball. Then she taught several plays that were practiced during scrimmages. Without the availability of a gymnasium, the basketball team was transported by school bus to Fisherman's Hall in Rockville to practice, and later to play its home games. Only two seniors, William B. Cooke and Warrick S. Hill, were members of the team.

The team's first opponent was Douglass High School in Upper Marlboro, Maryland. That game proved to be more than a challenge for Lincoln High's inexperienced players. Lincoln High's defense was no match for their fast-dribbling, sharp-shooting, more experienced Douglass High opponents. Principal Moore, observing the frustration on the faces of the players and eyeing the unbalanced scoreboard, proceeded to encourage the players during a time out. He promised each player a nickel for each basket that he made. However, Principal Moore's incentive, along with the support of the cheerleaders, did little to silence the big guns of the Douglass High Eagles.

Following the game, Mr. Moore and other faculty members transported the disheartened team and cheerleaders back to their respective communities in Montgomery County by car. Whereas the 1945 basketball team was displeased with the agony of defeat, it is worth noting that in 1949, Lincoln High's team, under the tutelage of Coach John Harvey, won the Maryland State Basketball Championship among the black high school teams.

Negro History Class

In February 1945, Mr. David W. Hazel gave an unforgettable Negro History class that focused on the impressive contributions that prominent Negroes made in American history.

Many blacks achieved prominence despite hardship and discrimination.

Although uneducated, for the most part, and in a few instances self-educated, black men and women rose above their inferior conditions and made significant contributions that helped to shape the course of American history. The black achievers studied included abolitionists, athletes, authors, educators, inventors, lawyers, musicians, performing artists, polar explorers and scientists.

Black people have a rich history, and the members of the senior class of 1945 were fortunate to acquire a greater knowledge of their heritage. They realized that those black achievers accomplished what they did partly because America's democratic system and ideals made it possible, although the price they paid in their struggle for equality in the United States was costly. They concluded that, in view of the notable achievements that have been made, black people should show a deep appreciation toward their predecessors and should strive with determination and integrity to continue to make advances.

Bernetta Hawkins graduated from Lincoln High School in 1947. Twenty-six years later, in June 1973, Bernetta and her daughter, Angela Ricks, both received their diplomas as graduates of the Opportunities Industrialization Course (OIC), which taught skills to the underemployed and the unemployed. They were among 83 Montgomery Countians who graduated, and for their diligence and optimism, this noteworthy achievement earned them jobs as clerk-typists.

During the 1930s and 1940s, there were student transfers out of Montgomery County. Some of the transferees were Lila Cole (Garnet Patterson Junior High School, Dunbar High School, Class of 1940), Helen Cooke (Dunbar High School Class of 1932), Margaret Cooke (New York, Class of 1932), Stanley C. Selby (Washington, Class of 1945), Thelma Smith (Central High School, Kalamazoo, Michigan, Class of 1945), Jane Hood (Banneker Junior High School, Dunbar High School Class of 1946), Thelma Ramey (New York Class of 1946), Elizabeth Ferrell (Cardozo High School Class of 1947), Mary E. Thomas (Dunbar High School Class of 1947), Florence Windear (Dunbar High School Class of 1946), Irene Snowden (Dunbar High School Class of 1948). This exodus from Montgomery County was due to such problems as family tradition, the failing health of a relative, the loss of a parent, and lack of transportation.

CARVER HIGH SCHOOL:
1950-1960

I n little more than a decade, the Lincoln High School enrollment nearly tripled. This rapid growth necessitated another series of petitions, by the United Trustees, to the Montgomery County Board of Education, for an even larger building than the second one. The School Board approved of a $750,000 structure, equipped with classrooms, a gymnasium, an auditorium, shops, a library, offices, restrooms and a cafeteria. The first section of the new Carver High School and Junior College was built at a cost of $380,000 on Norris Street Rockville Pike, Route 240 (now Rockville Pike, Route 355), one-half mile north of the Rockville courthouse. The new edifice was established on August 9, 1950. By persistent negotiation with the Montgomery County Board of Education, the community leaders made a significant difference in the lives of hundreds of teenagers who wanted to improve their standard of living via better education. In an increasingly complex, technological society, Carver High School, the last and most adequate of the three traditionally segregated buildings that served as high schools, was an answer to prayers. The building and equipping of Carver High School as a first-rate senior high school was indicative of some of the steps that Montgomery County made toward providing equal educational opportunities for black high school students.

As the first and only senior high school (grades 10-12) in Montgomery County for black students, it was fully accredited and offered four curricula—academic, commercial (typewriting, shorthand, office practice),

Carver High School

general, and vocational courses—that prepared some students for college placement and provided others with marketable skills for immediate employment.

Initially, Carver High School housed Carver Junior College, which, with 45-65 part-time enrollees, opened on August 9, 1950. Dr. Parlett L. Moore established the Junior College because the black high school graduates were not admitted to Montgomery Junior College in 1946 at that time.

In September of 1951, the Class of 1952 had the distinction of being the first senior class to enroll at Carver High School, and five new faculty members came aboard: John A. Jones, Calvin C. Rubens, Mrs. Blance T. Vessels, Mrs. Ruby E. Washington, and Lorenzo A. Woodward. The 1951-1952 faculty of 21 had 2 more members than that of the previous year and was responsible for 307 students.

The Class of 1952 broke the previous record of 74 graduates (established by the Class of 1950) in June 1952, with a total of 75 graduates who marched to "War March of the Priests" and "Pomp and Circumstance" at their commencement. This record remained unbroken for the next eight years until segregated public schools became history.

In Montgomery County, and throughout the seventeen Southern states, as well as the District of Columbia, boys and girls were separated by sex for certain subjects. But it was the rule, rather than the exception, that they were separated by race in educational facilities. The issues of inequality were challenged in courts until May 17, 1954, when the U.S. Supreme Court decided that separateness in education was in violation of the Fourteenth Amendment to the Constitution. However, immediate integration did not take place nationwide. Public schools in Maryland's Montgomery County did not integrate completely until the school year 1960-1961.

History of Segregation

The policy of race separation was practiced in the public arena—in education, entertainment, transportation, restaurants, and sporting events— only in white establishments. On the other hand, black businesses admitted white customers as long as they paid their admission fees. For instance, whenever big-name musicians (Lionel Hampton, Duke Ellington, Earl "Fatha" Hines, Louis Jordan, Cab Calloway, Count Basie, Louis Armstrong, Charlie "Bird" Parker, Fats Domino) and notable singers (Nat King Cole, Ella Fitzgerald, Ruth Brown, Lena Horne, Chuck Berry) came to the Howard Theatre on Seventh and T streets, in northwest D.C., both races mingled in the black facility, enjoying the entertainment together.

In the South, education had always been divided by race, as well as the churches (by the blacks' own desire). But before 1890, there was virtually no race separation in other public areas.

The editor of a Negro newspaper in New York went south looking for trouble, but found none. In general, white and black individuals mingled on railroad and street cars, at lunch counters, in theaters, at circuses, and in public parks.

Under Chief Justice Melville W. Fuller, the United States Supreme Court, in the 1896 Plessy v. Ferguson decision, gave legal sanction to the "Jim Crow" laws. The Supreme Court decided that a state law that required federal railroad trains to provide separate but equal facilities for Negro and white travelers neither infringed upon the Thirteenth (abolition of slavery) and Fourteenth amendments (citizenship for former slaves), nor violated federal authority to regulate interstate commerce. Thus, this rule gave birth to the "separate-but-equal" decision, which was effective until the 1954 Brown v. Board of Education decision brought about its reversal.

The "Jim Crow Laws" was the term applied to the new segregation mandates. The usage of the term "Jim Crow" began in the 1880s. Jim Crow, a white actor in black face in a popular minstrel show around 1855, performed a song-and-dance routine, the theme of which was "Jump, Jim Crow!" The name referred to a Negro character in an old song, and was used as an insult thereafter.

Jim Crow cars, on the passenger trains, were the first to have the term applied; followed by Jim Crow waiting rooms and lavatories, Jim Crow sections of street cars and buses, and Jim Crow entrances to circuses, factories, and the like.

White nurses were forbidden to attend Negro patients in hospitals, and vice-versa. Black individuals were not permitted (except as servants) at lunch counters, in bars, and in white-owned restaurants. Negro drivers, if they managed to obtain licenses, were not permitted to transport white passengers when taxicabs came into existence. For the most part, those restrictions began in the lower South and moved northward. On the other hand, the legal zoning of cities into black and white residential districts started in Baltimore in 1910 and spread southward. Segregation reached its peak in Washington, D.C., under President Woodrow Wilson (1913-1916), when all government offices, restaurants, and lavatories were segregated. For the most part, they were not integrated until the Franklin Delano Roosevelt administration.

Nominally, Jim Crow laws were passed for sanitary and sexual reasons, as Negroes were thought to be diseased, lousy, and lusting after white females. The hypocrisy of such claims lies in the fact that Negroes were in great demand as nurses and domestic servants, even when they refused to "live-in" and instead slept in their own homes.

In reality, the purpose of the Jim Crow laws was not sanitary and sexual protection, but work to instill a sense of inferior status in blacks. The Jim

Crow policy had an irresistible appeal to poor whites (who hired no domestic servants) because, even in their poor, illiterate, and diseased conditions, they could feel superior to their servants as a way to overcome their own self-loathing.

Jim Crow laws forced all black people, with hat in hand, to address even the most disreputable whites as "Sir," or "Ma'am." On the other hand, black individuals, no matter how respectable, had to be satisfied with "boy" or "girl," or if elderly, with "Uncle" or "Aunty."

The failure of a black male to remove his hat in the presence of white individuals or to step off a sidewalk when whites approached led to a nightmarish experience for him. Such an alleged act of insolence resulted in his being pulled out of his cabin and severely whipped. Moreover, lustful white males were at liberty to take advantage of Negro women without fear of punishment, but, on the other hand, if a Negro male glanced evilly at a white female, even one with a low reputation, he was liable to be lynched by a mob in defense of the alleged purity of "Southern womanhood."

Racial discrimination was practiced not only in the South, but in the North as well. Certain residential areas, usually overcrowded slums, were the only places in which Negroes who migrated to the North could find homes. For the most part, they were not accepted as members of labor organizations. The only jobs that they were assured of getting were as servants or as unskilled laborers.

By 1870, in Washington, D.C., black and white students were taught English grammar, geography, history, penmanship, spelling, and arithmetic in separate public schools. All students were administered oral and written tests on a regular basis.

In 1871, before students completed the ninth grade they were required to spell and understand a long list of words from "abridgement" to "zoophyte," as well as name four notable events that took place during Thomas Jefferson's first term of office as President of the United States.

Throughout the 1870s, Negro students between the ages of six and seventeen attended public schools in larger proportions than their white counterparts. In fact, the percentage of black students in that age group actually enrolled in public schools (which always exceeded 50 percent during the 1870s) rose to more than seventy percent by the 1878-1879 school year.

The curriculum for black adults lacked the elaborateness of that for white children, for it included only arithmetic, reading, spelling, and writing.

Despite local opposition, the education of Washington Negroes received adequate support from high levels of the federal government. Congress passed legislation to improve the schooling of Negroes and, in 1867, President Ulysses S. Grant approved the establishment of a federal bureau of education to assure the federal government's involvement in the education of the freed slaves.

Another glaring example of the separation of the two races occurred in the summer of 1951, when the white "school patrol (students selected, by a faculty member, to serve as safety monitors at the schools and on the school buses) was treated to a day at Glen Echo with lunch furnished by local businessmen. Jim Crow laws kept Glen Echo solidly white, and the black school patrol, sponsored by the police department, went to Emory Grove campgrounds. Glen Echo Park was a white-owned amusement park, while Emory Grove Campgrounds was a black-owned park in which, initially, annual religious services (camp meetings) were held on the last three Sundays in August. Later, it served primarily as a park where baseball games were played between local teams.

In Maryland's Montgomery County, prior to 1954, elementary and high school white students rode a bus to school free of charge; whereas, all black elementary school students walked to school, some as many as five miles each way. On the other hand, most black high school students rode a bus to the county high school for a monthly fee—some more than 20 miles each way.

Brown v. Board of Education

Prior to the 1953-1954 school year, there was unrest in many jurisdictions of the United States because of the segregation of schools. Various

Carver High School Marching Band, 1953 Memorial Day Parade

discrimination lawsuits were filed in state courts, but only one noteworthy case reached the United States Supreme Court—Brown v. Board of Education of Topeka, Kansas. Oliver Brown objected to his eight-year-old daughter, Linda, passing a white school just four blocks from her home en route to a black school that was twenty-five blocks from her Topeka home. When Linda questioned the rationale behind the practice, her father decided that it was time for him to act. He took her to the local school, but the principal denied her admission. Mr. Brown sued the Board of Education, and the Brown v. Board of Education of Topeka, Kansas case was one of five lawsuits that the NAACP used to fight segregated education across the nation.

The school year 1953-1954 was a very significant one for black students who resided in the District of Columbia and the seventeen southern states that practiced racial discrimination. It was during that year that the highest federal court in the United States, the Supreme Court (with three of the nine justices being southerners), voted unanimously, on May 17, 1954, that separate educational facilities were in violation of the Fourteenth Amendment.

In the *Brown vs. Board of Education of Topeka* case, Chief Justice Earl

Warren, with the approval of the other justices—Hugo Black, Harold H. Burton, Tom C. Clark, William O. Douglas, Felix Frankfurter, Robert H. Jackson, Sherman Minton, and Stanley F. Reed—said, "Segregation of white and colored children in public schools has a detrimental effect upon the colored children. The impact is greater when it has been the sanction of the law, for the policy of separating the races is usually interpreted as denoting the inferiority of the Negro group. A sense of inferiority affects the motivation of a child to learn. Segregation with the sanction of the law, therefore has a tendency to retard the education and mental development of Negro children and to deprive them of some of the benefits they would receive in a racially integrated school system."

On May 17, 1954, when the Supreme Court clearly ruled that segregation be terminated in a timely fashion, the reluctant transformation of individual attitudes about race made the enactment of the new legislation difficult. The passage of that law failed to consider the depth and the tenacity of the racial opinions that had shaped the attitudes of many Americans for over 300 years.

In the 1950s, the desegregation of public schools was met with strong resentment in the Slave States—Alabama, Arkansas, Delaware, Florida, Georgia, Kentucky, Louisiana, Maryland, Mississippi, Missouri, North Carolina, Oklahoma, South Carolina, Tennessee, Texas, Virginia and West Virginia. Some individuals exhibited a wait-and-see attitude, whereas state governors threatened to annul public schools rather than to permit black and white students to attend the same school.

Integration in Several Maryland Counties

At the inception of integration, Maryland black public senior-high schools ceased to be centers of academic development for senior-high school students. Some became headquarters for the local board of education, some became middle schools, others housed sixth-graders.

Anne Arundel County's Bates High School opened as a racially desegregated school in September 1966. It was designated as Annapolis Middle

School that accomodated all of the ninth-graders in Annapolis and some of the tenth-graders from nearby communities.

In Calvert County, public schools were completely integrated by 1969. In Howard County, was achieved by 1963. Both counties had black high schools that were converted to learning centers or educational service centers. In Prince George's County, Douglass High School and Fairmount High School were the only black senior high schools that retained their names.

At the closure of black high schools, the principals were demoted; some senior-high-school teachers were placed in previously white junior-high schools, while others were transferred to previously white senior-high schools.

Montgomery County Schools

The May 17, 1954 decision was met with mixed reactions, from full embracement to bitter opposition. The prophetic response of Montgomery County Superintendent of Schools Forbes H. Norris was: "Integration here will be a slow process." On August 17, 1954, the Montgomery County Board of Education organized an Advisory Committee on Integration (composed of five black and fourteen white individuals), that recommended gradual integration of one grade each year, starting with the first grade. However, an executive committee from the black Parent Teacher Associations, along with six local PTAs from black schools, favored total annulment of segregation in public schools by September 1955.

But when the board of education hired 12 non-degree and 116 inexperienced white teachers to fill the existing vacancies for the fall of 1955, waves were created in the black community. Blacks felt that this was a grossly inequitable action, especially when there was a large number of experienced black teachers, with college degrees, who were available.

One leading white citizen said, "I believe the Negro child and the white child would be better off in segregated schools because black youngsters are as much as three years behind whites and need problem classes. Integration will be resisted with every force at our command."

Moreover, many individuals were furious with the school administrators because they were either too fast or too slow, too harsh or too lenient, or too resistant or too tolerant in their response to integration.

Resistance to Integration

Even though black residents were scattered throughout Montgomery County, black students represented only six percent of the school enrollment and relatively few of them resided in the suburbs, except in the Clara Barton and Takoma Park areas. Consequently, for the most part, integration affected the up-county schools. In Poolesville, fourteen black pupils desired to attend the local previously all-white school. In response to this request, 200 white parents assembled in the schoolyard and demonstrated their objection to integration. In the process, they urged the white children to stay home. As a safety precaution, School Superintendent Norris requested that the Montgomery County police escort the black students through the door and into their classrooms. However, it was Dr. Norris who ended up holding open the door and escorting the fourteen students to safety.

Opposition to integration continued to escalate. The Montgomery County Chapter of the Maryland Petition Committee passed petitions around the county to seek more supporters of segregation. Petition advocates arranged an organizational and planning session at Poolesville Town Hall, through which more support was gained. The proponents of segregation, led by "outsider" John Kasper, were adamant in their zeal to stop integration at all costs.

John Kasper, a race agitator fresh from inciting prejudicial mob action in the Deep South, was welcomed by the Poolesville residents, since his plan of action—to withhold white children from school in protest—coincided with theirs. His large group of up-county followers drew national attention, in 1956, with their repeated demonstrations against integration. That bold opposition to integration ceased when Superintendent Norris threatened court action for illegal absences from school. The pro-segregationists did not stop at holding "non-race-mixing" meetings in the Poolesville Town Hall. They demonstrated against "race-mixing" at

Poolesville High School, and then proceeded to Rockville, where they declared their commitment to segregation in a crowded meeting with the Montgomery County School Board.

Everett Severe, another "outside" race agitator from the South, organized the white farmers in Montgomery County to oppose integration. They met in barns at night to formulate plans for the prevention of race-mixing. As a result of all of these acts of racist resistance, Dr. Norris tendered his resignation in 1957.

The attitudes of racial superiority of many white residents, along with the Montgomery County School Board's flagrantly unjust treatment of its black citizens, were primary factors in historians Nina H. Clarke and Lillian S. Brown concluding that "desegregation was an agonizing process all over the county."

As the integration process began, Hanley J. Norment reported that "all black school supervisors were systematically demoted; principals became assistant principals or counselors, and nearly all high-school teachers were reassigned to lower level schools." Although nearly all black teachers held degrees and some even had postgraduate degrees from prestigious universities, they were thought to be ineligible to teach in white or integrated schools.

The emergence of integration raised the ire of many white residents in Montgomery County, as well as in other Southern jurisdictions. Numerous protests and threats reached the School Board in the form of letters, resolutions, and fiery comments in hearings. The Montgomery County School Board received "ugly" letters from two communities. In some of those letters, white parents declared emphatically that their children would not attend the same school as their maids' children. In public hearings, many white parents vehemently stated that "they would never let their children sit in schoolhouse seats where blacks once sat." That comment was mainly in regard to Carver High School, which was relatively new and which white school administrators were surprised to find in excellent condition when it later became the school board headquarters.

School Integration Delayed

Because the majority of the Montgomery County School Board members were unwilling to comply with the 1954 Supreme Court decision, school integration was delayed several years.

Rose Kramer was a former teacher and a School Board member who led the movement to integrate the Montgomery County public schools. She said, "I began pushing my Board to take this decision very seriously and take it as an opportunity to improve our system." In the School Board's reluctance to approve a change, they formed a commission to bring recommendations to them. Based on these suggestions, the School Board proposed that integration start one grade at a time, biennially. This idea brought vehement objection from Kramer, who said, "It will take us 24 years to achieve this. School integration is the Christian thing to do, you know." After these statements, according to Mrs. Kramer, "They were really embarrassed."

School integration began, on a limited scale, in September of 1955, with a few black teachers integrating previously all-white elementary schools. It was a slow process, as it took five years to integrate the elementary and secondary schools.

Beginning in September 1956, African-American students were selected for enrollment in white schools on the basis of their standardized test scores. This criterion was used to determine whether African-American students could survive academically in the classrooms of their neighborhood white schools with their white counterparts. In the classroom, hand-picked students did perform well, but harassment from white students on the bus was a real problem.

However, in accordance with public objections, Carver High was not to remain a school. Instead, the School Board chose to build Julius West Junior High School, in Rockville, and to convert Carver High, in June of 1960, into the Montgomery County Public Schools Headquarters after a $2 million renovation.

Some School Board members used integration-delaying tactics to prevent black children from attending previously all-white schools. Those flagrant actions caused Mrs. Kramer to publicly label them as "legally and morally wrong" acts.

In spite of the racial discord, many individuals believed that all Mont-

Carver High School Football Team, 1956

gomery County residents would obtain equal rights in the 1960s. However, attempts to desegregate schools and other public facilities frequently resulted in open protests—crosses were burned in front of churches, and restaurants, recreational centers, and some public schools even remained racially separated. It is noteworthy that current United States Representative Constance A. Morella relocated to Montgomery County in 1956, the year the demonstrations opposing the integration of public schools were held at Poolesville. Her first teaching assignment was at Poolesvilie High School, where she taught English and civics. During that same year, she helped to temper local hostilities toward the integration of schools.

Her teaching career, which spanned nine years in county public schools and fifteen years at Montgomery College, was followed by a successful political career in the Maryland House of Delegates. Then, in 1986, she was elected to the United States House of Representatives, where she has been serving for the past twelve years. However, her political involvement has not overshadowed her support of the education of Montgomery County students.

On Sunday, January 25, 1998, Representative Morella, along with four other panelists, related her experience as a former teacher during the integration process, at a symposium on integration—*The Montgomery County Experience*—held at the Montgomery County Public Schools Headquarters. Her responses to questions from the audience revealed her continued interest in and support of the education of Montgomery County public school students.

Another panelist at the symposium was former teacher and School Board member, Rose Kramer. She recalled that some of the School Board members, at that time, realized that change needed to be made, but when uncomplimentary letters from the proponents of segregation arrived, they were overwhelmed. Nevertheless, she was undaunted and began urging the School Board members to take seriously the Brown v. Board of Education decision.

In September 1956, Major General Thomas Prather was among the first five students to integrate Gaithersburg High School. This transfer reduced his twenty-five-mile school bus ride (to Carver High) to a five-mile bus ride. Prather and the others were academically successful, but some communities had no black students, and to integrate those schools black teachers were appointed. Allison H. Claggett and Nina H. Clarke were two teachers who had that experience.

Other School Board panelists who were involved in the integration process included: Allison Claggett (former teacher and school liaison, Sandy

Carver High School: The school where parental involvement enhanced the teaching-learning process

Spring), John McGraw (former student, Gaithersburg), and Anita Summerour (former student, Rockville). Nina H. Clarke, former teacher and principal, paved the background for the discussion when she elaborated on the "Evolution of the Black Schools in Montgomery County." Afterward, Anita Neal Powell (President, Lincoln Park Historical Society) moderated the discussion.

By the fall of 1960, more than one-half of Montgomery County's public schools were integrated. Forty-two elementary and two high schools remained all-white, since "no Negroes lived in their immediate areas," related a School Board spokesman. Taylor Elementary School in Boyds and Rock Terrace Elementary in Rockville, two all-black elementary schools, were overcrowded and reportedly lacked adequate classroom space to be integrated. Later, Taylor Elementary was integrated.

Carver High School In The Fifties

The Carver High School Class of 1954 tied the record (75 graduates) set by the Class of 1952 and that record was never challenged thereafter. At the end of the school year, there were 309 students enrolled, 11 more than in June 1953.

At the end of the school year 1954-1955, there were 406 students on the roll, 97 more than there were in June 1954, and there were 8 fewer graduates (67). The following school year, there were 51 fewer students enrolled (355) and 11 fewer graduates (56) than in June 1955, under the instruction of 24 teachers.

The school year 1956-1957 concluded with 37 fewer students (318), fewer teachers (22), and 3 more graduates than the previous year. There was a decrease in the enrollment because of the implementation of a plan to transfer the high academic achievers to white schools near their homes. The first Carver High School students to integrate were Margaret Hawkins, Joyce Prather, Thomas Prather, Susie Smallwood, and Maurice Welsh, who were all assigned to Gaithersburg High School.

Margaret Hawkins was assigned a "buddy" to assist her in finding her way around in the new school. The students on the bus were quiet at first. She missed her former Carver High School classmates, but she "received fair treatment from (her) teachers and (her) classmates." As time passed, her fellow students became more relaxed and friendly toward her.

Thomas Prather, too, had to endure a difficult beginning at his new school. He recounted, "During the first two weeks, my classmates and bus students were quiet. When the information was disseminated among the students, 'He does not carry a knife,'" things improved. Thomas set out to disprove myths about African Americans to his white classmates, such as "(we) all carry knives, are confrontational, and can't cope academically." He also participated in the school band as first clarinet. Thomas later joined the U.S. Army and retired as a Major General in 1995.

Maurice Walsh "had no fear of being the lone black student on (his) bus or in (his) classes." He recalled that the "students became friendly and my teachers had a positive attitude." Still, Maurice missed his former classmates, and even attended the 1957 Carver High School Senior Prom. For all of the first Carver High School students to integrate, the experience was challenging.

Silas E. Craft (replaced Dr. Parlett L. Moore), Rufus Kelly (general science, chemistry, biology), Carrie B. Luck (physical education, graduate of Hampton Institute in Virginia, native of Annapolis), and Doris Mosley (librarian) were assigned to Carver High School that year. Six members of the faculty resigned: Dr. Parlett L. Moore (became president of Coppin State Teachers College in Baltimore), Bessie M. Hill (physical education, gradu-

*Carver High School
(East Enrtance)*

ate of Tuskegee Institute in Alabama, native of Montgomery County), Bernard E. Holsey (agriculture, graduate of Princess Anne College in Maryland, native of Montgomery County), John A. Jones, and Naomi Millender.

The school year 1957-1958 terminated with 55 more students (373), 2 more graduates (61) and 1 more teacher (23) than in June 1957. Mamie Clark (science) and George B. Thomas (replaced Mrs. Mosley as librarian) were recent arrivals.

The school year 1958-1959 ended with an increase of 123 students (496), 6 less graduates (55), and 5 more teachers (28).

The Last Year

In September 1959, the distinguished Class of 1960 walked the halls of Carver High School with mixed feelings. They were happy that they were soon to graduate, but also sad that their alma mater would no longer exist as an institution of learning where they could visit old friends and teachers in the future. As Carver High was slated to become the headquarters for the Montgomery County Board of Education, they had the distinction of being the last class to graduate from the school, and they vowed to be ever mindful to uphold its ideals and traditions.

When some Carver Alumni were interviewed, they gave mixed reactions to the U.S. Supreme Court's decision and to the closing of their alma mater. Some said that it was "too little, too late for their personal experience, but it would be beneficial to their younger relatives and schoolmates." Others said that they "accepted the challenge to be a part of the integrated process." On the other hand, one alumnus stated that she, among other alumni, considered it "a disadvantage to leave the instruction and guidance of the caring, well-qualified black teachers who were genuinely concerned about their students and who believed in their ability to achieve and excel." One alumnus said that he, along with other alumni, was "saddened by the closing of Carver," and he would miss his teachers who "were awesome in their ability to motivate and direct our thinking towards being the best that we could be." Still others mentioned that they would "miss the social bonding that prevailed at Carver."

At the end of Carver High's ninth and last year of existence (1959-1960), there were 50 fewer students (446), 2 fewer graduates (53), and 2 fewer teachers (26) than there were the previous year. The low student enrollment indicates that a larger number of high academic achievers transferred to the white schools that school year, which helped pave the way for total school integration.

The historic public school desegregation decision ruled separate educational facilities "inherently unequal," and set in motion a civil rights revolution that changed the nation forever. It brought about many changes in the educational and social lives of black students. For the most part, it was not readily accepted by the adult population; however, the students tended to be more amenable to it. It meant that most of the inequities —traveling long distances by bus, inadequate instructional materials, dilapidated buildings, unequal teachers' salaries—were history. The famous 1954 Supreme Court ruling denoted that the two races would learn together in the same classroom and would ride the same school bus. It also opened the door for public socialization between the two races. Finally, in paving the way for equality and justice in the education of Montgomery County students and the employment of teachers, it indirectly led to social integration of all theaters, restaurants, railroads, and other public facilities.

In 1960, at the closeure of Montgomery County's Carver Senior High, it became the headquarters for the Educational Services Center (now Montgomery County Public Schools) because of the strong opposition of some white parents who did not want their children to sit in seats that had been occupied by black children. It housed all of the administrative departments except Supporting Services and Reading Resources that were situated in the all-black Lincoln Junior High School. By 1961, Montgomery County's public schools were completely desegregated.

Despite the obstinate opposition to racial integration in public places, the desegregration of the 1960s brought about signs of social equality— entrance by the same door to public facilities, absence of signs which read "white only" or "colored," attendance to the same institutions, and the option of sitting where one chose on public conveyances.

UNSHAKEABLE PERSEVERANCE

A fter examining our history, it is obvious that life involves times of great accomplishment, despite the obstacles, interruptions, and pitfalls that present themselves to delay the progress of positive action.

Inasmuch as Maryland was considered a southern state, many Marylanders, including Montgomery Countians, were of the mindset that the American Negroes were second-class citizens with little need of an elementary school education, much less a secondary school education. Consequently, many blacks were forced to toil in the fields from sunrise to sunset with no hope for social advancement. Fortunately, there were a few Montgomery Countians who did not embrace that belief.

Prior to September 1927, when Montgomery County had no public high school for black students, some students migrated to localities where schools had been established. However, transportation to Washington posed a problem for those students who were desirous of a high school diploma. For that reason, many high school-aged students were denied education for the next sixteen years. They were faced with the decision between leaving their families behind to get an education, if their parents were financially capable of sending them, or staying at home to eke out a living as a domestic or a laborer. For the select few who were fortunate enough to attend high school, those were the best of times, despite the hardships and problems they faced, because they were conscious of the fact that their schooling would eventually enable them to obtain satisfactory employment. For the many students who did not have the opportunity to further their education, there was little optimism about the future, since they could only perform menial tasks.

In their quest for a better way of life, black students endured many hardships and inconveniences to obtain their high-school diplomas. They had strength of purpose and hope that even the odds against them could not shake, while the parents waited with hope and expectancy for the arrival of a high school in Montgomery County for their children.

The voices of the United Trustees could not be silenced in their meetings with the Board of Education. Eventually, their marathon performance resulted in the construction of Rockville Colored High School. Rockville

Lincoln High School Class of 1945 49th Anniversary Photo: presentation of tributes to living Rockville High Class of 1931 graduates-Ruize O. Tyler, and Celestine Prather-Hebron by James C. Offord, Warrick S. Hill and Betty Hawkins-Johnson.

High School was the fulfillment of the United Trustees' cherished dream, as it became a springboard for a better life for the students in the future.

The construction of Rockville High School was a major breakthrough for several reasons. It afforded the opportunity for more black high school-aged students to obtain a secondary school education in their home county; it provided an opportunity for the students to live at home, for the most part; it allowed some students to work during the evenings to earn money to pay their monthly bus fare; and it ultimately supplied an opportunity for more students to improve their quality of life.

Edward U. Taylor, being a product of Montgomery County's dual educational system (when there was no high school for black students), gladly accepted and ably met the challenge to pioneer the first high school for black students. When one has firsthand experience, one can more realistically identify with a particular situation. That was one of the reasons Mr. Taylor was able to persevere in his endeavor. His experience, strong faith in God, and levelheadedness, along with the support of his wife, Maude, and his resolute trustees, enabled him to succeed in spite of obstacles.

Even though a school was built, the Montgomery County black students were still faced with problems. Initially, 40 students had the privilege of only a half-day of instruction, and the problem of transportation was still tormenting them. Many students spent long hours on the buses because of the long routes. In the late 1920s, when transportation was unavailable in some communities, some students chose to remain in the public schools in Washington, whereas others chose to endure the inconveniences and attend Rockville High. Eventually, there was a bus to serve each community, resulting in a total of eight by the late 1930s.

In spite of the inconveniences and limitations, the students were ever mindful of their goals, and their teachers were attentive to their needs. Their teachers taught them lessons for living (civics, English, health, home economics, mathematics, physical education, science, and shop) and lessons for life (honesty, involvement, and integrity). The students realized that another useful lesson was how to identify genuine value in a world of uninspired imitations.

If any skeptics existed in Montgomery County during the early 1930s, they witnessed seven former students, from the Class of 1932, who successfully completed their college programs, four of whom were employed in Montgomery County, one in Calvert County, and two in Washington. The educational success stories, together with the immediate employment of those graduates, did not escape the notice of onlookers. It brought about an influx of students who enrolled at Rockville High School, and, consequently, a steady flow of enrollees at Bowie State Normal Institute. The dramatic increase in enrollment at the two aforementioned institutions must have made believers out of any skeptics who might have existed at that time. Rockville High School had an effective program.

Rockville Colored High School in Montgomery, like Central Colored High School in Calvert, Cookesville High School in Howard, Marlboro High School (initially for 5 years) in Prince George's, and Stanton High School in Anne Arundel, was the only high school for black students in the county.

With each decade following the opening of Rockville High School, black students witnessed barrier after barrier being removed to help improve their livelihood. The transportation problem was eliminated, the classroom space problem was solved, the course-offering limitation was improved, and the dual educational system was even eventually abolished.

From the 1920s through the 1950s, times were very difficult for black secondary school students, due to inconveniences, hardships, and racial barriers. The gravity of the situation was greatly magnified by temporary setbacks; however, the Rockville, Lincoln, and Carver high school students coped with the adverse conditions in which they existed. In their "separate but equal schools," they received an "adequate" education without new textbooks, without adequate instructional materials, and without equal salaries for their teachers. That is because they had caring and dedicated teachers who instilled strong values in them; they had supportive and God-fearing parents who instilled morals in them from early childhood, and they had strong will and unyielding spirit. Additionally, most adults had a genuine interest in the welfare of the black students in their community, which made for a solid home/school/church team. Considering the accomplishments of the alumni from the Class of 1931 through the Class of 1960, this cooperative effort was fruitful. Along with the trials came triumphs, as many of the alumni made their marks in society. Hence, one can conclude that an education is the key to making one's dream a reality.

During the first twelve years of the existence of a high school for black students in Montgomery County, there was frequent change in the administration. Fortunately, this continual shifting of principals had no negative impact on the curricular offerings or the education of the students. Realistically, the students expected that their teachers could prepare them academically and vocationally, and they were not disappointed.

Throughout the years, there was need for an improvement in the teaching environment. Whenever a need surfaced, Noah E. Clarke was the leading voice to stimulate the United Trustees into action. Frequently and persistently, they interacted with their communities and with the Montgomery County Board of Education. The capacity of these men to gain impressive victories was remarkable. They frequently took courage, in the face of overwhelming odds, to accomplish their mission.

From day one, the teachers, along with the parents of their students, stressed the importance of complying with rules and regulations, as well as mastering their subject matter. In addition to challenging academic studies, they provided a variety of extracurricular activities to enable the students to become well-rounded. From all indications, their efforts were not in vain, for reported accomplishments and known facts reveal that the Rockville, Lincoln, and Carver alumni were academically, personally, and vocationally prepared for their pursuit of satisfaction and security. Because they heeded the counsel of their trusted and respected teachers yesterday, they are disciplined, independent, law-abiding and productive citizens today.

In many cases, the alumni were unable to control the unfavorable circumstances that occurred in their lives, but they refused to accept the unfortunate predicaments in which they found themselves. Instead, they soared as high as they could fly. Following the wise counsel and hopeful

encouragement of their parents, they regulated their attitudes and they uti-
lized adversity as a stepping stone, to realize their dreams or to alleviate
their situations. Many black high school students who faced these unfavorable conditions are now rejoicing because they were able to overcome their
difficulties through adequate education, close-knit families, proper motivation, and positive thinking.

The individuals (students, teachers, trustees, parents) who trod the rug-
ged pathway through those trying years gained inner strength—the power to
endure to the end. Eventually, a school was built, a high school diploma was
earned, or an equal salary was won. Thus, success was attained through sheer
determination, strong work ethic, and dogged perseverance, in the search for
equality, justice, and a piece of the American dream.

The famous 1954 Supreme Court decision brought about many changes
in the educational and social lives of black children. For the most part, it
was not readily accepted by the adult population; however, the students
were more in favor of the change. It meant that most of the inequities that
existed up to this point—traveling long distances by bus, lack of instructional materials, dilapidated buildings, disproportionate teachers' salaries—
were history. It denoted that the two races would learn together in the same
classroom and would ride the same bus. It opened the door for public frat-
ernizing of the two races. Finally, it paved the way for equality and justice
in the education of the Montgomery County students and in the employment of the teachers.

Aftermath of Integration : Integration Process in Montgomery County Challenged in the 1990s

The integration process in Montgomery County, as well as in other
jurisdictions, got off to a slow and rocky start before total integration was
achieved in the late 1960s. The 1960s might be termed the "turbulent '60s"
with regard to integration, and three decades later, the 1990s might be called
the "unsettled '90s."

To alleviate racial imbalance in the public schools, Montgomery
County used two vehicles: the transfer policy and magnet programs. The

transfer policy has been challenged in court, because some parents felt that there may be other routes to integration and they wanted the best for their children.

The father of a white Glen Haven Elementary School student requested a transfer of his son to Rosemary Hills Elementary School, where a mathematics-science program (instituted in the 1980s) was offered. The Montgomery County Board of Education denied the parent's request, because it decided that Glen Haven Elementary School needed white students, whereas Rosemary Hills Elementary School did not. In retaliation, the parent started a lawsuit to obtain transfer permission, but the District Court ruled in favor of the Montgomery County Board of Education. Finally, however, the Fourth Circuit Court in "Eisenberg v. Montgomery County Public Schools" decided that the use of race in a transfer policy is unconstitutional.

Presentation of Proclamation by County Executive Neal Potter to Lincoln High School Class of 1945. Members: Annie Procton-Rhodes, James C. Offord, Warrick S. Hill, Dorothy Rhodes-Carroll (September 1993)

Former students from Rockville High School and Lincoln High School

Because the transfer policy is one of the chief devices that is used to maintain racial balance in the public schools, the members of the Montgomery County Board of Education have declared earnestly that they will fight to continue its usage, for fear that white students will transfer out of the integrated schools. Hence, the Montgomery County Board of Education is determined to appeal to the United States Supreme Court to reverse the Fourth Circuit Court decision.

Montgomery County's magnet programs are offered in predominantly African-American and Latino schools to attract white students from the surrounding areas. But the merits of the magnet schools have been debated, since the classes are composed primarily of white and Asian-American students, which suggests regression toward racial imbalance.

Allan J. Lichtman (an American University history professor) wrote an article that was published in the *Burtonsville Gazette* (November 17, 1999), in which he took a stand against segregation in our public schools. He mentioned several recent studies that reveal the efficacy of integrated schools. According to William T. Trent, "Desegregated schooling has important long-term benefits for minority students, especially in terms of its ability to open up economic opportunities for them. Taking an even longer view, improving economic and educational opportunities for one generation of minority individuals raised the socioeconomic status of the next generation."

110

Likewise, Jomills Henry Braddock II and James M. McPartland discovered that racially-varied instruction fosters interracial understanding, which, in turn, benefits black and white students. In their study, they declared: "School desegregation does create more positive reactions, among blacks and whites, to future interracial situations."

In conclusion, Professor Lichtman maintained that "A narrowly designed policy to promote racial balance, like that of Montgomery County, benefits whites and minorities by promoting understanding across races. It also provides minorities a chance they might not otherwise have to become successful and productive members of our communities."

In view of the study by Braddock and McPartland pertaining to the effectiveness of racially diverse instruction, it is noteworthy that Montgomery County has a high school whose student body is as diverse as the United Nations. Last school year (1998-1999), Montgomery Blair High School had a student body of almost 3,000 students from 100 different countries, and 60 different languages were spoken. It is also notable that Montgomery Blair High School is the largest high school in Montgomery County and the second largest in Maryland. Eleanor Roosevelt High School in Prince George's County has the top enrollment with 3,158 students.

Not only is the racially-diverse school worthy of note, but so is its principal. Phil Gainous (who is an African-American and has managed the school for sixteen years) won two prestigious awards—*The Washington Post* Distinguished Educational Leadership Award (the only Montgomery County principal to receive this honor in 1999) and the Mark Mann Excellence and Harmony Award—for his remarkable leadership. Mr. Gainous is a 1964 graduate of Morgan State University where he was named to the 1963 Pittsburgh Courier Black College All-American Team.

Besides having a racially diverse student body and teaching staff, Montgomery Blair High School has communication arts, a remedial program for students with learning disabilities, a special education program, magnet programs in mathematics and science, and students from a wide range of socio-economic backgrounds.

Dedicatory Presentation by Mayor Douglas M. Duncan to LHS Class of 1945 members: L to R: James C. Offord, Warrick S. Hill, Doris Plummer-Hackey, Annie Procton-Rhodes, William B. Cooke, Clarence R. Webster Jr. October 1993

In another southern state, integration had positive and negative effects. In the school-year 1993-1994, a white principal of Randolph County High School (Alabama) threatened to cancel a prom if interracial couples attended. His comments provoked heated protests, and the black students boycotted the school. Because blacks and whites had been involved in fights at the school, he alleged that his concern was for student safety. Later, the Justice Department reopened a desegregation case against the Randolph County school system and arsonists burned down the building. As a result, the principal lost his job. Two years later (1996), he was elected Randolph County School Superintendent, a position in which he proved to be more successful. Prior to his retirement from this office on January 1, 2000, he led a county-wide academic reversal and relieved the school system of a $650,000 debt.

Initially, the addition of black students to all-white schools alleviated the inconveniences as well as the unfairness and gave the black students a breath of hope for equality in education. However, integration was not a panacea, for it multiplied some black students' hardships by magnifying cultural differences and racial intolerance. It appears that whenever a new policy or practice was implemented, something of a limiting nature surfaced to counter it. Yet despite the hardships and controversy, better educational opportunities for black students have allowed them to pursue a better quality of life.

Progress for African-American high school students came slowly but not without unshakeable perseverance and unwavering determination. Initially, there was a struggle for a high school diploma outside Montgomery County until September 1927 when 40 eighth graders had the privilege of attending Rockville Colored High School and became the charter members of this long-awaited facility.

These pioneers and the next 11 classes participated in an 11-year system of education, whereas their white counterparts had been enjoying this privilege since 1891. The 12-year system had its inception in Montgomery County in 1931 for the white students but the African-American students had to wait until 1944 for the opportunity. For the white students, the 14-year system of education commenced with the establishment of Montgomery Junior College in 1946. Since the black students were not permitted to attend that institution, Dr. Parlett L. Moore, then-principal of George Washington Carver High School, founded George Washington Carver Junior College and became its dean in 1951. This dual system of education in Montgomery County was practiced on the public high school level, as well as the junior college level, until the total integration of schools in September 1960.

PART TWO

THE CLASSES

ROCKVILLE HIGH SCHOOL
CLASS OF 1931

Class Motto
"Before us lies the timber—let us build."

Class Colors
Orange & Blue

Class Flower
White Carnation

Class Song
Words by Beatrice Taylor, Tune "In the Gloaming"

Now the time has come, dear
Rockville,
When the seniors say good-bye,
With regret we'll have to leave
you
And to do our best we'll try—
For before us lies the timber:
Let us ever, ever, build,
If we thus obey our motto
We will always do our will.
In the future, friends and teachers,
When we each have gone our way,
Memories very oft will haunt us
Of our first Commencement Day.
Now we're making you a promise,
That we'll try to sow good seed
And when ever life permits us,
We'll not follow but we'll lead.
Dear Old Rockville, we'll be true
To ourselves and true to you.

Valedictorian
Beulah Mae Clarke

Salutatorian
Celestine Minerva Prather

GRADUATES
William Ernest Bishop
Beulah Mae Clarke
Sara Curtis
Richard Wesley Hall
King Solomon Hart
Celestine Minerva Prather
Beatrice Sophia Taylor
Ruize O. Tyler
Margaret Wood

FACULTY
Namon Allen, *Principal*
Ethel McDowell
Queene E. McNeill
Agnes Watson

Class Night Exercises
Friday, May 8, 1931, 8 P.M.

Processional
Negro National Hymn
High School Chorus

Invocation Salutatory
Celestine Prather

Class Roll
Margaret Wood

History
Ruize O. Tyler

Duet
Clara Luckett &
Dorothy Turner

Prophecy
Beatrice Taylor

Will
Solomon Hart

Gifts
William Bishop

Valedictory
Beulah Clarke

Class Song
Class

Music

High School Chorus Recessional

courtesy Ruize O. Tyler

ROCKVILLE HIGH SCHOOL
CLASS OF 1932

The Class of 1932 was the second and the largest class to graduate from Rockville High School during the Great Depression. Even though unemployment rates skyrocketed, the students managed to obtain money to stay in school.

In terms of academic achievement, Mary E. Johnson and Emma Holland stood at the top of the class, according to Dorothy (Turner) Bailey. In terms of athletic performance, Russell Awkard, Arthur Frazier, and Dewey Isreal were the baseball standouts. Other sports included basketball, dodge ball, soccer, and volleyball, as reported by Mr. Awkard and Mrs. Bailey.

Since secondary education, for black students was in its infancy in Montgomery County, one could not expect a full-scale academic or interscholastic athletic program to exist. The students were taught the basic subjects that were appropriate at that time, and that instruction was beneficial. The sports in which the students participated were for needed exercise.

In May 1931, there were 23 closely knit juniors who were looking forward to the arrival of May 1932. However, when September 1931 arrived, two members of the senior class—Helen and Margaret Cooke—relocated to Washington, D.C. and New York, respectively, where each graduated from high school, according to Helen Cooke Bonds. Edith Hill-Owens recalled that their 21 remaining classmates experienced "a very rainy graduation evening in Fisherman's Hall," and their diplomas were issued to them after graduation because Montgomery County Superintendent Edwin W. Broome had not signed them prior to commencement.

Valedictorian
Mary E. Johnson

Salutatorian
Emma Holland

GRADUATES
Corrie Alcorn
Russell Awkard
Melinda Baker
Alda Campbell
Sarah Davis
Arthur Frazier
Myrtle Hamilton
Zachariah Hart
Edith Hill
Emma Holland
Dewey Isreal
Mary Jackson
Ethel Johnson
Mary E. Johnson
Clara Luckett

119

Martha Marr
Mary Mercer
Leslie Plummer
Maggie Prather
G. Howard Thomas
Dorothy Turner

FACULTY
Thomas Kemp, *Principal*
Ethel McDowell
Queene E. McNeill
Agnes Watson

CONTINUED EDUCATION
Elizabeth Awkward
Raleigh, North Carolina
Alda Campbell
Helen Cooke
Washington, D.C.
Zachariah Hart
Edith Hill
Mary E. Johnson
Dorothy Turner

courtesy Clara (Luckett) Talley, Dorothy (Turner) Bailey

ROCKVILLE HIGH SCHOOL
CLASS OF 1933

Valedictorian
Mabel Dorsey

Salutatorian
William B. Duvall

GRADUATES
Raymond Clarke
Samuel Clarke
Mabel Dorsey
William B. Duvall
Katie Fuller
Melvin Hall
Watson Prather, Sr.
Annie Shelton
Henry Shelton
Warner Benjamin Smith
Herman R. Talley
Harry Thomas
Albert Warfield

FACULTY
Namon Allen, *Principal*
Henry Joyce
Queene E. McNeill
Agnes Watson

courtesy Mabel (Dorsey) Jackson, William B. Duvall, Herman R. Talley

ROCKVILLE HIGH SCHOOL
CLASS OF 1934

The Class of 1934 was the fourth graduating class of Rockville High School, and it had its share of scholars and athletes. Nina Honemond and Sarah B. Meads ranked first and second, respectively, in the class.

Allison H. Claggett, Claude N. Prather, and Paul F. Scott were the top baseball players in the class. These players, along with players from the other classes, pooled their talents to overwhelm and to surprise some of their big-city-high-school opponents. Their opponents included "Armstrong High School (Washington, D.C.), Douglass High School (Baltimore, Maryland), Dunbar High School (Washington, D.C.), Lincoln High School (Frederick, Maryland), and Highland Park High School (Prince George's County, Maryland)."

The baseball uniforms were purchased by the "Black businessmen of Rockville—George "Tee" Johnson, Robert L. "Mike" Snowden, and Edward "Beans" Johnson. The names of these businessmen were placed on the back of the uniforms."

Rockville High School also had a basketball team whose opponents were "Lincoln High School and Highland Park High School. There was no gymnasium or indoor facility, so Rockville's home games were played outdoors."

This class even had the opportunity to enjoy a night of socialization—the senior prom. But preparation for this memorable occasion was not without its difficulties and disappointments. "The senior girls had to make their prom dresses. Their instructor was a part-time home economics teacher who served both Montgomery and Prince George's counties. She visited Rockville only one day per week to assist the girls with their dresses. Unfortunately, she failed to stay for the completion of the dresses. The girls refused to accept defeat, so they took them home for their mothers to finish."

Baseball Team
Coach
Henry Joyce

Outfield
Russell Awkard ('32)
Samuel Clarke ('33)
Clarence "Pint" Isreal ('35)
Wilmore "Mo" Hill ('36)

Pitcher
Arthur Frazier ('32)

Catcher
Dewey Isreal ('32)

Shortstop
Watson Prather ('33)

First Base
Claude N. Prather ('34)

Second Base
Allison H. "Pickles" Claggett ('34)

Third Base
Paul F. Scott ('34)

Class Colors
Black & Gold

Class Motto
"Preparation is the keynote of success."

Valedictorian
Nina Elizabeth Honemond

Salutatorian
Sarah Bernice Meads

GRADUATES
Corrie Blanche Barks
Allison Hugh Claggett
Florence Cordelia Fisher
Sadie Matilda Fuller
Ellis Theodore Hackett
James Alphonso Hall
Lillian Rebecca Hart
Carlisle Blair Hill
Nina Elizabeth Honemond
Albert Henry Johnson, Jr.
Annie Elizabeth Johnson
Lorraine Griffin Johnson
Elijah Stanton McAbee
Sarah Bernice Meads
Hannah Louvina Moore
Claude Nathan Prather

Paul Freedman Scott
Allen Willis

FACULTY
Namon Allen, *Principal*
Henry Joyce, *Social Science, Mathematics*
Queene E. McNeill, *History, English*
Agnes Watson, *French, Mathematics*
Edwin W. Broome, *County Superintendent*
Edward U. Taylor, *County Supervisor*

Graduating Exercises
Friday, May 18, 1934, 8:30 P.M.

Processional
"War March of the Priests" (from *Athalia*)

High School Band Selection
"Lift Every Voice and Sing"

Audience Invocation
Reverend James W. Davis, Pastor of Mt. Calvary Baptist Church, Lincoln Park, Maryland

Negro Spiritual
"Deep River"

Class of 1934 Address
Mr. Campbell C. Johnson, Executive Secretary, Y.M.C.A., Washington, D.C.

High School Band Selection
"Trees" (Joyce Kilmer)

Presentation of Diplomas
Superintendent Edwin W. Broome

High School Band Selection
"Claudine"

Remarks
Supervisor Edward U. Taylor

High School Band Recessional
"March Progress"

Benediction
"Now the Day Is Over"

courtesy Allison H. Claggett, Nina
(Honemond) Clarke

ROCKVILLE HIGH SCHOOL CLASS OF 1935

Since the Class of 1935 had the distinction of being the last class to graduate from Rockville High School, it made history. It appeared to be a naturally history-oriented class because its field trips were to places of historical significance—the Capitol, the White House, the Washington Monument, and Gettysburg, Pennsylvania.

Edison Willis and Gertrude Johnson were the top scholars in the class, and Clarence "Pint" Isreal was the baseball giant.

The girls used their sewing skills to "make their dresses for Class Night Exercises, but they purchased their prom dresses."

Valedictorian
Edison Willis

Salutatorian
Gertrude Johnson

GRADUATES
Howard Brooks

Robert W. Duvall
Samuel Fisher
Irving Hackett
Evelyn Hamilton
Flora Hebron
Vicella Howard
Mamie Hutchison
Clarence Isreal
Gertrude Johnson
Lillian King
John Mercer
Marilyn Shelton
Charles Snowden
Leroy Snowden
Edison Willis

FACULTY
Namon Allen, *Principal*
Neil Cooper
Queene E. McNeill
Agnes Watson

CONTINUED EDUCATION
Howard University, Washington, D.C.
Howard Brooks
Charles Snowden
Leroy Snowden

courtesy Evelyn Hamilton-Snowden

125

LINCOLN HIGH SCHOOL
CLASS OF 1936

This class of 19 graduating seniors had the distinction of being the first class to graduate from Lincoln High School. Of those Montgomery County classes that held formal graduating exercises, it was the smallest class. It was the sixth class to graduate since a high school had been built in Montgomery County for the black high school students. It may have been the first class to have a prom given to them by the junior class for which some of the girls used their sewing skills to make their prom dresses, whereas others bought theirs.

Elsie Dorsey Kennedy remembered that she participated in an operetta entitled "Fashions in Paris," and that there was competition in volleyball and annual field meets.

Wilmore Hill recalled that he played baseball against Dunbar High School (Washington, D.C.), soccer against Lincoln High School (Frederick, Maryland), and participated in intramurals. He also remembered that Lincoln High School played basketball against Lincoln High School (Frederick, Maryland).

Class Motto
"There Is No Why Without a Because."

Class Colors
Orange & Black

Class Flower
Rose

Valedictorian
Elsie Dorsey

Salutatorian
Mary Burgess

Commencement Exercises
Wednesday, May 20, 1936, 8:30 P.M.

GRADUATES
William Barnes
Mary Burgess
Elsie Dorsey
Henry Dove
Theresa Duvall
Leslie Gaines
Richard H. Hill, Jr.
Wilmore Hill
Mary Lee
Howard Lyles
Bernice Martin
Clarence Mercer
Charles Nickens
Leslie Palmer
Lenora Sickles
Carlyne Smith
Eugene Surnmerour
Roland B. Talley
Rhetta L. Washington

FACULTY
Namon Allen, *Principal*

Neil Cooper
Queene E. McNeill
Alberta Mebane
Caleb Rhoe
Agnes Watson
Edward U. Taylor,
County Supervisor
Edwin W. Broome, *County*
Superintendent

CONTINUED EDUCATION
Elsie Dorsey
Theresa Duvall
Wilmore Hill
Rhetta Washington

courtesy Elsie (Dorsey) Kennedy

LINCOLN HIGH SCHOOL
CLASS OF 1937

Highlights

The Class of 1937 was a very active class in all aspects of the school's program. They exhibited their talents and skills in academics and athletics.

(Excerpts from *Rockville News*, Volume IV, No. 1, March 1937, Courtesy of Maurice F. Talley)

NEWSPAPER STAFF
Editor-in-Chief
Richard H. Tynes ('37)

Assistant Editor
Elsie V. Copeland ('37)

Business Editor
Leon F. Waters ('37)

Sports Editor
Maurice F. Talley ('37)

News Editor
Dorothy S. Washington ('37)

Joke Editor
Warren Q. Brooks ('37)

PATROL FORCE
Organized Monday, January 4, 1937

First Lieutenant
Leon F. Waters

Second Lieutenant
Richard H. Tynes

Secretary
Warren Q. Brooks

Treasurer
Andrew W. Howard

BASEBALL TEAM ORGANIZED
—Maurice F. Talley

On Wednesday, February 10, 1937, the boys of Lincoln High School met to organize a baseball team. Their coach was Neil Cooper.

In April 1937, Mr. Cooper, a Hampton Institute graduate, and two other drivers transported the team to Hampton Institute (now Hampton University) in Virginia. Mr. Cooper entered the Lincoln High School boys in a track meet at Hampton Institute, where they competed against teams from Baltimore, New Jersey, Pennsylvania, and Virginia.

The following day, Lincoln High's team competed against a rested Hampton Institute team in a game of baseball. The Hampton players watched the Lincoln High boys participate in a very competitive track meet on Friday, and they were posed to cruise to an easy victory over their tired high school opponents. But, they were unaware of their opponents' makeup—talented, undefeated, and confident. The college team proved to be no match for the powerful, senior-dominated Lincoln

High School team that won the game, 7-3.

During their senior year, their regularly scheduled opponents were Armstrong High (Washington, D.C.), Dunbar High School (Baltimore, Maryland), National Training (Baltimore, Maryland), and Phelps High School (Washington, D.C.). They played Armstrong High for the championship, and Lincoln High's team refused to yield to their big-city opponents. The game went into extra innings. In the tenth inning, Edward Awkward was moved from left field to shortstop, and Maurice F. Talley was shifted from shortstop to left field. Lincoln High won the game, and Maurice F. Talley was named the MVP (Most Valuable Player) of the game.

The 1937 baseball team is believed to be the only Lincoln High or Rockville High team to go undefeated during a season (twelve games).

Baseball Team
Manager & Second Base
William "Mickey" Prather

Secretary, First Base & Pitcher
Richard H. Tynes

Treasurer
Andrew W. Howard

Left Field
Edward Awkward

Catcher
John Brown

Center Field
Cecil Crawford

Pitcher
Leroy A. Hawkins

Third Base
Marshall Smith

Shortstop
Maurice F. Talley

Right Field & Pitcher
Leon F. Waters

The girls' volleyball team was also active. One of their opponents was a Tenleytown (Washington, D.C.) team.

Girls' Volleyball Team
Mildred Adams
Nettie Hood
Idella King
Gertrude Plummer

The boys and girls also had the opportunity to use their athletic abilities in competition at the annual field meets which were scheduled in the spring.

On field day, four senior boys were appointed by a playground official, to act as judges for the boys' dashes and track events. Richard Tynes picked the first runner, Maurice Talley selected the second runner, John Brown chose the third runner, and Maxwell Honemond selected the fourth runner. These boys were highly praised by the official for their work.

On Friday, February 12, 1937, the teachers and students gave a very interesting program in connection with Negro History Week. The program consisted of spirituals, recitations, readings, duets, several musical selections from the quartet, and a play entitled "The Two Races." Margaret Adams read the Scripture, and Juanita Awkard was mistress of ceremonies.

Under the direction of Mr. Herbert H. Norton, principal and agriculture teacher, the class in agriculture learned how to use the incubator and how to breed and select chickens for breeding.

The home economics girls scheduled four major projects—Easter Egg Hunt, Thursday, March 25, 1937; Shower for Home Economics Department, April 19, 1937; Fashion Show, May 3, 1937, 8:30 P.M.; and Mother's Day Banquet, May 17, 1937.

With the aid of their home economics teacher, Miss Alberta Mebane (now Mrs. Levingston), they made great progress in sewing this year, for they had lessons in knitting, crocheting, and other types of needle work.

LOOKING FOR A JOB
—Maurice F. Talley

When one looks for a job, when out of school, and the employer notices the low marks made in school, the employer will think that since the applicant fell down on the first job, he may fall down on him. The person, who makes good in school or out of school, is the one who overcomes distractions and obstacles and makes the most of every opportunity. One can rise above a poor record and can change his direction. Many do it. They go along rather badly for a while, then face about and do excellently.

To those who are near the end of school, I would certainly advise that attention be given to grades and even in the case of us seniors, I would say there is still a chance to make a "whirl wind" finish.

This advice is not only in order that the record be good and the jobs be easier to land, but because I think it will be a fine thing for your character, to buckle down and prove that you can go through with anything and everything you start. It is true, of course, that there are courses that you do not care for particularly. It is inevitable that this should be the case. School authorities, however wise they may be, cannot develop courses to interest every individual.

Some of the school work is particularly interesting and some of it is not. To master it is your job. It is probable there will be a time that the same qualities will make for excellent work elsewhere. It is very important, therefore, that each student makes his time count for all he can while he is in school and that he sees to it that his first job—that of a student—is mastered well.

A THEME
—Gertrude Plummer

Life is hard,
But I can take it.
After all, it's
What you make it.

DON'T GIVE UP
—Mildred C. Adams

Schoolmates, stand together.
Don't give up your grip.
In fair or stormy weather
We can't give up our grip.

Friends, and pals forever,
We've had a long, long trip.
It may require a licking,
But don't give up your grip.

SUCCESS
—Author Unknown
It's doing the job the best you can
And being just to your fellow man.

It's making money and holding friends,
And staying true to your odds and ends.
It's figuring how, and learning why
And looking forward and thinking high.
It's dreaming a little, and doing much,
And keeping us always in closest touch.

BRIGHT HIGH SCHOOL YEARS
—Elsie Cooper

Bright high school years with pleasure rife,
The shortest, gladdest days of life,
How swiftly you go gliding by.
Oh! why does time so quickly fly?
The seasons come, the seasons go,
The earth is green or white with snow.
But time and change shall never sigh
To break the memories of Lincoln High.

In after years when troubles rise
To cloud the blue and sunny skies,
How bright will seem through memory's haze
Those happy, golden, bygone days.
So let us ever strive that we
Shall ne'er forget those bygone days,
When we attended Lincoln High
And learned her truest, pious ways.

STUDENT'S ADVICE
—Richard H. Tynes

Everyone is born into this world with a definite type of work to do. Now is the time that you, the students of Lincoln High School, should find out what this work is in order that you will, in the future, be of worthy value to yourself, your race, and the world.

Set the goal today and let your aim be to reach it. On your way to the goal or top of success, always remember that it cannot be reached by taking two or more steps at a time. It can only be reached step by step.

To reach the goal, you will have to take patience, perseverance, honesty, knowledge, promptness, and courtesy along with you as companions. Others have reached it, why can't you? Do not lag behind or fail on your way because of your race, your color, and your looks.

Keep in mind that you, too, were born with a talent to lead or that you can be an expert in a certain field of knowledge. If you will keep these facts in mind, I am sure that you, too, will reach your goal.

TRAIN YOUR CHILDREN
—Mildred C. Adams

The training of your children is the most important step towards success that I know of. We, as people, know that the children are the coming generation, and it is the purpose of the older people to train them the way he should go and when he is older, he will not depart from it.

GRADUATION
—Unknown

Graduation is not a mere transference of a subject from high school out into life, but it shows that an individual has accomplished a four-year course of high school.

Graduation is a state of encouragement, a state of honor and exalted rank.

Graduation encourages a student to go farther on into colleges and universities. He is inspired by his accomplishment in high school.

Graduation elevates an individual in rank, it makes him become dignified and refined.

Graduation makes the graduator feel that he has maintained a point of efficiency in his life to obtain an academic degree, and it makes an individual want to go further on into higher institutions of education so that he may obtain a point of efficiency in his life greater than that he has maintained in his high school career.

SCHOOL IS OUT
—Elsie Copeland

And now our school is over
And we must say adieu
Good-bye, to all our classmates,
And our six teachers, too.
This time you will not see us
When lunch time comes at noon
Because, if you have not heard
We graduated in June.

Trials

Although most of the members of this class were transported to Lincoln High School, some did not have the privilege to ride a school bus. Margaret Adams, for one, walked approximately four miles from her home on Avery Road to Lincoln High School. She vividly recalled that one of her school mates amusingly greeted her daily as "Six Miles," because she had to walk such a great distance. Most students who walked lived closer to the school. Margaret walked an even greater distance when she was enrolled at Rockville High School.

Unfortunately, she did not have the convenience of transportation when she attended Norbeck Elementary School either. She braved the rain, snow, sleet, and hail for seven years when she walked, alone, nearly six miles. But she set a goal, and she reached it!

Lincoln High School
Class Of 1937

Commencement Program

Monday, June 7, 1937
Fashion Show, 8 P.M.,
School Auditorium

Wednesday, June 9, 1937
Senior Trip

Friday, June 11, 1937
Junior-Senior Prom

Sunday, June 13, 1937
Baccalaureate Sermon, 8 P.M.,
Jerusalem A.M.E. Church,
Reverend C. E. Hodges

Monday, June 14, 1937
Class Night Exercises, 8 P.M., School
Auditorium

Tuesday, June 15, 1937
Graduation Exercises, 8 P.M., School
Auditorium

Class Motto
"Finish What You Attempt."

Class Colors
Green & Orange

Class Flower
Rose

Valedictorian
Andrew W. Howard

Salutatorian
Margaret E. Adams

Historian
Richard H. Tynes

GRADUATES
Margaret Elizabeth Adams
Mildred Charlotte Adams
Edward Robert Awkward
Juanita Awkard
Mayfield Nannie Beverley
Warren Quinton Brooks
John Brown
Charlotte Rebecca Byrd
Laura Mabel Cook
Elsie Vernetta Copeland
Cecil Worthington Crawford
Anna Belle Fisher
Rebecca Nettie Hamilton
Leroy A. Hawkins
Maxwell Honemond
Nettie Virginia Hood
Georgianna Estelle Hopkins
Andrew Whitfield Howard
Pauline Isabelle Johnson
Idella Gertrude King
Dorothy Louise Lee
Milton Edward Moore
Virginia Louise Onley
Gertrude Viola Plummer
Darius Ellsworth Prather
William Henry Prather
Bessie Constance Simpson
Marshall William Smith
Maurice Fleming Talley
Richard Henry Tynes
Dorothy Sarah Washington
Leon Frederick Waters
FACULTY
Herbert H. Norton, *Principal*

Neil Cooper
C. H. Johnson
Queene E. McNeill
Alberta Mebane
Caleb Rhoe
Genevieve V. Swann

COMMENCEMENT PROGRAM

Tuesday, June 15, 1937
Lincoln High School Auditorium

Processional
"America The Beautiful"
Audience

Invocation
Reverend James E. Carter
"On the Road to Mandalay"
Chaffin

Address To Graduates
Jefferson Coage,
Former Recorder of Deeds

Negro Spiritual
Johnson High School Chorus

Remarks
Simon Smith,
Chairman, Board of Trustees

Negro Spiritual
Johnson High School Chorus

Remarks
J. W. Huffington,
State Supervisor of Maryland
Schools

Vocal Solo
Shelby Jackson

Lincoln High School Graduate Presentation Of Diplomas
Dr. Edwin W. Broome,
Superintendent of Montgomery
County Schools

Lamare High School Chorus
"Moonlight and Roses"

Benediction
Reverend J. W. Davis

Recessional

CONTINUED EDUCATION
Margaret Adams
Mildred Adams
Elsie Copeland
Maxwell Honemond
Gertrude Plummer
Dorothy Washington

courtesy Georgianna (Hopkins) Campbell

LINCOLN HIGH SCHOOL
CLASS OF 1938

Besides their regular academic work, many members of the Class of 1938 participated in extra-curricular activities, some of which were the Lincoln High School Glee Club and athletic teams.

The Glee Club members sang at school assemblies, commencement exercises, and at times for Jerusalem Methodist Church services in Rockville. Most of the members, including underclassmen, were Rosetta Davis, Alonzo Hackett, Bernard E. Holsey ('38), Emma Smith ('38), Dorothy Waters, and Harvey W. Zeigler ('38). Their director was home economics teacher Alberta Mebane.

The boys' and girls' athletic teams played teams from Bowie Teachers College (Bowie, Maryland), Douglass High School (Baltimore, Maryland), Dunbar High School (Washington, D.C.), and Storer College (West Virginia). The boys engaged in baseball and the girls contended in softball.

On field days, there was a larger student participation because additional games and track events were included on the schedule of events. The students competed against high school teams from the Western Shore of Maryland and eventually against Eastern Shore teams, if they were victorious in the initial competition.

Valedictorian
Louise Howard

Salutatorian
Deborah Awkard

GRADUATES
Deborah Awkard
John Beechan
James Carroll
Alice Claggett
Edith Claggett
Joyce Cook
Louise Copeland
Hilda Dixon
David Dorsey
John Duffin
Ethel Fisher
Catherine Gaither
Elizabeth Genus
Pearl Hallman
Saunders Hill
Thomas Hill
Bernard Holsey
Louise Howard
Thomas Jackson
Rosie M. King
Hewitt Lee
Sarah Lee
Elwood Matthews
Hattie Matthews
Russell McAbee
Naomi Mercer
Paul E. Moore
William Nickens
Viola Owens
Pauline Palmer
Margaret Plummer

*Pearl Hallman-Green, Lincoln High
School Class of 1938*

Lorenzo Plummer
Gladys Sims
Emma Smith
Florence Thomas
Ollie Thomas
Carroll R. Tynes
Evelyn Weedon
Harvey W. Zeigler

FACULTY
Herbert H. Norton, *Principal*
C. H. Johnson
Queene E. McNeill
Alberta Mebane
Caleb Rhoe
Genevieve V. Swann

*courtesy Phyllis (Awkard) Smith,
Harvey W. Zeigler*

LINCOLN HIGH SCHOOL CLASS OF 1939

A growing enrollment at Rockville High School soon caused it to be inadequate to accommodate grades 8-11. This lack of classroom space prompted the United Trustees, led by Mr. Clarke, to ask the Board of Education for a larger building. The request was honored with a brick-veneered building, situated in Rockville's Lincoln Park, that many believed to be a new building, which was named Lincoln High School.

The Class of 1939 made history by being the first freshman class to enroll at Lincoln High School. "In September 1935, there were 107 of them who were timid and scared and who had never met before but were not long in becoming acquainted."

Although they came with fear and shyness, they soon made a smooth transition from elementary school to high school. After gaining confidence in themselves, they "adopted an air of dignified freshmen and presented an operetta and a minstrel show in their auditorium."

Their freshman teachers were Namon Allen (Principal, English), Neil Cooper (algebra), Alberta Mebane (science), and Caleb Rhoe (civics).

When they became sophomores, they were more self-confident and more visible in school activities. During that year, they gave a program composed entirely of Negro spirituals and poems.

Not only was this a year for new faces in the sophomore class, but it was a year for new faculty members as well. "Herbert H. Norton, the new principal, came with high ideals and great enthusiasm, C. H. Johnson and Genevieve V. Swann" were the other first-time teachers who brought their expertise to the classrooms.

In September 1937, they entered their third year "as dignified juniors with a lot of things in view." This school year, "Allen T. Brown and Milton Turner came to Lincoln High School wholeheartedly and [they] worked diligently." Moreover, the junior class gave the senior class a prom, which provided a lot of excitement for the juniors. Further, Miss Mebane became Mrs. Levingston.

In September 1938, they were classified as seniors and this "was the most exciting and most strenuous year of all, because they were hoping and planning to graduate in June." They had "Queene E. McNeill, who strived to make them intellectual seniors, as their homeroom teacher." For further guidance, they had Parlett L. Moore, their new principal, "who did everything in his power to direct the students in the most profitable direction."

Along with the academic instruction, matrimonial vows were also taken. "In two successive years, Cupid made his appearance," this time it was Miss Swann and Mr. Brown who were united in holy matrimony.

Finally, only 33 students out of the 107 who entered in September 1935 endured to the end—*graduation.* "The total enrollment, grades 8-11, for this school year was 286, under the direction of seven faculty members in six classrooms and an annex."

Class Officers
President
Dorothy Waters

Vice-President
Carrie Hill

Secretary
June Butler

Treasurer
Albert Davis

Yearbook Staff
Editor-in-Chief
Albert Davis

Assistant Editor
D. Warner Dove

Business Managers
Carrie Hill &
Dorothy Waters

Sports Editor
Robert E. Hebron

Social And Literary Editor
Quo Vadis Brown

Art Editor
June Butler

**Lincoln High School
Patrol Force**
—James F. Onley, Class of 1939

Motto: "Society needs dependable boys and girls of today who will become the leading men and women of tomorrow."

Captain
Albert Davis ('39)

First Lieutenant
James F. Onley ('39)

Second Lieutenant
Andrew Doye ('41)

Secretary
Lloyd E. Branison ('39)

Treasurer
John Summerour ('39)

Sponsor
Herbert H. Norton
(Teacher of Agriculture)

Senior Officers
Charles A. Branison ('39)
Lloyd E. Branison ('39)
June Butler ('39)

Albert Davis ('39)
D. Warner Dove ('39)
Wade T. Mills ('39)
James F. Onley ('39)
J. Edward Riggs ('39)

Officers
Inez Addison ('41)
Janet Boston ('40)
Leroy Copeland
Vivian Copeland
Arthur Cross ('42)
Andrew Doye ('41)
George Green
Roland Harper
Hamilton Hawkins ('42)
John Owens ('42)
Hazel Phifer ('40)
Estella J. Pugh ('40)
John Sims ('40)
Edith Stewart ('40)
Harry T. Stewart ('42)
James Walker ('41)
Thelma Willis ('41)
Roland Wims ('41)

Girls Relay Team
Pearl Cooke ('42)
Carrie Hill ('39)
Mary Nolan
Madeline Palmer ('40)

Girls Volleyball Team
Helen P. Awkard ('39)
Clarice Awkward ('39)
Mabel Awkward ('41)
Janet Boston ('40)
Catherine Johnson ('40)

Estella Pugh ('39)
Edith Stewart ('40)
Edna Thomas ('38)
Dorothy Waters ('39)

The Boys Athletic Association
Manager
Lloyd E. Branison

First Captain Of Volleyball Team
Allen W. Plummer

Second Captain Of Volleyball Team
D. Warner Dove

First Captain Of Softball Team
William Summerour

Second Captain Of Softball Team
John Summerour

Softball Team
Catcher
William Summerour ('39)

Pitcher
Coleman Thomas ('40)

First Base
Thomas Jackson ('40)

Second Base
James Jackson ('41)

Third Base
Mack Isreal ('39)

Right Field
William Foster, Jr. ('40)

Left Field
Roland Gray ('41)

Center Field
Charles Offord

Left Shortstop
John Summerour ('39)

Right Shortstop
Albert Williams

Lincoln High

Dear Lincoln High we're stepping
out
To continue the spirit you gave us
no doubt.
We are very, very sorry to leave
But yet we know we must not
grieve.

Four years we've toiled both day
and night
Obtaining knowledge in the fight
Four years we've been within
your walls
Obtaining strength to meet life's
calls.

These helpful years we spent
with you
Receiving knowledge and courage too
Were kindred years we'll never
forget
Even though we have a long road
yet.

Dear Lincoln High we leave in
sorrow
But we pray that you toil on
tomorrow

And as we leave with dripping
eyes
May you continue to win the
prize.

1939 Class Will

(Excerpts from *Le Memoir*, Class
History by Quo Vadis Brown and
Carrie Hill, Courtesy of Margaret
Foreman, Class of 1951)

We, the members of the Senior
Class of 1939, are having the honor
of receiving our diplomas from dear
old Lincoln High School in a short
time. Before the last few hours speed
away, we, presumably in sound
minds, wish to make our last will
and testament.

To our respected and well-beloved
principal, Mr. Moore, we leave our
difficult guidance problems so that
the oncoming classes will have the
pleasure of solving them. We also
leave with him a peace of mind that
he will not see any member of our
group wandering in the hall during
class hours.

To Mr. Brown, we leave our
French and history books and our
good behavior during class periods.

To Miss Mebane, we leave our
cookbooks and patterns so that she
may use them for the future classes.

To Mr. Norton, we leave our agriculture equipment for the oncoming
classes.

141

To Miss Swann, we leave our good behavior during chemistry period and the 1939 field ball team.

To Mr. Turner, we leave our difficult math problems so that the oncoming classes will have the pleasure of solving them.

To the Junior Class, we give an inestimable possession the rank of a 'dignified senior' with the hope that they acquire our quiet ways, our privileges, and a full appreciation of the school.

To the Sophomore Class, we leave our brilliant record so that they may profit by our mistakes and make Lincoln High School one of the best schools possible.

To the Freshman Class, we leave our hope that they will have ambition and strength enough to reach the goal we have attained; (this) requires study and hard work.

To Mr. Martin, the janitor, we leave our dusty desks and torn-up notes.

Senior Superlatives
Thoughtful & Industrious
Helen P. Awkard

Modest with a Clear Outlook
Clarice Awkward

Future Economics Teacher
Nettie V. Bowles

To Know Him Is to Like Him
Charles A. Branison

Best Dressed Young Man
Lloyd E. Branison

Lives for Dancing
Catherine Brown

On the Road to Success
Quo Vadis Brown

Artistic Personality
June A. Butler

Gay, Though Serious "en francais"
Marie Contee

Straight as an Arrow
William S. Copeland

Oh Captain, My Captain, May Be on a Ship Someday
Albert Davis

Faithful Classmate
Cora E. Davis

Meek & Neat
Florence G. Dorsey

Good Sport, Avocation: the Stage
D. Warner Dove

Comical, But May Become a Great Musician
Robert E. Hebron

Very Serious
Carrie Hill

His Frankness Makes It Pleasant to Know Him
F. Mack Isreal

Song Bird, Orator
Shelby Jackson

Worthy Senior
T. Hortense Lyles

Old Stand-by, Never a Deserter
Wade T. Mills

Future Mathematician
James F. Onley

Petite Mademoiselle
E. Louise Owens

Free-hearted, Good Sport
Marjorie C. Prather

Athlete
J. Edward Riggs

Quiet, But Friendly
Lucille E. Robinson

Just a Kid Named "Joe"
John Summerour

Agreeable, Future Mechanic
William Summerour

Popular in Social Life
Carl Timbers

*Studious, Good Spirit &
All-Around Girl*
Dorothy Waters

Conscientious
Ella L. Wims

Class Motto
"Preparation is the Keynote to
Success."

Class Colors
Blue & Gold

Class Flower
Rose

Valedictorian
Dorothy Waters

Salutatorian
Carrie Hill

GRADUATES
Helen Porter Awkard
Clarice C. Awkward
Nettie Viola Bowie
Charles Alexander Branison
Lloyd Elijah Branison
Catherine Brown
Mabel Bernice Brown
Quo Vadis Brown
June Audrey Butler
Marie Contee
William S. Copeland
Albert Davis
Cora Elizabeth Davis
Florence Gertrude Dorsey
David Warner Dove
Robert Ellis Hebron
Carrie Irene Hill
Frank Mack Isreal
Shelby Farra Jackson
Thelma Hortense Lyles
Wade Thomas Mills
James Fenton Onley
Ethel Louise Owens
Allen W Plummer
Marjorie Constance Prather
James Edward Riggs
Lucille Elizabeth Robinson
John Summerour

William Summerour
Mary Elizabeth Terry
Carl Timbers
Dorothy Bartella Waters
Ella Louise Wims
FACULTY
Parlett L. Moore, *Principal*
Allen T. Brown
Queene E. McNeill
Alberta Mebane
Herbert H. Norton
Genevieve Swann
Milton Turner

Class Night Exercises
June 16, 1939

Song
"America the Beautiful"

Prayer
Leslie I. Gaines, Class of 1936

Song
"Juanita"

Play
"Youth Marches On"

Giftorian
Ella Wims-Smith

Class Song
"Farewell Lincoln High"
(Composed by Shelby Jackson and
June Butler)

Sermon To The Graduates
June 19, 1939

Processional
Hymn
"Come, Thou Almighty King"

Hymn
"My Faith Looks Up to Thee"

Announcements

Sermon
Reverend C. E. Hodges,
Pastor, Jerusalem M. E. Church,
Rockville, Maryland

Hymn
"Work, for the Night Is Coming"

Benediction

Recessional

Graduating Exercises
June 19, 1939, 8:30 P.M.

Processional

Chorus
"Lift Every Voice and Sing"

Invocation
Reverend Gordon Grant, Pastor,
Clinton A.M.E. Zion Church,
Rockville, Maryland

Salutatory
"The School's Debt to the
Community"
Carrie Hill

Solo
"Beautiful Dreamer"
Shelby Jackson

Valedictory
"What the Community Owes Its School"
Dorothy Waters

Chorus
"On the Road to Mandalay"
(Speaks)

Address
Dr. Charles H. Wesley, Dean
of the Graduate School, Howard
University, Washington, D.C.

Chorus
"Dere's No Hidin' Place Down Dere"

Presentation of Diplomas
Edwin W. Broome,
Superintendent of Instruction
Rockville, Maryland

Remarks

courtesy Alma (King) Ridgely

LINCOLN HIGH SCHOOL
CLASS OF 1940

Class Motto
"Today We Follow, Tomorrow We Lead."

Class Colors
Blue & White

Class Flower
Rose

Valedictorian
Edith Stewart

Salutatorian
Bernice Mason

GRADUATES
John Francis Beverley
Janet Loutine Boston
Doris Ovella Budd
Mary Catherine Budd
Delores Olivia Copeland
Ernest Clayton Dorsey
Iola Elsie Dorsey
Lillian Ciniours Dorsey
Lorraine Katherine D. Dorsey
Mildred Coretta Dorsey
William Foster, Jr.
Evelyn Virginia Gant
Roland Gray
Eugene Handy Jackson
James Thomas Jackson
Elbert Murray Johnson, Jr.
Mary Katherine Johnson
Lona Frances Johnson
Mabel Elizabeth Johnson
Novella Christine Lee

Virginia Jennie Martin
Bernice Virginia Mason
Anna Augusta Owens
Mary Madeline Palmer
Hazel Lorraine Phifer
Pauline Catherine Plummer
Leona Hyacinth Polk
William A. C. Polk
Wesley Harrison Posey
Estella Jean Pugh
Margaretta Elizabeth Ramey
John Arthur Sims
Gladys Cornelia Snowden
Edith Catherine Stewart
Edgar Coleman Thomas
Edna Marguerite Thomas
Lester W. Wims

Sermon to the Graduates
June 9, 1940

Processional
Hymn

The Graduating Class

146

"Going Home"

Responsive Reading
Gloria Patri

Hymn
"Jesus, Lover of My Soul"

Scripture

Prayer

Announcements

Hymn
"My Faith Looks up to Thee"

Sermon
Reverend S. A. Gordon Grant,
Pastor, Clinton A.M.E. Zion
Church, Rockville, Maryland

Class Night Exercises
June 11, 1940

Song
"America the Beautiful"

Prayer
William Polk, Class of 1940

Song
"God Bless America"

Play
"Out of the Past"

Class Poem
"Farewell Classmates
and Lincoln High"
(Composed by Iola Dorsey)

Duet
"Whispering Hope"

(Iola Dorsey and Madeline Palmer)

Giftorian
Margaretta Ramey

Class Song
"Forget Me Not"
Class
(Composed by Coleman Thomas
and William Polk)

Graduating Exercises
Processional

Chorus
"Swing Along"
(Cook)

Invocation
Reverend C. E. Hodges, Pastor,
Jerusalem M.E. Church,
Rockville, Maryland

Salutatory
"Our School, a Laboratory of
Citizenship"
(Bernice Mason)

Quartette
"Water Boy"
(Robinson)

Valedictory
"Character Building, a Factor in
Our School Curriculum"
(Edith Stewart)

Chorus
"Trees"
(Rasback and Deis)

Address
Dr. Dwight O. W. Holmes,

147

President, Morgan State
College,Baltimore, Maryland

Chorus
"Bells of St. Mary's"
Presentation Of Diplomas
F. K. Metzger, Member of
Montgomery County Board of
Education, Rockville, Maryland

Awards
Edward U. Taylor,
County Supervisor, and
Others To Be Announced

Chorus
"Joshua Fit the Battle of Jericho"

Benediction
Reverend W. H. Polk Pastor,

Poolesville M.E. Church,
Poolesville, Maryland

Recessional
(The audience is requested to remain
seated until after the recessional.)

FACULTY
Parlett L. Moore, *Principal*
Allen T. Brown
Queene E. McNeill
Alberta Mebane-Levingston
Herbert H. Norton
Maso P. Ryan
Genevieve Swann-Brown

*courtesy John Francis Beverley, Mary
Catherine (Budd) Swann, Madeline
(Palmer) Jackson, Edith (Stewart) Banks*

LINCOLN HIGH SCHOOL
CLASS OF 1941

Class Motto
"Not Finished, Just Begun."

Class Colors
Blue & White

Class Flower
Rose

Valedictorian
McAdoo Ramey

Salutatorian
Kathline Johnson

GRADUATES
Academic Course
Mabel Awkward
Justine Cole
Florence Davis
Maurice C. Genies
Thompkins W. Hallman
Bertha Lee
Marie Lyles
Pearl Luckett
*McAdoo Ramey
Mary Robey
Evelyn Snowden
Arthur W. Talley
Thelma Willis
*Roland Wims

General Course
Inez Addison
Alice Bowie
*Jerelene Clipper
Ernest Cooper

Helen Dimmie
Christine Dorsey
Marie Dove
Frances Fisher
Robert Greene
Grace Hebron
Margaret Jackson
Rebecca Jones
Preston L. Matthews
Charles Moore
Margaret Pinkett
Earnestine Prather
Marie Thomas
James Walker

Vocational Course
Adeline Bowles
Andrew Doye
Maude Hopkins
Walker I. Hill
Thelma Jackson
James Jackson
*Kathline Johnson
Florence King
Olivia Lee
Marjorie Lee
Frances Lyles
Charles F. Pendleton
Mamie Pratt
Ella Mae Sims
Selah Warren
Lucille White
Edith Windear

* *Member of National Honor Society*

FACULTY
Parlett L. Moore, *Principal*
Allen T. Brown

S. Eloise Levister
Queene E. McNeill
Alberta Mebane-Levingston
Herbert H. Norton
Maso Palmer Ryan
Martha A. Settle
Genevieve Swann-Brown

Edward U. Taylor,
County Supervisor
Edwin W. Broome,
County Superintendent

Graduating Exercises
Processional
"Priest March"
(from *Athalia* by Mendelssohn)

Choral Selection
"The Old Refrain"
(Kreisler)

Invocation
Reverend C. E. Hodges Pastor,
Jerusalem Methodist Church,
Rockville, Maryland

Choral Selection
"We Are Climbing Jacob's Ladder"
(Spiritual)

Dramatic Sketches

Introduction
Kathline Johnson

Character
Maurice C. Genies, Pearl Luckett,
and Roland Wims

Leadership
Kathline Johnson,
Evelyn Snowden, Jerelene Clipper,
and Others

Solo
"In the Garden of
Tomorrow"
(Graffe-Deppen)

Vocations
Maude Hopkins, Adeline Bowles,
Walker I. Hill

Citizenship
McAdoo Ramey, Florence Davis,
and Frances Lyles

Recapitulation
McAdoo Ramey

Choral Selection
"Finlandia"
(Sibelius)

Address to Graduates
Carrington L. Davis, Principal,
Dunbar High School,
Baltimore, Maryland

Chorus
"Dream Song"
(Brahms)

Presentation of Diplomas
Fern D. Schneider,
County Supervisor
of High Schools

Awards
Edward U. Taylor,
Supervisor of Colored Schools

Class Song
"Class of 1941"
(by Kathline Johnson)

Benediction
Reverend W. H. Polk, Pastor,

Poolesville Methodist Church,
Poolesville, Maryland

Recessional
"Pomp and
Circumstance"
(Elgar)

courtesy S. Eloise Levister

LINCOLN HIGH SCHOOL
CLASS OF 1942

The Class of 1942 set a record for having the largest number of students (51) to graduate from either Rockville or Lincoln High. Those seniors were enrolled in three curricula—academic, general, and vocational course.

A group of Juniors and Seniors

Class Motto
"We Have Crossed the River, and the Ocean Lies Ahead."

Class Colors
Red & White

Class Flower
Red Rose

GRADUATES
Academic Course
Ella Louise Awkard
*Muriel G. Baker

1941-1942 National Honor Society Kneeling, L to R: Norman Ridgeley, Virgie Stewart, Annie Procton, Bessie Hill, Warrick S. Hill. Standing, L to R: S. Eloise Levister, Helen Baker, Dorothy Rhodes, Marie Washington, Sylvia Waters, Mable D. Thomas, Betty Prather

Mary Anna Cole
Emma Virginia Cooke
Pearl Elsie Cooke
Charles Herbert Dorsey
Mable Louise Gray
Otelia Viola Hayes
*Bessie M. Hill
*Esther Williams Hill
Carolyn Melvyna Johnson
Myrtle Virginia Jones
Grace Etta Norris
Jack M. Quiller
Ulysses M. Taylor
Janie Ophelia Washington
*Sylvia Wynella Waters

General Course
Allen W. Brooks
Ralph Kenneth Brooks
Loretta Laverne Brown
Lucille Copeland
Arthur J. Cross
Edith Bell Frazier
Charles C. Gaither
Daniel Edward Gaither
Earl Hatcher
Hamilton Allen Hawkins
Juanita Corrine Lyles

Virginia Beatrice Moore
Merrel Thornton

Vocational Course
Lester Prather Bagley
Augustus Budd
Phoebe Anna Chaney
James S. Copeland
Melvin Lorenzo Crawford
Mildred M. Estep
Charles Raymond Jackson
Corrine Jackson
Gloria Cecelia Mae Jackson
Pauline Jackson
James Edward Johnson
Donald Thomas King
John Franklin Marr
Dorothy Onley
John Owens
John Russell Palmer
*Norman Briscoe Ridgley
William Henry Morice Ridgley
Blanche Louise Riggs
Harry Thomas Stewart
Seymour Thomas, Jr.

* *Member of the National Honor Society*

FACULTY
Parlett L. Moore, *Principal*
Genevieve S. Brown
Elsie Dorsey
S. Eloise Levister
Queene E. McNeill
Mary C. Moore
Ruby E. Morris
Herbert H. Norton
James T. Robinson

Lincoln High School 1941-1942 Chorus Chorus Director, Mrs.Sarah E. Levister-Shelton. Front Row: Mable D. Thomas, Mary Mason, Mildred Estep, Loretta Brown, Emma Cooke, Carolyn Johnson, Blanche Riggs, Katrine Copeland, Virgie Stewart, Bessie Hill. Second Row: Sylvia Waters, Maxine Claggett, Ella Awkard, Otealia Hayes, Myrtle Jones,___, Juanita Lyles, Dorothy Onley. Third Row: Norman Ridgeley, Harry T. Stewart, John R. Owens, Charles C. Gaither, Jack M. Quiller, Augustus Budd,___,___,Donald T. King,___C. Herbert Dorsey, Merrel Thorton, William H.M. Ridgely.

Graduating Exercises
June 8, 1942
Lincoln High School Auditorium

Processional
"War March of the Priests"
From *Athalia*
(Mendelssohn)

Flag Salute
National Anthem

Invocation
Reverend C.E. Hodges, Pastor,
Jerusalem Methodist Church,
Rockville, Maryland

Choral Selection
"Go Down Moses"
Spiritual
(Burleigh)

Dramatic Sketches

Introduction
Sylvia Waters

Safety and Protection
Muriel Baker,
Ralph K. Brooks, Augustus Budd,
Emma Cooke,
James S. Copeland,
Lucille Copeland,
Herbert Dorsey, Charles C. Gaither,
Otealia V. Hayes,
Grace Norris,
and Norman B. Ridgley

Musical Selection
"Moonlight and Roses"
(Lemare)
Senior Girls' Sextette

1942 Senior Girls Sextette
L to R: Bessie Hill, Juanita Lyles, Sylvia Waters, Carolyn Johnson, Myrtle Jones, one member not pictured.

*Experiences and Services to Our
Government*
Jack M. Quiller,
Mable Gray,
Esther W. Hill, Virginia B. Moore,
and Ophelia Washington

Conservation and Production
Loretta L. Brown,

Ella Awkard

Mildred Estep,
Daniel E. Gaither,
and Harry T. Stewart

Physical Fitness and Health
Arthur J. Cross,
Phoebe Chaney,
Donald T. King,
Juanita Lyles, John Owens, and
Blanche Riggs

Choral Selection

"Deep River"
Spiritual
(Burleigh)

Sustaining Morale
Ella Awkard,

Some of the Senior boys.
First Row: __,Ralph K. Brooks, Hamilton A. Hawkins, Earl Hatcher. Second Row: C. Herbert Dorsey, Harry T. Stewart, John F. Marr. Third Row:__,__,__, John R. Owens, Merrel Thorton. Rear Row: Ulysses M. Taylor, Jack M. Quiller, Augustus Budd, William H.M. Ridgley.

Bessie Hill,
Carolyn Johnson,
Myrtle Jones,
and Ulysses M. Taylor

Recapitulation
Sylvia Waters

Choral Selection
"Lift Every Voice and Sing,"
Negro National Anthem
(Johnson)

Presentation of Diplomas
Dr. Edwin W. Broome, County
Superintendent of Schools

Awards
Edward U. Taylor,

County Supervisor of Colored
Schools

Class Poem
"Our Love for Lincoln High
School," Blanche Riggs

Class Song
"Memories,"
Charles C. Gaither &
William H.M. Ridgley

Benediction
Reverend J.W. Dockette, Pastor,
Sharp Street Methodist Church,
Sandy Spring, Maryland

Recessional
"Pomp and Circumstance"
(Elgar)

1942 Senior Girls
L to R: Esther W. Hill, Emma Cooke, Ella Awkard

LINCOLN HIGH SCHOOL
CLASS OF 1943

Victory Corps 1943

Since this was the year that the twelfth grade was added, there were no formal graduating exercises. At the end of the school year, the two students—Gladys Owens and Betty Prather—who had fulfilled their Maryland State requirements for graduation were merely handed their diplomas without pomp and ceremony.

Even though those young ladies used second-hand books, they were fortunate to have certified teachers who made the difference, in spite of the fact that they had few instructional materials with which to work.

On the other hand, their counterparts at all-white Montgomery Blair High School in Silver Spring had a somewhat different story to relate. John R. Benedict, Class of 1943, revealed some eye-opening disclosures in an article that he wrote for the November 10, 1943 issue of the *Gazette*, after the class celebrated its 50th anniversary reunion at the Bethesda Marriott Hotel:

"The Class of 1943 was drastically short-changed by World War II. Blair archives are almost completely void of any information about it.

"Because of wartime shortages, its teachers included University of Maryland students. The class was prohibited from having a formal yearbook, so members made their own mimeographed typewritten pages and pasted-down snapshots.

"There were less than 200 in the graduation ceremony at the Silver Theatre in Silver Spring on June 8, 1943, and more than 50 are known to be deceased."

Whereas the Blair High students experienced a deprivation of certain things due to wartime shortages, it was customary for the Lincoln High students to be short-changed.

LHS National Honor Society

L to R: Annie Procton, Maxine Claggett, Doris Plummer, NHS Adviser S. Eloise Levister, Warrick S.Hill, Helen Baker, Mable D.Thomas, Thelma Ramey

1943-1944 Transportation Committee Standing L to R: Florence Windear, Dorothy Rhodes, Mrs. Armentris Hooks-Evans (sponsor) Kneeling, L to R: Vaughn Johnson, Warrick S. Hill

As of this writing, both Class of 1943 Lincoln High School graduates are very active in their respective communities.

FACULTY

Parlett L. Moore, *Principal*

Genevieve S. Brown

Doris M. Greene

Armentris P. Hooks

S. Eloise Levister

Queene E. McNeill

Maynard E. McPherson

Mary C. Moore

Ruby E. Morris

Herbert H. Norton

James T. Robinson

Lemuel A. Thomas

E.V. Elizabeth Slade

LINCOLN HIGH SCHOOL
CLASS OF 1944

The Class of 1944 began its high school career in September of 1939 with an enrollment of 122 students. Due to the largeness of the class, it was divided into two sections with Queene E. McNeill and Maso P. Ryan as the home-room teachers, who endeavored to help their charges become representative students of Lincoln High School.

In the year 1940, we were no longer freshmen but sophomores with a never-to-be-forgotten freshman year behind us. We now had to adjust ourselves to the new five-year curriculum which most of us accepted willingly. During this year, one new teacher was added to the faculty, Miss Levister, teacher of English and music. We owe her great credit for helping to organize the National Honor Society. Annie Mae Jackson, Betty Prather, Maude Smith, and Mable Thomas were inducted into the National Honor Society during this year.

During our junior year, the girls presented a play in the assembly entitled *The Ghost of a Freshman*. Mable Thomas was student director. It was during this year that Helen Baker, Merrel King, Virgie Stewart, and Marie Washington became members of the National Honor Society. We were fortunate in having four new teachers added to the faculty: Miss Elsie Dorsey, Miss Mary C. Moore, Miss Ruby Morris, and Mr. James T. Robinson.

Entering our fourth year, it was amazing to observe the decrease in our enrollment; nevertheless, those of us who returned worked diligently to help in the war effort as well as to make definite academic progress. The homeroom was then under the supervision of Miss Ruby E. Morris.

With the closing of our fourth-year term, we had two graduates, Gladys Owens and Betty Prather, who completed the vocational course.

1944 Lincoln High School May Queen Virgie Stewart

*Helen Baker,
Class of 1944*

Mrs. Genevieve S. Brown, our present homeroom teacher, has worked hard with us. She has manifested a great interest in each of us and has exerted every effort to develop us into worthwhile citizens.

Our class has greatly decreased in number because of the war. Many have gone to work in important war industries, others have joined Uncle Sam's fighting forces. Among the latter are George Clipper, Charles Frazier, and Euell Owens in the Marines; Carlton Garrison and Louis Payne in the U.S. Army; and Rudolph Lee in the U.S. Navy.

The remaining members of the senior class have participated in many school events. Ethel Awkard, Thomas Foreman, Bernice Jackson, Virgie Stewart, and Mable Thomas, members of the Safety Patrol Force, attended a baseball game at Griffith Stadium in Washington, D.C. The Lincoln High newspaper has also been well represented.

The National Honor Society added another member to its list in 1944—Mae Mitchell. With the good spirit of our homeroom teacher, Mrs. Brown, we presented a short skit in assembly on the lives and accomplishments of famous American Negroes. Also on the program was featured a Negro History quiz, in which members of the audience participated."

The Class of 1944 made history in more than one way at Lincoln High School. It was the first class to graduate from the twelfth grade, and it was the second smallest class ever to graduate. But, what it lacked in class size, its members made up for with

*May Queen & Her Attendants
L to R: Bernice Jackson, Ethel Awkard,
Catherine Timbers, Queen Virgie Stewart,
Helen Baker, and Mable D. Thomas*

May Queen 1944 Virgie Stewart

1944 May Queen Attendants L to R: Helen Baker, Mable D. Thomas

their intellectual powers. More specifically, three members of this class—Helen Baker, Mae Mitchell, and Mable D. Thomas—along with two sophomores, Lillian Hayes and Violet Isreal, participated in an Americana Quiz Broadcast over Station WMAL in Washington, D.C., on Sunday, March 26, 1944, against an Armstrong High School team. Mrs. Genevieve S. Brown, Mrs. Armentris P. Hooks, and Miss S. Eloise Levister (now Mrs. Shelton) were the coaches."

Because of the lack of transportation to the radio station and the lack of space at the broadcast station, most Lincoln High School students sat by their radios to listen to the battle-of-the-brains contest. The few students who were able to make the trip witnessed Lincoln's team trailing a very confident Armstrong team through two rounds. Following the second round, Lincoln valedictorian

Mable D. Thomas displayed her brilliance of mind to electrify the Lincoln High School spectators and listeners when she correctly answered a ten-point bonus question and thereby led her team to a stunning victory over a strong and confident Armstrong High team.

This class was not only composed of academically talented students, but it had some athletically inclined ones as well, which made it a complete class of students.

Five young ladies in this class—Emma Jane Dorsey, Dorothy Fisher , Della Gray, Mary Kelly, and Virgie Stewart—were considered to be standouts in softball. Emma Jane, Dorothy, Della, and Mary were powerful batters, accurate fielders and throwers, and intelligent base runners, whereas Virgie was overpowering on the pitcher's mound with her fastball and errorless pitching. She also used great skill in getting on base safely.

Two young men in this class—Charles E. Frazier and W. Marshall Lyles—let their presence be felt on the softball field and on the baseball diamond. Not only did they bat the ball hard and far, but they denied many batters the privilege of getting on base safely with their flawless catches and their bullet-like throwing. In track, three young ladies—Bernice Jackson, Mae Mitchell, and Mable D. Thomas—were forces to be dealt with on a relay team, as they swiftly carried the baton to their waiting teammate.

Newspaper Staff

Editor-in-Chief
Mable Thomas

Assistant Editors
Helen Baker
Virgie Stewart

Art Editor
Robert Sellman

Business Editors
Mary Mason
Mae Mitchell

Exchange Editor
Catherine Timbers

Class Motto
"Not at the Top, but Climbing."

Class Colors
Red & White

Class Flower
Red Rose

Valedictorian
Mable D. Thomas

Salutatorian
Helen Baker

GRADUATES
Academic Course
Ethel McKay Awkard
Helen Virginia Baker
Clara Katrine Copeland
William Elgar Hood
Mary Elizabeth Mason
Mae Ellen Mitchell
Robert H. Sellman
Virgie Elizabeth Stewart
Mable Drusilla Thomas

General Course
Thomas Worthington Foreman
Charles Edwin Frazier
Carlton Ulysses Garrison
Bernice Virginia Jackson
William Marshall Lyles
Paul Garnett Payne
Sarah Catherine Timbers

Vocational Course
Pauline Delores Beverley
Dorothy Elizabeth Fisher
Martha Atle Gunn
Annie Mae Jackson
James Phillip Johnson
Merrel Lee King

Class Officers

President
Mable D. Thomas

Vice-President
Annie Mae Jackson

Secretary
Martha Gunn

Assistant Secretary
Virgie Stewart

Treasurer
Merrel King

NATIONAL HONOR SOCIETY
Helen Baker
Annie Mae Jackson
Merrel L. King
Mae Mitchell
Virgie Stewart
Mable D. Thomas

FACULTY
Dr. Parlett L. Moore, *Principal*
Clarence L. Bond
Genevieve Brown
Jessie M. Drummond
Thelma L. Gray
Doris M. Greene
Armentris P. Hooks
S. Eloise Levister
Queene E. McNeill
Maynard E. McPherson (part-time)
Ruby E. Morris
Herbert H. Norton
E. V. Elizabeth Slade
Lemuel A. Thomas

Edward U. Taylor, *Supervisor*
Dr. Edwin W. Broome,
Superintendent

GRADUATING EXERCISES
Wednesday, June 14, 1944

Theme
"We Build the Ladder by Which
We Climb"

Processional
"War March of the Priests"
(Mendelssohn)

Flag salute
National Anthem

Invocation
Reverend W. E. Williams, Pastor,
Jerusalem Methodist Church,
Rockville, Maryland

Choral Selection
"Lift Every Voice and Sing,"
Negro National Anthem
(Johnson)

Dramatic Sketches
Class of 1944

Prologue
Helen Baker
"Our Heritage Our Career"

Class Poem
Virgie Stewart

Class Song
"Our Challenge"
Class of 1944

May Queen Virgie Stewart on her throne surrounded by her senior class attendants.

Epilogue
Mable D. Thomas

Choral Selection
"Recessional"
(Kipling-Dekoven)

Presentation of Diplomas
Dr. Edwin W. Broome,
Superintendent of Instruction

Awards
Edward U. Taylor, Supervisor of
Colored Schools

Selection
"Double Octette"

Benediction
Reverend R. E. Burnett, Pastor,
Sharp Street Methodist Church,
Sandy Spring, Maryland

Recessional
"Pomp and Circumstance"
(Elgar)

(The audience is requested to remain seated until after the recessional.)

courtesy Virgie Stewart-Prather

1944 Senior Boys Quartet
L to R: Harry T. Stewart, Ulysses M. Taylor, William H.M. Ridgley, Donald T. King

LINCOLN HIGH SCHOOL
CLASS OF 1945

Reflections
The Best Years of Our Lives,
1940-1945

Our Freshman Year
Transition Period

Although more than 50 years have passed, our high school memories still linger in our minds. We fondly reminisce of the early 1940's when we attended classes at good old Lincoln High School in Lincoln Park (Rockville, Maryland) with its competent and caring teachers, who taught us moral values, honesty, and personal integrity, as well as the required subject matter. Former President Theodore Roosevelt embraced the idea that "To educate a person in mind and not in morals is to educate a menace to society." Education-wise, our former teachers and former President Roosevelt were on the same wave length. Allow us to escape 55 years back to Lincoln High School where education was a top priority, and our teachers were educators, who rose to the occasion to carry us to greater heights.

As we turn back the hands of time to September 1940 to revisit our high school days, we recall that there were 154 of us who enrolled as eighth graders at Lincoln High School. We remember "listening to inspiring words of welcome by our principal," Mr. Parlett L. Moore, and being assigned homerooms alphabetically.

With the thousands of students who have enrolled in the Montgomery County public schools, it was impracticable to keep an annual list of these students on file, in addition to an alphabetical file on every entrant. Such a practice would create a space problem.

Since the Central Records Office, Montgomery County Public Schools, only keeps an alphabetical file on each student, it would be next to impossible for the personnel there to determine the names of the eighth

Doris Plummer and Clarence R. Webster Jr.

Juanita Washington and Robert Ross

graders who entered Lincoln High School in September 1940, unless the names of the students were given to them first. This being the case, Central Records personnel verified the 138 names of students that our finite memories permitted us to recall. According to historical records, there are 16 of our former classmates who are unaccounted for out of the recorded 154.

HOMEROOM 8A
(A-He), Room 2,
Miss Queene E. McNeill
Millie L. Adams
Lucy Addison
Basil Alcorn
James Baker

M. Louise Beckwith
Mabel Bowins
Lawrence Boyd
John Braxton
Dorothy V. Brown
Madeline A. Brown
Clifton N. Burgess
Bernice Byrd
Virgie Campbell
Helen Carroll
Rowena Chambers
Walter Christian
Calvin Claggett
E. Maxine Claggett
James H. Claggett
Thomas E. Clark
Doris Cole
William B. Cooke
McRein Cooper

Doris Cole

William Elgar Copeland
Arie Crawford
Eleanor Cross
Emanser Crutchfield
Eula Mae Crutchfield
Sarah L. Davenport
Margaret DeMar
Paul W. Diggs
Ernestine Dorsey
Glendora Dove
Marguerite Dove
Mary Dove
Edward Doyle
Anna Ellis
Julia Foreman
Charles E. Frazier
Gladys Frazier
Dorothy Fulmore
Eva Gaither
Carlton U. Garrison

Calvin Genies
Rentha Genies
George Gibson
Arthur Green
Mildred Hackey
Evelyn Hall
Howard H. Hall
Julia Mae Hall
Upton M. Hallman
Viola Hamilton
Betty Hawkins

HOMEROOM 8B
(Hi-P), Room 3,
Mrs. Genvieve Swann
Warrick S. Hill
Clarence Holland
J. Everett Holland
J. Barbara Hood
Virgil J. Hood
Ollie Hopkins

Mary Snowden,
Paul Payne

Dorothy Wims

Isobel Howard
William Hyson
David Isom
Beatrice Isreal
Catherine Jackson
Clifton Jackson
Edward W. Jackson
Mary Jackson
Sarah Jackson
Theodore Jackson
William Jackson
Beatrice L. Johnson
Pauline E. Johnson
Pauline L. Johnson
Sarah Kelly
Margaret King
Regeane Lancaster
Freeman Lee
Willie H. Lee
Philip Lewis
Reed Logan
Charles N. Lyles
Russell Lyles
Dolly Lyons

James H. Lyons
Mable Martin
Leroy Matthews
Mable Matthews
Grace Mercer
Norman Miller
John Moore
Helen Naylor
James C. Offord
N. Louise Ogburn
Viola Parker
Paul G. Payne
Leona V. Pendleton
Robert Penn
Doris E. Plummer
Garnett S. Plummer
Shirley M. Plummer
Lillian Prather
Sylvester Pratt
Annie L. Procton
Bernice Pumphrey
Gladys Pumphrey

HOMEROOM 8C
(Q-Z), Room 5,
Dr. Parlett L. Moore
Annie Randolph
Florence E. Randolph
Dorothy M. Rhodes
Wilbur A. Ricketts
Bernice Ricks
Dallas Ricks
C. Louise Robinson
Robert Ross
Stanley C. Selby
Roland F. Sims
George Slater

Wilbur A. Ricketts

Bernice Smallwood
Thelma Smith
Charles Snowden
Mary I. Snowden
James Stevenson
Ernest Stewart
Roy Summerour
John Talley
Mae Talley
John Thomas
Alice Thompson
Susie Thompson
Cleveland Tucker
Charles Washington
Dorothy Washington
Juanita Washington
Leon Washington
Carl R. Webster
Clarence R. Webster, Jr.

Annie Procton and Dorothy Rhodes

Dorothy Wims
Charles E. Wood

We hailed from 19 elementary schools, the principals of which are indicated in parentheses, to become the prospective Class of 1945:

Clarksburg-Boyds (Lillian Jiles); Emory Grove (Helen Aiken Bryant); Germantown (Lillian B. Offord Brown); Ken Gar; Laytonsville (Mattie B. Simpson); Linden; Norbeck (Katherine Gaither); Poolesville (James H. Waters); Quince Orchard (Grace Richardson Billingsley); River Road; Rockville (Thomas W. Cornish); Sandy Spring (Ross J. Boddy); Scotland (Margaret Taylor Jones); Sellman (Samuel Jones); Smithville

Grace Mercer

(Gladys Challenger Boston); Spencerville (Inez H. Smith); Stewarttown (Alda Campbell Taylor); Takoma Park (Alicebelle V. Allen); Sugarland (Nellie Watts Brown).

Our Second Year
Academic Achievement,
Extra-Curricular Activities,
Popularity Contest

During our second year, we recall that "many of our classmates made the honor roll, and we were fortunate to have Warrick S. Hill and Dorothy Rhodes inducted into the National Honor Society" on December 5, 1941. In the latter part of "the school year 1941-1942, the National

Shirley Plummer

Ethel Awkard, Maxine Claggett

Honor Society inductees were Maxine Claggett, Doris Plummer, and Annie Procton."

Along with our scholastic achievements, "many of our classmates participated in sports and other school activities. Along the line of popularity, William B. Cooke and Annie Procton were crowned May King and May Queen" at our May Day festivities because they sold the most war stamps.

Because we were so occupied with our schoolwork and war-time activities, we hardly noticed that the school year would terminate soon, and we would be separated from our teachers, classmates, and friends again.

Unfortunately, it was the rule

rather than the exception for black students, both on the elementary and high school levels, to receive secondhand supplies from their Caucasian counterparts, but the condition of the books did not hinder our learning. This trend was broken when some members of the Class of 1945 were ninth graders who received new biology books, and for others when they were tenth graders who took Spanish. Our competent, caring teachers made the difference between our success and failure, and instilled those values that enabled us to become productive, law-abiding citizens in our communities.

Marguerite Dove

These poems were composed by the indicated students and were published in the school newspaper "Lincoln High News" in April 1942.

OLD GLORY

"Old Glory" is our own dear flag
That waves for you and me;
We must strive to keep her ever
Waving, sailing for liberty.

We must never shame "Old Glory,"
Or cease to give her fame;
She is of our own U.S.A.,
And proud to bear the name.

She is our most prized possession.
So value her with pride;
Every one must do his part
To keep her waving high.
We must honor her in earnest
To keep her always free;
Old Glory! may she forever wave,
As the symbol of our liberty!

—Virgie Stewart, Class of '44

HOME

Home is the place I love to be
When things aren't going right;
Home, my home is the place for me
In the darkness of the night.

When the way gets lonely
And I long for a friend,
I look toward home
And find peace within.

Clifton N. Burgess

In that home where my mother
Is waiting for me,
There is no other place
I love, so, to be.

So when you feel lonely
And oh! so blue —
Just go back home
And find peace there, too.

—Dorothy Rhodes, Class of '45

MY PRAYER

I pray thee, oh God, today
to bless us in every way;
I pray thee, oh God,
To bless the ground we trod.

I pray thee, oh God, today
To bless the bird up in the tree,
To bless him on his flight each day,
And bless the song he sings to
You and me.
—Wilbur Ricketts, Class of '45

Our Third Year
Enlightenment,
Foreign Language Involvement,
Popularity Contest

We recall when our third school year, 1942-1943, arrived, just 76 of us returned to continue our educational pursuit as tenth graders. We learned that our class would make history for being the second class to graduate from the twelfth grade at Lincoln High School. We would receive five years of high school instruction, instead of the traditional four years. We were in store for yet another surprise—the boys and girls were assigned separate homerooms for the first time. The boys were under the leadership of Mr. Herbert H. Norton in the Shop, and the girls were under the supervision of Mrs. Doris Greene in the Cottage.

Class Officers

President
Howard H. Hall

Secretary
Dorothy Rhodes

Treasurer
William B. Cooke

Student Council Representatives
Warrick S. Hill,
Doris Plummer,
Dorothy Rhodes

Annie Procton

Class Motto
"What you are to be you are now becoming, so do your best."

Class Colors
Green & Gold

Class Flower
Gardenia

Some of us were chosen by the faculty to serve on various school committees.

Activities Program Coordinating Committee
Sponsors
Mrs. S. Eloise Levister & Mr. Parlett L. Moore

Maxine Claggett
Warrick S. Hill
Annie Procton

Emergency Adjustment
Sponsors
Miss Ruby Morris &
Miss S. Eloise Levister

Annie Procton

Pupil Transportation
Sponsor
Mrs. Armentris Hooks

Warrick S. Hill
Dorothy Rhodes

War Adjustment Committee
Sponsor
Miss Ruby Morris

Annie Procton

Welfare And Safety
Sponsors
Mrs. Genevieve Swann Brown &
Mr. Herbert H. Norton

Clifton N. Burgess

Some of us held offices in the Lincoln High School student organizations.

Marguerite Dove, Doris Plummer

Boys Club

Sponsors
Mr. Lemuel A. Thomas
Mr. Herbert H. Norton

President
Warrick S. Hill

Vice-President
William B. Cooke

Secretary
Wilbur A. Ricketts

Dramatic Club

Sponsors
Mrs. Ruby Morris
Miss Queene E. McNeill

President
Annie Procton

Assistant Secretary
Doris Plummer

Girls Club

Sponsor
Mrs. Armentris Hooks

Secretary
Annie Procton

Home Economics Club

Sponsor
Miss Doris Greene

Secretary
Dorothy Rhodes

Treasurer
Grace Mercer

National Honor Society

Sponsors
Miss S. Eloise Levister
Dr. Parlett L. Moore

Assistant Secretary
Doris Plummer

Treasurer
Warrick S. Hill

New Farmers of America

Sponsor
Mr. Herbert H. Norton

Treasurer
Howard H. Hall

Newspaper Staff

Sponsor
Miss Queene E. McNeill

News Editors
Maxine Claggett
William B. Cooke
Warrick S. Hill
Doris Plummer
Annie Procton
Dorothy Rhodes

Art Editor
Howard H. Hall

Joke Editor
Rentha Genies

Business Editor
Leona Pendleton

Sports Editor
Virgil J. Hood

School Patrol
Sponsor
Mr. Herbert H. Norton

Second Lieutenant
J. Everett Holland

Victory Corps
Sponsor
Miss Mary C. Moore

President
Sarah Davenport

Secretary
Maxine Claggett

Treasurer
James Baker

Those of us who took the academic course, along with the eleventh graders who took the academic course, comprised the first and only class that took Spanish in the history of Lincoln High School. We enjoyed the competent and dynamic instruction of Mrs. Ruby E. Morris Wiley for two consecutive years. She obtained the names and addresses of high school students in the Spanish-speaking countries of South America who would correspond with us, so that we could become fluent in their language, and they, in ours. This correspondence was both practical and interesting. Not only was there an exchange of letters, but also an exchange of photographs by some.

We remember Mrs. Wiley to be small in stature, but what she lacked in size, she more than compensated for with excellent instruction in her English and Spanish classes, as well as her 90-words-per-minute typing. We were fortunate to have her for English when we were tenth graders and for Spanish when we were tenth and eleventh graders.

In a different vein, the "Home Economics Club, with the help of the Girls Club, sponsored a popularity contest in which votes were sold.Juanita Washington, our classmate, sold the most votes and was crowned Miss Lincoln High School by Mr. Moore on May 21, 1943. In addition, Mable D. Thomas (Class of 1944) presented a corsage of carnations, donated to the club by Gude Florist in Rockville, to Juanita Washington, and Phyllis Awkard (Class of 1947) presented envelopes containing defense stamps to her and to the other contestants."

Scholastically speaking, we were still achieving academically as "Mae Talley was inducted into the National Honor Society." At this point in time, our third year rapidly came to an end.

Our Fourth Year
Memorable Events

In our junior year, some of us were relocated to the main building with first-year teacher Thelma L. Gray as our homeroom teacher, and others were assigned to Herbert H. Norton in Shop I. At this point in our high-school career, only 43 of us remained.

The decrease in our enrollment was due partly to the induction of some of our classmates into the armed forces. Joining the army were Clifton N. Burgess, Carlton U. Garrison, and Clarence Holland; joining the Marines was Charles E. Frazier; and joining the Navy were Calvin Genies, Howard H. Hall, and Clarence R. Webster, Jr.

Three of our classmates–Charles E. Frazier, Carlton U. Garrison, and Paul G. Payne–graduated a year earlier than expected, thanks to the wisdon of our caring principal, Parlett L. Moore. Since Charles, Carlton, and Paul would reach their 18th birthday nearly a year before graduation, Mr. Moore designed an accelerated course which would permit them to take their required junior and senior year subjects simultaneously, to fulfill their Maryland State requirements before becoming eligible for the United States military draft.

"One of the most successful programs of our junior year was the Armistice Day program, on November 11, 1944, that included original speeches, patriotic songs, poems, and recitations, as well as taps. Another highlight of the program was the presentation of a service plaque to the school." Later in the year, "the 11B English class presented a guidance play, 'The Pursuit of Happiness,' during an assembly."

Socially, we were not neglected, as the culminating activity was the Annual Junior-Senior Prom that we gave for the seniors. "It was a spectacular success since we had a variety of people who participated. The girls invited 25 servicemen from nearby Fort George G. Meade in Anne Arundel County, Maryland, to share this memorable event with them and the senior girls."

Our Senior Year
Mission Accomplished

Finally, we rejoiced at the arrival of our fifth and most significant year at Lincoln High School, happy that we would be graduating but sorry that we would be departing from friends and teachers who had become a part of our lives.

We gained two classmates, Thomas W. Jackson and Paul M. Lee, who like their predecessors Charles E. Frazier, Carlton U. Garrison, and Paul G. Payne, were encouraged to take the accelerated course to ensure them of graduation from high school before being drafted into military service.

In November of 1944, second-year teacher Thelma Gray Barnum took on the monumental task of starting a boys' basketball team which was composed of all inexperienced players and with no gymnasium in which to practice or play. The players had to be bussed to Fisherman's Hall in Rockville to practice and play their home games. Seniors William B. Cooke and Warrick S. Hill played on the team and did little to defend their more experienced, fast-dribbling, sharp-shooting opponents. Although the team's win-loss record was unimpressive, the players learned a valuable lesson in teamwork, as well as important life lessons.

During the month of May, Mary I. Snowden was crowned May Queen; and Maxine Claggett, William B. Cooke, Warrick S. Hill, Doris Plummer, Annie Procton, Dorothy M. Rhodes, Wilbur A. Ricketts, Bernice Ricks, Mae Talley, and Juanita Washington participated in an oratorical contest. Juanita Washington won the contest and received a $25 savings bond for her performance, and Bernice Ricks was the runner-up and was the recipient of a bronze pin.

The final weeks prior to commencement teemed with activities. The juniors gave us a royal sendoff with the annual Junior-Senior Prom; Class Night planning was in full swing as class themes, class songs, and class poems filled the air, as well as thoughts of what to give each classmate that would be characteristic of his/her high-school life; we took our final examinations; and then we rehearsed many hours for our commencement exercises in the assembly hall.

Finally, we reached the milestone for which we had been striving–graduation. Graduation was an end-ing and a beginning in our lives. It was a steppingstone from the past, with its countless hours of study and its numerous moments of contentment, to a new and slightly different life that was filled with temendous challenges and responsibilities. It was a sad as well as a cheerful time of life when we said "Farewell" to classmates, teachers, and friends, and looked forward to start a new chapter of our lives when we would meet new friends and acquaintances in our careers.

Class Motto
"Today Decides Tomorrow."

Class Colors
Blue & White

Class Flower
Red Rose

Valedictorian
Dorothy Mae Rhodes

Salutatorian
Warrick Samuel Hill

GRADUATES

Academic Course
Millie Lucretia Adams
James Baker
*Ethel Maxine Claggett
*William Branson Cooke
McRein Mary Ellen Cooper
Margaret Louise DeMar
Gladys Elizabeth Frazier
Rentha Viola Genies

Upton Montgomery Hallman
*Warrick Samuel Hill
Virgil Jackson Hood
Leona Virginia Pendleton
*Doris Emogene Plummer
*Annie Lucinda Procton
*Wilbur Allen Ricketts
Bernice Elaine Ricks
*Dorothy Mae Rhodes
*Mae Lucille Talley

* *National Honor Society*

- *Vocational Course*
Arie Virginia Crawford
Marguerite Lucille Dove
Dorothy Bernice Fulmore
Julia Mae Hall
Betty Elizabeth Hawkins
Thomas Wade Jackson
Paul Melvin Lee
Willie Hortense Lee
James Henry Lyons
Charles Neiper Lyles
John Henry Moore
Garnett Sylvester Plummer
Shirley Markell Plummer
Catherine Louise Robinson
Robert Leonard Ross
Roland Franklin Sims
Mary Irene Snowden

Charles Lee Washington
Dorothy Mary Washington
Juanita Theresa Washington
Dorothy Beatrice Wims

FACULTY

Dr. Parlett L. Moore, *Principal*
Clarence L. Bond
Genevieve Brown
Nettie V. Chappell
Edna R. Evans
Jessie Drummond
Thelma Gray
Doris M. Greene
S. Eloise Levister
Maynard E. McPherson
Julia H. Miller
Mary C. Moore
Ruby E. Morris
E. V. Elizabeth Slade
Lemuel A. Thomas
Naomi E. Waller

GRADUATING EXERCISES
Wednesday, June 13, 1945

Theme
"Today Decides Tomorrow"

courtesy Betty Prather, Virgie Stewart

LINCOLN HIGH SCHOOL CLASS OF 1945 50th ANNIVERSARY CELEBRATION

The Lincoln High School Class of 1945 celebrated its golden anniversary at the Gaithersburg Hilton Hotel on Saturday night, July 15, 1995. Of the 154 members who enrolled in September 1940, thirty of them attended the celebration, along with their spouses, relatives, and friends. One member journeyed from Philadelphia, Pennsylvania; another member traveled from Portsmouth, Virginia; three others came from Washington, D.C., and 25 members were already here in Maryland.

Lincoln High School Class of 1945 50th Anniversary, July 1995
Seated, L to R: Thelma Smith-Porter, McRein Cooper-Thompson. First Row, L to R: Charles L. Washington, Garnet S. Plummer, Paul M. Lee, Beatrice L. Johnson, James Baker, Doris Plummer-Hackey, Bernice Ricks-Joppy, Mary Snowden-Contee, Annie Procton-Rhodes, Louise Beckwith-Hoes, Shirley Plummer-Lyles, Margaret DeMar-Awkward, James H. Lyons, Dorothy Wims-Onley, James C. Offord. Second Row, L to R: Clarence Holland, Charles E. Frazier, Mildred Hackey, Clifton N. Burgess, Clarence R. Webster,Jr. Maxine Claggett-Phillips, William B. Cooke, Dorothy Rhodes-Carroll, Warrick S. Hill, Leona Pendelton-Ramey, Mae Talley-Peterson, Betty Hawkins-Johnson

Many members felt that this affair would be the culminating activity following their 50-year departure from historically all-black Lincoln High School (Rockville, Maryland), which closed in June 1958. There will be plans for other events, but those events will be anticlimactic.

This 50th-year anniversary was planned for the attendees to meet, greet, reflect, and enjoy as the celebration took place and the forgotten memories rekindled.

Following the social hour, Doris (Plummer) Hackey emceed a program during which Class Valedictorian and Reunion Committee Assistant Secretary-Treasurer Dorothy (Rhodes) Carroll gave the welcome address and Leona (Pendleton)

Mrs. Armentris P. Hooks, our commendable U.S. history teacher

Ramey read the Lincoln High School Class of '45 Reunion Poem.

Prior to eating a delectable meal, Dorothy (Wims) Onley led the singing of the Negro National Anthem, then Reunion Committee Co-Chair William B. Cooke gave the invocation. After the dinner hour, each member of the Reunion Committee participated in the program.

Public Relations Person James C. Offord introduced the committee members, as well as the family of deceased classmate William Jackson. This introduction was made because Tracy, the younger of two sons of William and Roxanna, had been a prominent basketball player. In fact, he starred on the Paint Branch High School basketball team (Grades 9-12) and played a leading role on the Notre Dame University basketball team (1977-1981). In 1981,

Tracy Jackson, Austin Jackson(in rear)

179

Lincoln High School Class of 1945 47th Anniversary, Rockville, Maryland, May 23, 1992. Seated: Madeline Brown-Washington, Maxine Claggett-Phillips, Mary Snowden-Contee, Barbara Hood-Broadus

Tracy was drafted by the Boston Celtics (National Basketball Association) and due to a surplus of guards, he was later traded to the Chicago Bulls with whom he played for two years before being selected to play with the Indiana Pacers. Subsequently, he played with the Athletes in Action for two years, which proved to be a rewarding experience.

Besides the introduction of Tracy and his mother Roxanna, his older brother Austin and his younger sister Gwendolyn were also recognized.

After these introductions, Secretary-Treasurer Annie (Procton) Rhodes introduced the National Honor Society members; Betty (Hawkins) Johnson and Bernice (Ricks) Joppy introduced the class members, and Clarence R. Webster, Jr., introduced the Class Valedictorian and Class Salutatorian.

Prior to the singing of the Class Song, Class Salutatorian and Re-union Committee Chair Warrick S. Hill gave some reflections upon the years 1940-1945 and later introduced J. Richmond, who created the unique designs for the printed programs.

At times, the room was as busy as a beehive. John C. Kelly was videotaping; C. Arthur Eubanks was photographing; the attendees were socializing, and the Young Bucks Band was providing the music.

Not only did the all-Black Lincoln High School alumni and their guests enjoy the affair, but six Caucasian alumni, who wandered in from their five-year reunion and requested to participate, had a delightful time as well.

Much to the surprise of many of the Lincoln High School alumni, the celebration was taped and televised on cable Channel 8 that night. The members, who witnessed it, called others to share the experience.

S. Eloise Levister, our remarkable English & music teacher

Many of the members of the Class of '45 expressed their gratitude for living to celebrate their 50th anniversary. They considered it a real blessing to have such a privilege. Judging from the compliments that have been paid, the attendees will cherish the memories of this occasion for many years to come.

The following members of the Class of '45 participated in this celebration: James Baker (Lillian), Louise Beckwith-Hoes, Clifton N. Burgess (Elsie), Maxine Claggett-Phillips (Harry), William B. Cooke (Theresa), McRein Cooper-Thompson (Howard), Emanser Crutchfield, Margaret DeMar-Awkward, Charles E. Frazier (Mavis), Mildred Hackey, Betty Hawkins-Johnson (Arthur), Warrick S. Hill (Christine), Clarence Holland (Margie), Beatrice L. Johnson, Paul M. Lee (Mary Ellen), James H. Lyons (Mary Bell), James C. Offord (Charlotte), Leona Pendleton-Ramey, Doris Plummer-Hackey (George), Garnett S. Plummer (Shirley), Shirley Plummer-Lyles (Marshall), Annie Procton-Rhodes (Lewis), Dorothy Rhodes-Carroll, Bernice Ricks-Joppy (Melvin), Thelma Smith-Porter, Mary Snowden-Contee, Mae Talley-Peterson, Charles L. Washington (Mary Jane), Clarence R. Webster, Jr. (Patricia), Dorothy Wims-Onley.

Lincoln High School Class of 1945 50th Anniversary.Warrick S. Hill & wife, Christine, July 15, 1995

Lincoln High School Class of 1945, 50th Anniversary Reunion, July 15th, 1995, Gaithersburg Hilton Hotel

Class of 1945 Reunion Committee, Spring of 1992 after meeting at Residence of Annie Procton-Rhodes. L to R: James C. Offord, Virgil J. Hood, Dorothy Rhodes-Carrol, Warrick S. Hill, Annie Procton-Rhodes, William B. Cooke, Leona Pendleton-Ramey, Clarence R. Webster, Jr, Bernice Ricks Joppy. Absent: Betty Hawkins-Johnson, Doris Plummer-Hackey

L to R: Warrick S. Hill, Doris Plummer-Hackey, Clarence R. Webster, Jr. (face hidden), J. Richmond

Seated: Thelma Smith Porter. Standing: Betty Hawkins Johnson, Clifton N. Burgess, Dr. Jacquelyn Porter (daughter of Mrs. Porter), Leona Pendleton Ramey (bending over), Clarence R. Webster, Jr. (partially hidden), Warrick S. Hill

Standing: William B. Cooke, Maxine Claggett-Phillips, James Baker, Betty Hawkins-Johnson

Charles E. Frazier & Mavis Zeigler Prather

L to R: Austin Jackson, Tracy Jackson, Clarence R. Webster, Jr., Warrick S. Hill

Warrick S. Hill and Betty Hawkins-Johnson

Standing: Roxanna Jackson, wife of former classmate William Jackson, mother of Austin, Tracy, & Gwendolyn

L to R: Betty Hawkins Johnson, Clifton N. Burgess, Mary Snowden-Contee, Paul M. Lee, Shirley Plummer-Lyles, Doris Plummer-Hackey

183

Lincoln High School

Mrs. Elsie Dorsey-Kennedy

Seated:Mrs. Elizabeth Slade-Childs, Mrs.Eloise Levister-Shelton, Mrs. Thelma Gray-Barnum. Standing: Mrs. Jessie Drummond-Holmes, Mrs. Armentris Hooks-Evans, Mrs. Alberta Mebane-Levingston.

Mr. Maynard E. McPherson (on the right) & Wife, Pauline (on left), Their son Calvin and his wife (in the middle)

L to R: Clarence R. Webster, Jr, Thomas E. Clark, Virgil J. Hood, William B. Cooke, Warrick S. Hill

Virgil J. Hood with his wife Genevieve (L) and former English teacher Mrs. Eloise Shelton (R)

Patricia Manson, Clarence R. Webster, Jr

Class of 1945
47th Anniversary

L to R: Sarah Davenport-Riddick, Christine C. Hill (wife of Warrick S. Hill)

L to R: N. Louise Ogburn, Thelma Smith-Porter

L to R: Amelia Marshall-Sewell, Willie Lee Marshall

L to R: Beatrice L. Johnson, Mary Belle Hawkins-Lyons, Lillian Hayes-Baker, Clarence R. Webster, Jr.

L to R: Beatrice L. Johnson, Sarah Jackson-Adams

L to R: Sarah Jackson-Adams, Wilbur Adams

L to R: Barbara Hood-Broadus, Thelma Smith-Porter, Betty Hawkins-Johnson

L to R: Dorothy Wims-Onley, Shirley Plummer-Lyles, C. Louise Robinson-Moore

47th Anniversary Lincoln High School Class of 1945 Reunion Committee Front L to R: Betty Hawkins-Johnson, James C. Offord, Leona Pendleton-Ramey, Doris Plummer-Hackey, Annie Procton-Rhodes, Dorothy Rhodes-Carroll, Bernice Ricks-Joppy, William B. Cooke Rear, L to R: Clarence R. Webster, Jr. Warrick S. Hill, Virgil J. Hood

Mrs. Jessie Drummond, our knowledgeable Physics teacher

Charles E. Frazier & Mavis Zeigler Prather

Lincoln High School Class of 1945 30th Anniversary Picnic at Lake Needwood on October 26, 1975

L to R: Annie Procton-Rhodes, daughter, Dana and husband Lewis

L to R: Charles N. Lyles, Dorothy Washington

L to R: McRein Cooper-Thompson and sons, Louis and Robert

L to R: Mrs. Genevieve S. Brown, Dr. Parlett L. Moore, George Contee

L to R: Margaret DeMar-Awkward and husband, Daniel

Bernice Ricks-Joppy's son, Alan; Conversing: Mrs. Genevieve S. Brown, Dr. Parlett L. Moore and Mrs. Thelma Moore (wife)

Benice Ricks-Joppy and family: Alan (in front), Leah, Melvin Jr. and Edythe

Marguerite Dove-Johnson, William B. Cooke, Mary Snowden-Contee, Virgil J. Hood, Shirley Plummer-Lyles, James C. Offord

L to R: Betty Hawkins-Johnson, Doris Plummer-Hackey

LINCOLN HIGH SCHOOL
CLASS OF 1946

"On September 8, 1941, the Class of 1946 entered the portals of Lincoln High School as eighth graders with an enrollment of 162 students. Some of the notable members of that eighth grade class were:

1. Hannah Duvall, Lois Plummer, and Lorraine Thomas, who won prizes for the most courteous pupils in their respective homerooms;

2. Evelyn Johnson, Norma Hill, and Hazel Rhodes, who were members of the Student Council;

3. Hellyn Johnson and Nathan Mayes, who participated in Garnet Masque (Dramatic Club) plays;

4. Alice Lincoln, Lois Plummer, Mary Powell, and Aloise White, who were members of the School Safety Patrol;

5. Jean Mason, who was on the winning team of the Highland Park softball tournament;

6. Thelma Ramey, who led the class on the honor roll; and

7. Lorraine Thomas, who won third prize in an essay contest and received $2 for her performance.

On September 14, 1942, 104 ninth graders returned to Lincoln High School and were assigned to two homerooms.

Room 4 Homeroom Officers

President
Walter Adams

Vice-President
William Coates

Secretary
Lorraine Thomas

Treasurer
Caroline Genus

Student Council Representative
Delores Braxton

Adviser
Mr. Lemuel A. Thomas

Room 6 Homeroom Officers

President
Nathan Mayes

Vice-President
Jessie Moore

Secretary
Thelma Ramey

Assistant Secretary
Mildred Hackey

Treasurer
Elbert Isreal

Student Council Representative
Jean Mason

Adviser
Miss S. Eloise Levister

Homerooms 4 and 6 won the attendance banner several times during the year.

There was also noticeable success among these ninth graders:

1. Hannah Duvall and Jessie Moore participated in the 'Miss Lincoln High' popularity contest;

2. Ianthia Gray, Nathan Mayes, and Aloise White were members of the School Safety Patrol;

3. Norma Hill, Alphonzo Jackson, Nathan Mayes, and Thelma Ramey did notable work in the music classes;

4. Nathan Mayes became a member of the electricity and aeronautics pre-induction classes; and

5. Thelma Ramey was inducted into the National Honor Society.

This school year, the physical education program was greatly modified and expanded to meet the demands of the war situation. Miss Mary C. Moore and Mr. James T. Robinson planned a program which provided for participation in basketball, broad jumping, chinning the bar, drills (simple mass movement), soccer, softball, volleyball, weightlifting, and similar 'hardening-up' activities." Unfortunately, Mr. Robinson resigned and was replaced by Mr. Lemuel A. Thomas.

"During the second semester, Miss Moore and Mr. Thomas further developed the program which had been started. A tennis court was built; basketball goals, soccer goals, parallel bars, and chinning bars were erected to provide for participation in these sports, and archery was introduced.

Class Motto
"Enter to learn; go forth to teach."

Class Colors
Blue & Gold

Class Flower
White Gardenia

"On September 13, 1943, eighty-two tenth graders entered Lincoln High School and were assigned to two homerooms.

Room 4 Homeroom Officers

President
Lillian Hayes

Vice-President
Walter Adams

Secretary
Edna Crawford

Treasurer
Gladys Garrett

Student Council Representative
Norma Hill

Adviser
Mr. Lemuel A. Thomas

Room 5 Homeroom Officers

President
Florence Windear

Vice-President
Jean Mason

Secretary
Edith Warfield

Treasurer
Alma King

Student Council Representative
Lorraine Thomas

Adviser
Miss Jessie M. Drummond

The tenth grade class gave a Christmas play in the school auditorium entitled *A Child is Born* which was sponsored by Mr. Lemuel A. Thomas.

Some of the notable members of the tenth grade were:

1. Hadassa Campbell, Gladys Garrett, Ianthia Gray, Paul Lee, Nathan Mayes, and Aloise White, who were members of the School Safety Patrol;

2. Walter Adams and Myrtle Fisher who were members of the Garnet Masque (Dramatic Club);

3. Thomas DeMar, Paul Hardy, and Ernest Stewart who served in the United States Navy, and James Moten who served in the United States Army, all of whom were former members of this class;

4. Seward Dimmie and Fletcher Snowden who operated the school movie projector;

5. Lillian Hayes who represented the tenth grade at the Youth Conference at Upper Marlboro, and won first prize in a quiz contest there;

6. Lillian Hayes and Violet Isreal who participated in the Americana Quiz over radio station WMAL with members from the twelfth grade who were victorious over Armstrong High with a score of 46-36, and received five silver dollars each as prizes;

7. Norma Hill, Phyllis Hopkins, and Lorraine Thomas who were inducted into the National Honor Society;

8. Violet Isreal who was elected secretary of the Girls' Club;

9. Jean Mason who was a clarinetist in the school music organization;

10. Fletcher Snowden who was elected secretary for the NFA (New Farmers of America); and

11. Florence Windear who was a member of the Transportation Committee, and Treasurer of the Home Economics Club."

Class Colors
Red & White

Class Flower
Rose

In the fall of 1944, 53 members of the eleventh grade were assigned to two homerooms under the supervision of Mrs. Thelma Gray and Miss S. Eloise Levister (Shelton).

The junior class culminating activity was a prom which they gave to the seniors on June 1, 1945, in the school auditorium. Fred Wims's orchestra furnished the music. During the evening, shrimp salad sandwiches, canapes, cookies, ice cream, and punch were served.

Junior Class Officers
President
Lorraine Thomas

Vice-President
Gladys Garrett

Secretary
Violet Isreal

Assistant Secretary
Edna Crawford

Treasurer
Walter Adams

Student Council Representatives
Gladys Garrett
Lorraine Thomas

The class listed as its notable members:

Artists
Walter Adams
Paul Lee
Evelyn Slaughter

Captain of Girls' Basketball Team
Florence Windear

Members of Girls' Octette
Mary Askins
Myrtle Fisher
Mary Frazier
Caroline Genus
Norma Hill

Members of the National Honor Society
Norma Hill
Phyllis Hopkins
Jean Mason
Lorraine Thomas

Members of the School Safety Patrol
Gladys Garrett
Ianthia Gray
Paul Lee
Ollie Powell
Evelyn Slaughter
Aloise White

Operator of School's Movie Projector
Seward Dimmie

Former members of this class who served in the armed forces included Alphonzo Jackson, Raymond Johnson, Winfield Johnson, James Moten, Edward Simpkins, and George Slater.

"On September 10, 1945, 38 self-confident, enthusiastic seniors entered LHS. This was their most prominent year which was filled with many extra-curricular activities." Their first task was to elect class officers who eventually led them through the year's activities.

Class Officers
President
Lorraine Thomas

Vice-President
Myrtle Fisher

Secretary
Lois Plummer

Assistant Secretary
Alma King

Treasurer
Walter Adams

Assistant Treasurer
Jean Mason

Student Council Representatives
Gladys Garrett
Alma King

Social-Welfare Committee Member
Mary Frazier

In November, the seniors "presented an Armistice Day program," and in February, they "presented a program in celebration of Negro History Week."

During the second part of the school year, "Evelyn Slaughter entered a popularity contest for 'Miss Lincoln High,' and Gladys Garrett

was inducted into the National Honor Society."

As seniors, the members of the Class of 1946 were quite active in extra-curricular activities.

NATIONAL HONOR SOCIETY

Senior Officers
President
Lorraine Thomas

Vice-President
Norma Hill

Treasurer
Phyllis Hopkins

Advisers
Miss S. Eloise Levister
& Mr. Parlett L. Moore

ATTENDANCE COMMITTEE

Norma Hill was the lone senior officer on this committee which was under the sponsorship of Mrs. Genevieve S. Brown and Miss Daisy M. Wright.

NHA
The New Homemakers of America Club was "organized in December 1945 and took the place of the old Home Economics Club. It was an improvement over the former organization since it offered state and national affiliations for its members. Its purpose was to help

promote a healthy, happy home life for all."

Officers
President
Gladys Garrett

Vice-President
Doris Honemond

Secretary
Alice Matthews

Assistant Secretary
Mavis Zeigler

Treasurer
Clemmie Garrett

Historian
Alice Nolan

Reporter
Evelyn Slaughter

Chapter Mother
Mrs. Ruth Slaughter

Advisers
Mrs. Doris G. Jackson,
Miss Elizabeth Slade,
and Miss Daisy M. Wright

NFA

The New Farmers of America Club was "composed of boys in the vocational and general courses. Seniors Dorsey Addison and Harvey Awkard, along with four junior boys, went to Princess Anne College in Princess Anne, Maryland, to a State Judging Contest. Harvey Awkard was successful in winning second place in judging poultry."

"The club sponsored swine and poultry projects that resulted in four pigs and 100 fryers."

Officers
President
William Coates

Vice-President
Dorsey Addison

Secretary
George Jackson

Assistant Secretary
Walter Adams

Treasurer
Harvey Awkard

Reporter
William Bright

Adviser
Clarence L. Bond

GARNET MASQUE

"In September 1945, Garnet Masque held its organizational meeting to elect officers and to prepare for the presentation of plays."

"On December 20, 1945, the club presented two one-act plays—*The Candle in the Window* and The *Lost Carol.*"

"On May 17, 1946, the club presented a three-act play, *Strike Three,* in which most of the members participated."

Officers
President
Walter Adams

Vice-President
Alice Waters*

Secretary
Patsy Lyles*

Assistant Secretary
Alice Matthews*

Treasurer
Phyllis Awkard*

Reporter
Myrtle Fisher

Advisers
Mrs. Edna R. Evans
Miss Naomi E. Waller

* *Junior*

OTHER

Seniors "Walter Adams, Norma Hill, and Jean Mason were Art Editor, Sports Editor, and News Editor, respectively, on the LHS News Staff."

Seniors "Gladys Garrett, Ianthia Gray, Doris Honemond, Alma King, Evelyn Slaughter, Lorraine Thomas, and Aloise White served as members of the School Safety Patrol."

Seniors "Harvey Awkard, Myrtle Fisher, Norma Hill, Violet Isreal, and

Lorraine Thomas were members of the Grounds Committee, Program Committee, Attendance Committee, Building Committee, and Health and Safety Committee," respectively.

"At the close of the year, graduation planning moved swiftly. The juniors gave them a royal send-off" prior to the big event—*graduation.*

They vowed to "always remain true to the high ideals and traditions of LHS."

COMMENCEMENT

Class Motto
"In Unity There Is Strength."

Class Colors
Blue & White

Class Flower
Red Rose

Valedictorian
Lorraine Thomas

Salutatorian
Phyllis Hopkins

GRADUATES
Academic
Anna Elizabeth Bailey
Seward Joseph Dimmie
Hannah Louise Duvall
Myrtle Virginia Fisher
Mary Carletha Frazier
*Mabel Norma Hill
Violet Ethel Isreal
Alma Arleen King

Norma Hill

Edna Margaret Crawford
Ianthia Brooks Gray
Sarah Beatrice Hawkins
*Phyllis Laurett Hopkins
Armiter Beatrice Jackson
Nellie Idella Lee
Georgia Lorraine Palmer
Grace Augustine Plummer
Marjorie Jeanette Prather
Annie Elizabeth Thomas
Aloise White

Certificate
Dorsey Wedington Addison

*Member of National Honor Society

*Shirley Jean Mason
Marjorie Lois Plummer
*Doris Lorraine Thomas
Margrette Virginia Wims

General
Walter Gordon Adams
Dorothy Elizabeth Bishop
*Gladys Louise Garrett
Doris Rebecca Honemond
Thelma Juanita Kelly
Alice Virginia Lincoln
Ollie Isabel Powell
Hazel Elizabeth Rhodes
Evelyn Steward Slaughter

Vocational
Hazel Clarice Adams
Mary Ellen Askins
Harvey Maurice Awkard
William Henry Coates

Gratuating Exercises
June 12, 1946
Theme
"Building the World We Live In"

Processional
"War March of the Priests"
(Mendelssohn)

Flag Salute
National Anthem

Invocation
Reverend Morris F. Wallace, Pastor,
Clinton A.M.E. Zion Church,
Rockville, Maryland

Choral Selection
"Lift Ev'ry Voice and Sing"
(Johnson)

Dramatic Sketches

Introduction
Phyllis Hopkins
"Yesterday's Builders, Today's
Challenge, Tomorrow's World"

Recapitulation
Lorraine Thomas

Chorus
"Finlandia"
(Sibelius)

Presentation of Diplomas
Mrs. Elizabeth P. Hauck, Member,
Montgomery County
Board of Education

Awards

Musical Selection
"Where'er You Walk"
(Handel)

Thelma Ramey

Benediction
Reverend J. Virgil Lilly, Pastor,
Rockville Christian Church,
Rockville, Maryland

Recessional
"Pomp and Circumstance"
(Elgar)

FACULTY
Dr. Parlett L. Moore, *Principal*
Clarence L. Bond
Mrs. Genevieve Swann Brown
Nettie V. Chappell
Mrs. Dorothy H. Cunningham
Mrs. Jessie M. Drummond Holmes
Mrs. Edna R. Evans
Mrs. Doris M. Greene Jackson
S. Eloise Levister
Mrs. Julia H. Miller
Myra L. Pharr
Rozelle S. Silvey
Beverly E. Sinkford
Mrs. E. V. Elizabeth Slade
Wilhelmina E. Smith
Naomi E. Waller
Daisy M. Wright

Edward U. Taylor, *Supervisor*
Dr. Edwin W. Broome,
Superintendent

*courtesy Betty Prather-McKenzie, Alma
King-Ridgley, Virgie Stewart-Prather*

LINCOLN HIGH SCHOOL
CLASS OF 1946 CELEBRATES

The Lincoln High School Class of 1946 was the second class to reach and observe the commemorative milestone of 50 years after high school graduation. They celebrated this notable event on Friday, September 20, 1996, at the Golden Bull (in the Grand Ball Room) in Gaithersburg. The members and their guests had a delightful time renewing old friendships.

Norma Hill Duffin presided over the evening's activities, and Phyllis Hopkins Dutton welcomed the attendees. Subsequently, Reverend Douglass M. Force (pastor of the Fairhaven United Methodist Church) gave the invocation and blessed the meal.

Following a buffet-style dinner, the program was resumed with the presentation of the classmates and singing of the class song. Thereafter, Lorraine Thomas Driver and Seward Dimmie lit a candle in remembrance of their deceased classmates and teachers.

In recognition of individuals who made a contribution toward the implementation of their anniversary plans, Norma Hill Duffin presented certificates of appreciation to a few alumni, teachers, and civic organizations.

The members of the Lincoln High School Class of 1946 thanked their teachers, relatives, and friends for spending a festive evening with them and helping to make this an enjoyable and memorable occasion.

Prior to the entertainment session, Hazel Adams Hammond concluded the program with remarks.

Then, John Taylor (a former teacher in Montgomery and Baltimore counties, known throughout Maryland as "Kinderman") was their special guest. He led participants in the macarena dance and later taught the members of the Class of 1946 how to do an exercise-dance routine that he had created. Overall, he added a special touch to the activities of the evening.

To further provide for audience participation, Paul D. Young (of the D and M DJ Productions) furnished the music for the young-at-heart to put their feet in motion.

The Class of 1946 attendees included Harvey M. Awkard, Lillian Hayes Baker, Seward J. Dimmie, Idella Lee Dorsey, Lorraine Thomas Driver, Norma Hill Duffin, Phyllis Hopkins Dutton, Ollie Powell Fontaine, Gladys Garrett Fox, Ianthia Gray, Hazel Adams

Hammond, Sarah B. Hawkins, Myrtle Fisher Jackson, Anna Bailey James, Jean Mason Johnson, Marjorie Prather Johnson, Doris Honemond Lyles, Hazel Rhodes Masterson, Mary Askins Myers, Margrette Wims Nolan, Elizabeth Thomas Peterson, Violet Isreal Raby, Hannah Duvall Stewart, Evelyn Slaughter Strauss, Lois Plummer Waggoner, and Alice Lincoln Webster.

Mrs. Armentris Hooks Evans was the only former teacher who was able to share in this celebration.

LINCOLN HIGH SCHOOL
CLASS OF 1947

"On September 14, 1942, 150 (eighth graders) enrolled at Lincoln High School." Initially, the class was assigned to four separate homerooms.

Room 2 Homeroom Officers
President
Alice Cooke

Vice-President
Benjamin Awkward

Secretary
Phyllis Awkard

Assistant Secretary
Mae Coates

Treasurer
Benjamin Budd

Student Council Representative
Margaret Brooks

Adviser
Queene E. McNeill

Room 3 Homeroom Officers
President
Bernetta Hawkins

Vice-President
Ethel Norris

Secretary
Alice Matthews

Assistant Secretary
Patsy Lyles

Treasurer
Barbara Isreal

Student Council Representative
Bernetta Hawkins

Adviser
Mary C. Moore

Science Building I Homeroom Officers
President
Alice Waters

Vice-President
George Stewart

Secretary
Mary Thomas

Treasurer
Louise Talley

Student Council Representative
Althea Wims

Adviser
Mrs. Genevieve S. Brown

Science Building II Homeroom Officers
President
Elizabeth Ferrell

Vice-President
Edith Driver

Secretary
Evelyn Wood

Treasurer
Clement Martin

Student Council Representative
Edna Ellis

Adviser
Mrs. Armentris P. Hooks

Class Mottol
"Whatever you do, do it with all
your might; Things done by halves,
are never done right."

Class Colors
Green & White

Class Flower
Orchid

Besides taking their required academic load, "many of the freshmen were members of the Dramatic Club, Girls Club, Home Economics Club, the NFA (New Farmers of America), and the Victory Corps.

On March 25, 1943, Science Building I homeroom gave a program entitled 'Information Please,' which the whole school enjoyed very much."

On May 21, 1943, the Home Economics and Girls Clubs sponsored a "Miss Lincoln High" contest in which freshmen Kathleen Johnson and Alice Offord were contestants.

On September 13, 1943, 116 ninth graders were assigned to three homerooms.

Room 2 Homeroom Offciers
President
Emanser Crutchfield

Vice-President
Edith Driver

Secretary
Phyllis Awkard

Assistant Secretary
Mae Coates

Treasurer
Benjamin Budd

Student Council Representative
Elizabeth Ferrell

Adviser
Queene E. McNeill

Science Building II Homeroom Officers
President
George Stewart

Vice-President
Regina Wood

Secretary
Alice Waters

Treasurer
Mary Thomas

Student Council Representative
Ella Sidney

Adviser
Mrs. Armentris P. Hooks

National Honor Society Member
Alice Waters

Musician
James Ridgley

Newspaper Staff
Alice Bowles
Patsy Lyles
Alice Waters

TRI-HI-Y
Phyllis Awkard
Margaret Brooks
Mae Coates
Irene Cole
Elizabeth Cooper
Cornelia Jackson
Kathleen Johnson
Patsy Lyles
Alice Matthews
Marie Stewart
Alice Waters
Althea Wims

"The junior class gave the seniors a prom on May 24, 1946, in the school's assembly room. The music was furnished by Fred Wims' orchestra. During the evening, chicken salad sandwiches, assorted cookies, punch, and ice cream were served in the cafeteria."

In the fall of 1946, 58 seniors were anxious for the arrival of an important event—*graduation.* Already, years had become months prior to that milestone, and then they had to wait for months to become weeks, and weeks to become days and days to become hours for this occasion to become a reality.

In the meantime, they had to pass their senior subjects to meet the Mary-land State Department of Education requirement for graduation, as well as plan for their senior activities.

Soon, it was a matter of hours, then the arrival of the long-awaited day was at hand. On June 13, 1947, the graduating seniors marched in step with the School Band playing "War March of the Priests" and "Pomp and Circumstance" in an academic procession and eventually received their academic diplomas.

LINCOLN HIGH SCHOOL GRADUATING EXERCISES

Class Motto
"Before us Lies the timber; Let us Build."

Class Colors
Blue & White

Class Flower
American Beauty Rose

Valedictorian
Alice Waters

Salutatorian
Vaughn Johnson

GRADUATES
Academic
Alice Virginia Bowles
David BenjaminBudd
Irene Cole
Elizabeth Havana Cooper
Cornelia Jackson

Vaughn Thomas Johnson
Patsy Louise Lyles
Florence Marie Stewart
George McKinley Stewart
Alice Romona Waters
Althea Wims

General
Louis Alexander Adams
Gladys Virginia Bishop
Ethel Estelle Brown
Rosetta Alverta Cross
Mary Jane DeMar
Calvin Coolidge Garrett
Robert Ellis Jackson
Kathleen Helen Johnson
Florence Jeanette Lomax
Ethel Geraldine Norris
William Stanley Parrott
Calvin Thomas Payne
James Ellsworth Ridgley
Richard Edward Simms
Edward Simpkins
Stephen Henry Slaughter, Jr.
Branson Scott Smith
Myrtle Virginia Thomas
Ella Madeline Tibbs
Samuel Andrew Turner
Julian Howard Washington, Jr.
Regina Ernestine Wood
Mavis Bernice Zeigler

Vocational
Rosie Ionia Addison
Phyllis Alicia Awkard
Clifton Neil Burgess
Dories Mae Clarke
Mae Louise Coates
Bertha Calvin Crawford

Luther Reed Crutchfield
Gladys Louise Davis
Cassius Julius Dorsey
Clara Mae Dorsey
Lucille Elizabeth Dorsey
Edith Elizabeth Driver
William Norman Frazier
Dennis Augustus Holland
Barbara Louise Isreal
Rudolph Theolius Lee
Robert Joseph Lewis
Lilly Martha Mahoney
Robert Francis Marr
Alice Virginia Matthews
Euell Howard Owens
Mary Helen Prather
Ella Louise Sidney
Evelyn Mae Wood

SENIOR CLASS OFFICERS
President
Robert Marr

Vice-President
Calvin Garrett

Secretary
Mae Coates

Assistant Secretary
Phyllis Awkard

Treasurer
George Stewart

Student Council Representative
Benjamin Budd

FACULTY
Parlett L. Moore, *Principal*
Mrs. Mary Ann Buie

Martha R. Campbell
Nettie V. Chappell
Alta M. Clarke
Mrs. Edna R. Evans
Mrs. Edith S. Gordon
John A. Harvey
A. Frances Higgs
Mrs. Jessie D. Holmes

Barbara Isreal

Bernard E. Holsey
D. Christine Jackson
Rozelle S. Silvey
Wilhelmina E. Smith
Louise W. Stewart
Mrs. Bernice J. Sutton
Alice M. Wanzer
Mrs. Clarice M. Wilson
Daisy M. Wright

Edward V. Taylor, *Supervisor*
Dr. Edwin W. Boome,

Superintendent

Graduating Exercises
Processional

Flag Salute
National Anthem

Invocation
Reverend Walter E. Williams,
Pastor, Jerusalem Methodist
Church, Rockville, Maryland

Musical Selection
School Band
Theme
"Pillars of Democracy"

Dramatization

Prologue
Alice Waters

Freedom
Vaughn Johnson

Loyalty
Benjamin Budd

Brotherhood
Mae Coates

Cooperation
Evelyn Wood & Others

Unity
Louis Adams & Others

Choral Selection
"One World"
(O'Hara)

Presentation of Diplomas

James W. Gill, Member,
Montgomery County
Board of Education

Awards

Class Song

Benediction
Reverend Ernest E. Arter, Pastor,

Mount Zion Methodist Church,
Brookeville, Maryland

Recessional
(The audience will please remain
seated until after the recessional.)

*courtesy Virgie Stewart-Prather, Betty
Prather-McKenzie, Phyllis (Awkard) Smith*

LINCOLN HIGH SCHOOL
CLASS OF 1948

"On September 13, 1943, one hundred sixty-eight freshmen entered Lincoln High School. They were assigned to four homerooms where they elected homeroom officers."

Room 1 Homeroom Officers
President
Ruby Hawkins

Vice-President
Rudolph Edmunds

Secretary
Doris Jackson

Assistant Secretary
Pearl Holland

Treasurer
Charlotte Holston

Student Council Representative
Irene Gray

Adviser
Miss Ruby E. Morris

Cottage I Homeroom Officers
President
Betty McPherson

Vice-President
Alice Nolan

Secretary
Delores Prather

Assistant Secretary
Kermit Prather

Treasurer &
Student Council Representative
Perry Martin

Adviser
Miss Doris M. Greene

Cottage II Homeroom Officers
President
Irene Sidney

Student Council Representative
Edward Taylor

Adviser
Miss Elizabeth Slade

Shop I Homeroom Officers
President
Prather Dorsey

Vice-President
Betty Beckwith

Secretary
LaRue Clay

Treasurer
Walter Butler

Student Council Representative
Estelle Brown

Adviser
Mr. Clarence L. Bond

Anxious to make their high school life worthwhile, the members of this class participated in various extracurricular activities, such as Dramatic Club, Girls Club, Home Economics Club, New Farmers of America, Victory Club, to name a few. They also let their presence be known by making the honor roll after each marking period and by participating in various assembly programs.

On March 24, 1944, Cottage I students presented the annual Maryland Day program under the guidance of Miss Doris M. Greene.

Like other classes, the Class of 1948 experienced a decrease in their class size. "On September 9, 1944, one hundred thirty-four ninth graders enrolled at Lincoln High School and were assigned to three homerooms."

Cottage I Homeroom Officers
President
Rudolph Edmunds

Vice-President
Edwin Cunningham

Secretary
Louise Clipper

Treasurer
Betty Beckwith

Student Council Representative
LaRue Clay

Adviser
Miss Elizabeth Slade

Science Building II Homeroom Officers
President
Jean Thomas

Vice-President
Edward Taylor

Secretary
Delores Prather

Assistant Secretary
Eudora Sellman

Student Council Representative
Irene Snowden

Adviser
Mr. David W. Hazel

Shop II Homeroom Officers
President
Pearl Holland

Vice-President
Callie Matthews

Secretary
Ruby Hawkins

Treasurer
Alice Nolan

Student Council Representatives
Frances Gray
Perry Martin

Adviser
Mrs. Doris G. Jackson

During the year, members from all

sections were quite involved academically and athletically, as well as being involved in an assortment of extra-curricular activities.

During the year, "they recognized some of their weaknesses. With the assistance of their teachers during several activity periods, these needs were addressed to help make them worthy citizens in the school and in the community."

"On September 10, 1945, the Class of 1948 enrolled as sophomores and were assigned to three homerooms."

Shop I Homeroom Officers
President
Clara Smith

Vice-President
Kermit Prather

Secretary
Julian Washington

Treasurer
Delores Prather

Student Council Representative
Irene Sidney

Social & Welfare Committee Member
Eudora Sellman

Adviser
Mr. Clarence L. Bond

Science Building II Homeroom Officers
President

Janie Furbush

Vice-President
Estelle Brown

Secretary
Louise Clipper

Student Council Representative
LaRue Clay

Social & Welfare Committee
Agnes Claggett

Adviser
Miss Wilhelmina L. Smith

Room 8 Homeroom Officers
President
Ruby Hawkins

Secretary
Clemmie Garrett

Treasurers
Russell Jackson
Marion Mahoney

Student Council Representative
Marion Mahoney

Adviser
Mrs. Julia H. Miller

During the year, a number of tenth graders participated in various activities.

Boys Basketball Team
DeWayne Arter
Earl Claggett

Edwin Cunningham
Francis Moore
Kermit Prather
Purvice Summerour
Edward Taylor

Girls Basketball Team

Betty Beckwith
Janie Furbush
Ruby Hawkins

Yearbook Staff

LaRue Clay
Louise Clipper
Delores Prather
Irene Sidney
Clara Smith
Elsie Talley
Jean Thomas

School Patrol Force

Edwin Cunningham
Evelyn Jackson
Alice Nolan
Edward Taylor

LaRue Clay, Evelyn Jackson, and Alice Nolan were candidates for the popularity contest that was held on February 8, 1946, as a part of the mid-term festivities.

Louise Clipper won first prize in a talent program on May 10, 1946, when she sang her version of "Crying Blues."

Rudolph Edmunds, Clemmie Garrett, and Ruby Hawkins participated in a Negro History quiz.

Eudora Sellman and Elsie Talley were inducted into the National Honor Society. '

With their first three high school years behind them, the Class of 1948 prepared to meet the challenges of their junior and senior years. At that point, not only were their academic programs more difficult, but their extracurricular activities were more demanding as well.

Making plans for the greater responsibilities, meeting deadlines, and passing tests soon brought them to the close of another chapter in their lives. In other words, their calendars indicated that their days at Lincoln High School were numbered. Having been served notice that their time had almost run out, 48 seniors returned to Lincoln High School to embark on their senior year and prepared for their eventual departure. To meet the numerous challenges that were ahead of them, they elected class officers and selected heads of the various committees.

Senior Class Officers
President
William Bright

Vice-President
Louise Clipper

Secretary
Eudora Sellman

Assistant Secretary
Clara Smith

Treasurer
Clemmie Garrett

Assistant Treasurer
Evelyn Jackson

Advisers
Mrs. Genevieve S. Brown
Miss Martha R. Campbell

Assistant Copy Editor
Jean Marbley

Photo Editor
William Prather

Written Layout Manager
Clara Smith

Assistant Copy Editor
Emma Thomas

Faculty Adviser
Miss Geraldine E. Jackson

"Jean Thomas (Annual), Louise Clipper & Clemmie Garrett (Class Prophecy), Mildred Kelly & Eudora Sellman (Class Will) Estelle Butler & Mary Carter (Giftorians), Carolyn Waters (Invitations), DeWayne Arter and Jean Marbley (Pin and Ring), and Rudolph Edmunds (Senior Week)" were the deciders of each of the indicated committees.

Yearbook Staff
Editor-in-Chief
Jean Thomas

Assistant Editor
William Bright

Copy Secretary
Louise Clipper

Business Manager
Clemmie Garrett

File Clerk
Bernice Holland

The Senior Class "dedicated the 1948 annual to their parents in appreciation of their faithful endeavor to secure a high school education for them." They hoped that their parents would "recapture some of the glamour of their own school days and, at the same time, gain a fuller understanding of the studies and recreations of Lincoln High School" when they read this book.

Their principal, Parlett L. Moore, penned a very informative and inspiring message for their yearbook. "With the publication of this annual, we find ourselves entered upon a new era in secondary education for Negro youth in Montgomery County. This period is characterized by (1) a tremendous expansion in school plants and a marked reorganization of our curriculum and high school units of administration; (2) a state of uncertainty in practically every pursuit of life; (3) a tremendous increase in vocational opportunities and requirements; (4) an ever increasing demand for efficient, socially competent, productive and creative students.

The next few months will probably bring forth a type of school plant and equipment heretofore unknown to our students. Such an achievement will impose a tremendous responsibility upon the student personnel (present and future) to maintain and utilize a modern edifice properly. Patrons, alumni, and out-of-school youth will face the responsibility of utilizing the available services provided by a new plant as well as to share in preserving the aesthetic features of a modern building and to keep it as a monument to the community.

The high school students of today cannot hope to conquer the obstacle and cope with the uncertainties of the future with the type of educational preparation appropriate to situations which existed in Colonial America or in the Reconstruction days. Life interests and activities of yesterday were largely confined to local communities or certain sections of one state. Today, transcontinental flyers, giant clippers, and jet-propelled craft render the automobile and old express trains obsolete. In bygone days, communication by telephones, telegraph, and mail met the needs of our populace; today, the radio makes communication with the distant continents more convenient than inter-city communications were a few decades ago. The control of atomic energy spells even greater uncertainty for the future. Families, once separated by miles of open space, are now concentrated in one apartment, to further complicate the problem of human relations. These and multitudes of other changes and uncertainties demand a type of secondary education that will equip the individual to meet these eventualities as they are encountered.

This equipment will include (1) a carefully formulated value system, (2) the ability to meet novel situations with fortitude and poise, (3) the power to analyze complex social and scientific problems or situations, to collect and organize data, to formulate tentative hypotheses and to test those hypotheses, (4) the ability to live and work together in large groups with wholesome attitude and respect for the rights, opinions, tastes, and feelings of all people, (5) mastery of social techniques and skills, (6) skill in communication and computation, and (7) proper use of leisure time and perhaps a number of other related and similar items.

To the end that every student might become equipped with these attributes, our school included in its program of offerings, in addition to the organized classes distributed among the five courses, a variety of extra class experiences—arts and craft activities, creative dancing, interscholastic athletics, school band, and numerous others. To the task of presenting a brief sketch of the nature and scope of those experiences, the 1948 yearbook is dedicated with the hope that it might serve in print and pictures as a source of information and inspiration to the students now in school, to those who once passed this way, to those yet to come, and to the multitude of loyal patrons.

To the editorial staff, who labored tirelessly and diligently to accomplish the publication, the words of Emerson are appropriate: 'The reward for a thing well done is to have done it.'"

SENIOR SUPERLATIVES
Best Couple
Louise Clipper & DeWayne Arter

Best Dancers
Evelyn Jackson & William Prather

Best Dressed
Ella Fisher & Francis Moore

Best Figure & Physique
Betty Olney & Robert Scott

Best Looking
Jean Thomas &
Edwin Cunningham

Best Speaker
Carolyn Waters &
Rudolph Edmunds

Most Athletic
Jean Thomas & Edward Taylor

Most Amusing
Louise Clipper &
Purvice Summerour

Most Friendly
Louise Clipper & William Prather

Most Likely to Succeed
Louise Clipper & Perry Martin

Most Studious
Eudora Sellman & William Bright

Most Talkative
Clara Smith & Rudolph Edmunds

Most Pleasing Personality
Rosalie Diggs & Perry Martin

Quietest
Carolyn Waters & Jerome Wade

Shortest
Ella Fisher & Russell Jackson

Tallest
Estelle Butler & DeWayne Arter

Most Popular
Clemmie Garrett & Edward Taylor

Most Modest
Mildred Kelly & Robert Gaither

Lincoln High School Athletics
The boys basketball team—composed of "Edward Taylor (Captain),

DeWayne Arter, Edwin Cunningham, Rudolph Edmunds, Robert Gaither, Charles Lenoir, Perry Martin, Francis Moore, Russell Palmer, and Purvice Summerour"—compiled a season's record of 3 wins and 7 losses." Although their playing record indicated that they were losers, the "excellent sportsmanship and positive attitude that they displayed" on the basketball court made them winners. Their coach was John A. Harvey.

"The girls basketball team, with Edith Smith as captain, had a very successful season this year, not because they won a great majority of games but because of the value this experience had for each member." Other members of the team included Ruth Hall, Mildred Kelly, Jean Thomas, and Rebecca Williams.

The Lincoln High School students exploded with unbridled joy when "a plaque for the Western-Shore Girls championship was presented to the team on March 20, 1948, at the tournament held in Cambridge, Maryland." The team was coached by Virginia E. Henderson.

The Lincoln High School field ball team was "built up from scratch this year." Although their record was unimpressive, they gained a wealth of experience which was beneficial the following year. "Edith Smith served as captain of the team and Virginia E. Henderson was the coach."

Lincoln's "touch football team played a six-game schedule this year. At the close of the season, it had a record of 3 wins, 2 losses, and 1 tie. Perry Martin was the team captain, and the team members were William Brown, Earl Claggett, Edwin Cunningham, Robert Gaither, Charles Lenoir, Francis Moore, Herbert Payne, Oliver Riggs, Purvice Summerour, Edward Taylor, and Paul Thompson. John A. Harvey was the coach of the football team."

Social Welfare Committee

This committee commenced its activities with a Halloween Social presented in the school auditorium. "Roses are Red, Violets are Blue" was the sentiment behind their Valentine Matinee. A Talent Show was given to enhance enjoyment and to add variety. Lois Offord won first prize among the singers and Evelyn Jackson and William Prather, among the dancers.

Doctors, dentists, nurses, and the school staff, along with the Montgomery County Health Department, worked cooperatively in the schools for prevention and control of communicable diseases. "Lincoln High School had the resources for consultation and diagnostic services. Mass procedures were used in testing vision and hearing."

The 1947-1948 school year was the "second year for a regular school nurse at Lincoln High School. The students were more conscious of their health problems and felt free to take them to the nurse."

Building And Ground Committee

This committee "worked very diligently this school year to make the grounds attractive. The grounds were kept clear of waste and paper." It was impressed upon the student body that is was their "individual responsibility to keep the school and grounds as beautiful as they could." Finally, 48 jubilant seniors reached their long-awaited milestone on June 23, 1948. They donned caps and gowns, marched in procession to their designated area, participated in their graduating exercises, received their academic diplomas, and marched out with gleeful hearts. This was the last time that these students, as a group, were in a Lincoln High School setting.

GRADUATING EXERCISES

Class Motto
"Tonight we Launch, Where Shall we Anchor?"

Class Colors
Blue & White

Class Flower
American Beauty Rose

Valedictorian
Eudora Sellman

Salutatorian
Perry Martin

GRADUATES
Academic
DeWayne Blackwell Arter
Earl Asbury Claggett
*Martha Louise Clipper
Edwin Hartsworth Cunningham
Charles Rudolph Edmunds
Ella Juanita Fisher
Russell Smith Jackson
MildredVirginia Kelly
Thomas Perry Wilson Martin
Francis Julian Moore
Betty DeLain Olney
*Eudora Belle Sellman
Clara Virginia Smith
James Purvice Summerour
Edward Valentine Taylor
Jean Elizabeth Thomas
Carolyn Virginia Waters

General
Seleno Edward Clarke
Rosalie Diggs
Joseph Irving Dorsey
Nathaniel Edward Dove
Robert Harold Gaither
Pearrie Hawkins, Jr.
Bernice Evelyn Holland
Harold Eugene Jackson
James Robert Kelly
Jean Frances Marbley
James Braxton Moten

Linwood Emory Norris
William Alonzo Prather
Mary Ann Pumphrey
Robert Augustus Scott
Derose Jerome Wade

Vocational
William Morris Bright
Margaret Estelle Butler
Mary Ellen Carter
Agnes Irene Claggett
Georgia Cordelia DeMar
Milford Clem Dove
Charles Harris Frazier
*Edith Clemintine Garrett
Barbara Elizabeth Hill
Vernon McKinley Hill
Evelyn Corrine Jackson
Harold Rufus Payne
Elaine Mattie Beatrice Prather
Emma Corrine Thomas
Ronald Tilghman

*   *National Honor Society*

FACULTY

Parlett L. Moore, *Principal*
Frank P. Bolden
Mrs. Genevieve S. Brown
D. Winifred Byrd
Martha R. Campbell
Nettie V. Chappell
Alta M. Clarke
Mrs. Edna R. Evans
John A. Harvey
Virginia E. Henderson
Bernard E. Holsey

Geraldine E. Jackson
Mrs. Rowena C. Johnston
Julia U. Magwood
Louis S. Monk
Mrs. Daisy W. Myles
Marie N. Platte
Rozelle S. Silvey
Wilhelmina E. Smith
Louise W. Stewart
Mrs. Bernice J. Sutton
John E. Swanson
Mrs. Clarice M. Wilson
Alberta J. Withers

Edward U. Taylor, *Supervisor of Colored Schools*
Maxwell E. Burdette, *High School Supervisor*
Dr. Edwin W. Broome, *Superintendent*

Graduating Exercises

Theme
"We Have a Date with the World"

Processional

Flag Salute
National Anthem

Invocation
Reverend J.H. Holland, Pastor, Good Hope Methodist Church, Colesville, Maryland

Band Selection
"Pomp and Circumstance"
(Elgar)

Dramatization

Introduction
Perry Martin

Preparation for Date

Selection of Equipment

Departure

Conclusion
Eudora Sellman

Choral Selection
"One World"
(O'Hara)

Presentation of Diplomas
H. Stanley Stine, President,
Montgomery County
Board of Education

Awards

Benediction
Reverend C.E. Smallwood, Pastor,
John Wesley Methodist Church,
Clarksburg, Maryland
Recessional
(The audience is requested to remain seated until after the recessional.)

Senior Calendar
May 8
Senior Trip to Luray Caverns

May 21
Junior-Senior Prom

June 18
Class Night-Closing Day

June 20
Sermon

June 23
Graduation

We thank the faculty and students who have contributed willingly and tirelessly to our effort to make this yearbook a success. We hope that this souvenir will serve to lighten the burdens of the heavily ladened and enrich many of our leisure hours in years to come.

The Yearbook Staff expresses its appreciation also to A & N Photo Service, Washington, D.C., for group and division pictures.

courtesy Virgie Stewart-Prather, Earl Claggett, Edward V. Taylor

LINCOLN HIGH SCHOOL
CLASS OF 1949

"On September 9, 1944, the orange clipper planes (buses) arrived at the Rockville airport (Lincoln High School) with 175 shaky enlisted people (8th graders) on board. This battalion was divided into four companies and was stationed in barracks (rooms).

"Company A had an enrollment of 43 students under the supervision of Mrs. Newberry, then Mr. Froe, later Miss Battle, and last Mrs. Evans. Under Mrs. Evans, they strove to make an improvement in their personal lives as well as an improvement in the beautification, cleanliness, and neatness of their homeroom.

"They considered their most successful event to be the assembly program which was given on May 15, 1945, to the students and faculty.

"Company B had an enrollment of 43 students who were stationed in barracks 1 (room 1) under the supervision of Mrs. Ruby E. Morris-Wiley. Mrs. Wiley departed after nearly two months to be with her military husband, and she was replaced by Miss Naomi E. Waller.

"The 8B students participated in the Frederick Douglass Fund, the Community War Fund, and the March of Dimes drives as well as a drive for a new piano in the assembly room."

8B Homeroom Officers
President
Ethel Hansborough

Vice-President
Faye Foreman

Secretary
Elizabeth Holston

Treasurer
Helen Hawkins

Student Council Representative
Ethel Hansborough

Company C had an enrollment of 46 students who were under the supervision of Mr. Herbert H. Norton.

8C Homeroom Officers
President
Jacqueline Lowery

Vice-President
Ann Miles

Secretary
Melvin Joppy

Assistant Secretary
Elizabeth Moore

Treasurer
Theodore Jackson

Student Council Representative
Ann Miles

"The 8C students participated in the War Fund drive, gave an exciting program during an assembly, and raised money for the annual.

"Company D had an enrollment of 43 students who were stationed in barracks 5 (room 5) under the guidance of their commanding officer (homeroom teacher), Miss Jessie M. Drummond.

8D Homeroom Officers
President
Thomas Ross

Vice-President
Edith Riggs

Secretary
Helen Thompson

Assistant Secretary
Sarah Thomas

Treasurer &
Student Council Representative
Grace Scott

"During first semester, Grace Scott and Sarah Thomas were on K.P. (lunch orders), and James Stemley and Francis Weedon replaced them during second semester.

"Homeroom 8D brought in the most money toward the Frederick Douglass Memorial Fund and, consequently, won first place in the drive for a new assembly room piano.

"They participated in the March of Dimes drive, the Red Cross rally, and the War Loan drive. They sold tickets for a turkey dinner given for the benefit of the school and made donations toward new supplies for the girls restroom.

"Company 8D participated in class projects, clubs, and socials. On April 30, 1945, they gave an assembly program which featured a play entitled *School's Out at Tater Hollow*.

"The eighth-grade battalion worked very hard with one purpose in mind—an honorable discharge (high school diploma) in June 1949."

"On September 10, 1945, one hundred twenty-nine ninth graders were assigned to four homerooms under the supervision of Miss Naomi Waller, Mrs. Cunningham, Miss Nettie V. Chappell, and Miss Elizabeth Slade, respectively.

"Room 1 homeroom had an enrollment of 37 pupils who had been very cooperative in carrying on the various school activities. Nine of these pupils performed admirably:

1. Edith Riggs as homeroom president, as a member of the Social-Welfare Committee, as a candidate for 'Miss Lincoln High,' and as soloist on Talent Hour when she sang 'Symphony,'

2. Oliver Riggs as a member of the

school band and Dramatic Club,

3. Thomas Ross as a member of the Dramatic Club and as a Student Council Representative,

4. Grace Scott as a member of the News Staff, school Annual Committee, and Girls Octette,

5. Edith Smith as a homeroom secretary, as a member of the girls basketball team, as a member of the News Staff, and as a member of the school band,

6. Marion Smith as homeroom treasurer, as manager of the girls basketball team, as a member of the News Staff, as a member of the school Annual Committee, as a member of the Girls Octette, and a member of the Dramatic Club,

7. Sarah Thomas as homeroom assistant secretary, as a member of the News Staff, as a member of the school Annual Committee, as a member of the Girls Octette, and as a member of the Dramatic Club,

8. Maria Twyman as homeroom vice-president, and

9. James H. Williams as a member of the Dramatic Club and school band.

"Room 5 homeroom had an enrollment of 29 pupils under the supervision of Mrs. Cunningham. They participated in all of the school drives and programs. Two of these students made the rest of them very proud--Ethel Hansborough who sang 'Sentimental Reasons' on the Talent Hour and Eliza-beth Holston who was elected to represent room 5 homeroom in the 'Miss Lincoln High' contest and who raised $21.50."

Room 5 Homeroom Officers
President
Mary Daye

Vice-President
Bruce Hill

Secretary
Helen Hawkins

Assistant Secretary
Barbara Hansborough

Treasurer
Delois Hackey

Student Council Representative
Helen Hawkins

Room 7 Homeroom Officers
President
Theodore Jackson

Secretary
Lorraine Prather

Assistant Secretary
Elizabeth Moore

Treasurer
Ann Miles

Adviser
Miss Nettie V. Chappell

"Lorraine Prather was the supervisor for the clean-up campaign that was conducted in room 7 during

Health Week. They did everything possible to make their room the most attractive one in the building. Their motto was 'One step at a time, but always forward.'"

Cottage II Homeroom Officers
President
Marjorie Burriss

Vice-President
Barbara Copeland

Secretary
Margaret Carter

Assistant Secretary
Cornelius Awkard

Treasurer
Gladys Claggett

Student Council Representative
Josephine Carroll

"Cottage II homeroom appreciated the splendid work carried on by homeroom president Marjorie Burriss. She was chosen to represent Cottage II in the 'Miss Lincoln High' contest.

"Cottage II homeroom had many talented pupils, who hoped to become musicians, nurses, stenographers, and teachers someday."

During the year, many of the students were members of the school Annual Committee, Girls Octette, News Staff, and Social-Welfare Committee.

Their motto was 'We Can Try.'

Senior Class Officers
President
Edward Norris

Vice-President
Alberta Driver

Secretary
Helen Hawkins

Assistant Secretary
Edith Riggs

Treasurer
James Williams

The Senior Committee was composed of Edith Riggs (Annual), Alice Washington (Class Prophecy), Betty Foreman (Class Will), Barbara Copeland and Helen Hawkins (Giftorians), Faye Foreman (Invitations), and Helen Hawkins (Pin & Ring).

Yearbook Staff

Chief Editor
Edith Riggs

Business Manager
Bruce Hill

Department Editor
Alberta Driver

Class Editor
Edward Norris

Reporter
Jean Starke

Typing Assistants
Mary Smith
Mary Taylor
Hattie Thomas

Faculty Adviser
Geraldine E. Jackson

The Lincoln High School boys basketball team "won the 1949 State Championship in its third year of participation under Coach John A. Harvey."

In the play-offs, the team "defeated Douglass High of Upper Marlboro, 46-17, Bates High School of Annapolis, 39-30, and St. Clair High of Cambridge, 23-12."

Five team players—Howard Claggett, Charles Lenoir, Russell Palmer, Herbert Payne, and Carl Turner—appeared in the local newspaper for their role as Maryland State Champions.

It is noteworthy that "Charles Lenoir and Russell Palmer were the only players from the 1948 squad" to help lead "this comparative new team" to the Maryland State Basketball Championship. It goes without saying that the team was well-coached.

During the regular season, the team compiled a 7-6 record.

January 15
Piedmont, *lost*

January 21
Upper Marlboro, *lost*

January 25
Frederick, *won*

January 28
Cambridge, *lost*

January 31
Armstrong, *lost*

February 5
Martinsburg, *won*

February 8
Upper Marlboro, *won*

February 11
Frederick, *lost*

February 15
Martinsburg, *won*

February 18
Cambridge, *won*

February 25
Leesburg, *won*

March 4
Phelps, *lost*

March 11
Leesburg, *won*

"The school press (Newspaper Staff) served as a medium of news exchange for the student body, the community, and other schools."

Newspaper Staff
Editor-in-Chief
Helen Hawkins

News Editor
Edith Riggs

Features
Naomi Garner
Ruth Genies
Maria Twyman

Sports Editor
Isaiah Harriday

Exchange Editor
Barbara Copeland

Art Editor
Kenneth Awkward

Humor
Marion Smith

Reporters
Vivian Dorsey
Frances Driver
Blanche Harris
LaVerne Posey
Sarah Thomas

Typing Editor
Barbara Copeland

Faculty Adviser
Mrs. B.J. Williams

The Hi-Y held its meetings "twice a month and three topics were discussed—'The Right Relationship between Boys and Girls,' 'Study of Atomic Energy,' and 'Getting at the Roots of Race Prejudice.'"

Hi-Y Officers
President
Edward Norris

Vice-President
James Williams

Secretary
Stanley Owens

Assistant Secretary
James Stemley

The NHA (New Homemakers of America) met twice a month. It included in its program "celebration of St. Patrick's Day, Good Grooming Week, National Negro Health Week (clean-up projects in school and in the community), Easter social (dyed eggs for hospitalized children), and stuffed toys (for hospitals), Mother & Daughter Banquet, attendance to State NHA meeting in Baltimore installation service, and school-closing party."

NHA Officers
President
Betty Hawkins
Vice-President
Mary Williams
Secretary
Lillian Smallwood
Treasurer
Lois Honemond
Sponsor
J. Gaither Dixon

After a year of active involvement in academic work, extracurricular activities, and senior projects, 69 seniors were ready to reap the benefits of their labors. By this time, they had met the Maryland State Department of Education's requirements for graduation and were anxious to participate in the culminating activity of their high school career—graduating exercises. On June 20, 1949, their dream was fulfilled.

Senior Calendar

June 4
Senior Trip

June 1
Class Night

June 19
Sermon to Graduates

June 20
Commencement

GRADUATING EXERCISES

Class Motto

"Mighty Oaks from
Little Acorns Grow."

Class Colors
Navy Blue & White

Class Flower
Red Rose

Valedictorian
Alberta Driver

Salutatorian
Edward Norris

GRADUATING CLASS

June 20, 1949
Cornelius Awkard
Eleanor Bell
Edward Beverley
Edward Bishop
Virginia Boyd
William Brown
Virginia Budd
Margaret Carter
Isaac Claggett
Evelyn Cole
Catherine Cooper
Barbara Copeland
George U. Copeland
Thomas Copeland
Della Crockett
Harold Dorsey
Alberta Driver
Faye Foreman
Annie Frazier
Lennie Garrett
Delois Hackey
Eugene A. Hallman
Ethel Hansborough
Samuel Harper
Helen V. Hawkins
Ethel Hebron
Bruce Hill
S. Margaret Hill
Doris Holland
Doris Hopkins
Eldridge Jackson
Maria Jackson
Odel Jackson
Theodore Jackson

Maurice Jordan
Tilghman Lee
Mary Ann Lyles
Elizabeth Moore
Virginia Moore
Edward Norris
Stanley Owens
Charlotte Parrott
Raymond Plummer
Arthur Prather
Ethel Prather
LaVerne Prather
Edith L. Riggs
Oliver A. Riggs
Grace Scott
Lillie Selby
Kenneth Shelton
Francis Smith
Marian Smith
Jean Starke
James Stemley
Donald Stewart
Betty Talley
Aubrey Taylor
Sarah A. Thomas
John Twyman
Maria Twyman
Alice Washington
Corrine Weedon
Francis Weedon
Charles White
James Williams
Rebecca Williams
Helene Wilson
Lillie Mae Wilson

FACULTY

Parlett L. Moore, *Principal*
Frank P. Bolden
Mrs. Genevieve S. Brown
D. Winifred Byrd
Alta M. Clarke
Mrs. Edna R. Evans
John A. Harvey
Virginia E. Henderson
Mrs. Margaret H. Hill
Bernard E. Holsey
Geraldine E. Jackson
Mrs. Rowena C. Johnston
Julia U. Magwood
Louis S. Monk
Marie N. Platte
Romaine F. Scott
Rozelle S. Silvey
Wilhelmina E. Smith
Louise W. Stewart
John E. Swanson
Mable D. Thomas
Mrs. Jennie M. Walburg
Mrs. Lillian J. Williams
Mrs. Clarice M. Wilson
Alberta J. Withers

Edward U. Taylor,
Supervisor of Colored Schools

Maxwell E. Burdette,
Supervisor of High Schools

Dr. Edwin W. Broome,
Superintendent

Graduating Exercises

Theme
"Strong Trees Have Deep Roots"

Processional

Flag Salute
National Anthem

Invocation
Reverend W.R. Brodgen, Pastor, Mt. Calvary Congregational Church, Spencerville, Maryland

Vocal Solo
Alberta Driver

Dramatization
"Good Citizenship Requires a Firm Foundation"

Choral Selection
Girls' Glee Club

Presentation of Diplomas
Mrs. Durward V. Sandifer, President, Montgomery County Board of Education

Awards

Benediction
Reverend Morris F. Wallace, Pastor, Clinton A.M.E. Zion Church, Rockville, Maryland

Recessional
(The audience is requested to remain seated until after the recessional.)

courtesy Virgie Stewart-Prather, S. Margaret Hill, Marie (Stewart) Neal, Helen V. Hawkins

LINCOLN HIGH SCHOOL
CLASS OF 1949 CELEBRATES

The Lincoln High School Class of 1949 celebrated its golden anniversary at the Marriott Hotel in Gaithersburg on Friday, June 25, 1999. Thirteen members of that class met for more than a year to plan the activities for this festive occasion. The committee members were Faye Foreman Hackey, Eugene Hallman, Samuel Harper, Betty Talley Hawkins, Helen V. Hawkins, Elizabeth Holston Hill, S. Margaret Hill, Eldridge Jackson, Mary Daye Johnson, Raymond Plummer, Ethel Hansborough Riggs, Oliver A. Riggs, and James Williams.

The program was comprised of the following: a welcome; silent prayer for the sick; immobile, and deceased classmates and faculty members; blessing of the food; reflections; acknowledgment of guests; and remarks. In addition, the following were also on display: class theme, "Strong Trees Have Deep Roots"; class motto, "Mighty Oaks from Little Acorns Grow"; class colors, navy blue and white; class flower, red rose; class song; and class poem.

Prior to partaking of a delicious dinner (prepared by Esther Hallman Curtis, Class of 1957, and her husband, Curtis), Betty Talley Hawkins welcomed the attendees, and James Williams blessed the food.

Following the catered meal, Ethel Hansborough Riggs read reflections composed by Samuel Harper and Betty Talley Hawkins. They reflected on the way things were during their high school days in the 1940s and the tremendous improvement that has been made in the education of black high school students in Montgomery County since the 1940s. The reflections were amusing, as they recognized some members of the class with humorous titles according to their current community involvement.

Mary Daye Johnson read a poem that she composed and acknowledged the alumni that were in attendance from each class. Each invited class was assigned a table. Out of a graduating class of 69 students, the Class of 1949 had 33 members present. The Class of 1956 had the largest number of members present, and for her efforts in rallying her former classmates, Ruth Taylor Frazier was given roses. Nine classes ('38, '41, '45, '49, '50, '51, '54, '56, '57) from Lincoln and Carver high schools participated in this festive event.

Another feature of the program was the issuance of numbered tickets at the door. At appointed times, the holders of the randomly selected ticket numbers were given door prizes.

Following remarks by Betty Talley Hawkins, many of the attendees "kicked up their heels" as they danced to the music (oldies but goodies) played by local disc jockey Darryl Foreman (relative of Faye Foreman Hackey). While some watched the rhythmic movement of the bodies on the floor, others socialized.

The Class of 1949 attendees were elated that they were able to reach this milestone in their lives, and other attendees were happy that they could share in the celebration of such a memorable occasion.

LINCOLN HIGH SCHOOL
CLASS OF 1950

Besides being the largest senior class to graduate from Lincoln High School, the Class of 1950 was the next to last class to graduate from it prior to its becoming a junior-high school. To coincide with such significance, the members elected officers who provided quality leadership for conducting their senior activities.

They elected Geraldine Barbour (President), Mary Smith (Vice-President), Irene Isreal (Secretary), Ruth Genies (Assistant Secretary), and Carl Turner (Treasurer) as class leaders under the sponsorship of Mrs. Genevieve S. Brown, Julia U. Magwood, and Daisy W. Myles.

The Lincoln High School Annual Staff dedicated the 1950 *Eagle* to Supervisor Edward U. Taylor with "heartfelt gratitude and appreciation for his untiring efforts and work." They dedicated the annual to Mr. Taylor because he accomplished much toward improving school standards during his 27 years of service in Montgomery County.

During the school year 1949-1950, the seniors were actively involved in many activities.

1. "Assembly programs were very entertaining. "

2. Lincoln Chapter of Hi-Y sent three delegates to Hi-Y Conference December 2-4 in Wilmington, Delaware.

3. Eaglette Staff visited Murray Brothers Printing Office, 920 U Street, N.W., Washington, D.C.

4. PTA heard student forum 'Problems of the High School Student.'

5. National Honor Society held 'Miss Lincoln' popularity contest.

6. Morgan State College Band was presented in concert by the Lincoln Choral Club.

7. NHA & NFA held Mother & Daughter, Father & Son Banquet.

8. Lincoln alumni Bessie Hill and Maurice Genies returned to become faculty members.

9. PTA Program Committee gave a variety show.

10. Garnet Masque produced a riotous, three-act comedy, *A Gift from Uncle Henry*, on December 16. The play was one of a series of annual Christmas plays staged by the dramatic group.

11. NHA gave a Pre-Halloween Dance.

12. United Nations Trip on December 2, 1949.

13. For five consecutive advisories, the 8C Class of 1949-1950 had the largest number of students on the honor roll and thereby merited the National Honor Society Award."

Before long, the seniors were faced with final examinations to determine whether they would 'make it' as was the common expression. Then, the wheels were put in motion with plans and rehearsals for class night and graduation.

GRADUATING EXERCISES
Lincoln High School, Monday, June 19, 1950

Class Motto
"The Past Forever Gone, the Future Still Our Own."

Class Colors
Blue & White

Class Flower
Red Rose

Valedictorian
Ruth Genies

Salutatorian
Geraldine Barbour

GRADUATES

*Geraldine V. Barbour
Marguerite Yvonne Beverley
Emily Elizabeth Bishop
Winifred Mable Bishop
Juanita Delores Boxley
John E. Brown
Mary Romaine Budd
Paul Edward Claggett
James Reynold Clarke
Agnes Marie Coates
Susie Ellen Coleman
Joseph David Cooper
Lewis Denton Cross
Pauline Charlotte Crutchfield

Barrington Lee Davis
William David Diggs
Agnes Vivian Dorsey
Bertha Mae Dorsey
Leon Dorsey
Calvin Lorenzo Dove
Frances Rebecca Driver
Norris Upshard Duvall
Ella Mae Edmunds
Gordon Dale Frazier
James Marshall Frazier
Wilma Darene Frazier
*Naomi A. Garner
Bernard A. Gassaway
Milton Fred Gassaway
*Ruth Genies
Roland Cole Harper
Isaiah Warfield Harriday
*Betty Marie Hawkins
*Mary Belle Hawkins
Cero Saunders Hayes
*Beatrice Virginia Hebron
James Vernon Hill
James Clifton Hoes
Kelly Edward Hoes
Frederick Rudolph Howard
Irene Elizabeth Isreal
*Frances Louise Jackson
*Gloria Venecia Jackson
Jacqueline Adele Johnson
Joyce Marie Lee
Madeline Cecilia Lee
Charles Thomas Lenoir, Jr.
Barbara Ann Marbley
William Douglas Marbley
Arnold Eugene Martin
James Maurice Miles
Lois Virginia Offord

Myrtle Louise Owens
Russell Carlton Palmer
Herbert Ricarte Payne
*William Henry Powell
Charles Ernest Prather
*Edythe Dorothea Pratt
James Daniel Ross, Jr.
Elenora Marie Russell
Melvin H. Shelton
Mary Jeanette Smith
George Robert Snowden
Pauline Elizabeth Summerour
*Joan Felicia Taylor
Alta Louise Thomas
Constance E. Thompson
Marion E. Thompson
*Martha Aureline Tibbs
Carl Lavelle Turner
Melvin Glenwood Washington
Martha Alice Williams
Daniel A. Withers
Milton E. Young

* *Member of National Honor Society*

Graduating Exercises
Theme
"A Backward Glance
and Now Tomorrow"

Processional

Flag Salute
National Anthem

Invocation
Reverend Walter Williams, Pastor,
Jerusalem Methodist Church,
Rockville, Maryland

Musical Selection

Dramatization

Prologue
Geraldine Barbour
"Reviewing the Past, Living in the
Present, Challenging the Future"

Epilogue
Ruth Genies

Presentation of Diplomas
Mrs. Herman M. Wilson,
President, Montgomery County
Board of Education

Awards

Benediction
Reverend C.E. Smallwood, Pastor,
John Wesley Methodist Church,
Clarksburg, Maryland

Recessional
(The audience will please remain
seated until after the recessional.)

FACULTY
Parlett L. Moore, *Principal*
Mrs. Genevieve S. Brown,
Vice-Principal
Frank P. Bolden, *Driver Training,
Biology*
D. Winifred Byrd, *Home
Economics*
Mrs. Louise S. Carpenter, *Music*
Alta M. Clarke, *Counselor,
Sociology*

Mrs. Marjorie B. Edwards, *English, Core*
Mrs. Geraldine J. Elliby, *Art, Business*
Mrs. Edna R. Evans, *English, Core*
Maurice C. Genies, *Industrial Arts*
John A. Harvey, *Physical Education*
Bessie M. Hill, *Physical Education*
Mrs. Margaret H. Hill, *Core, Art*
Bernard E. Holsey, *Agriculture*
Mrs. Rowena C. Johnston, *Cafeteria Manager, Home Economics*
Julia U. Magwood, *Mathematics, English*
Louis S. Monk, *Core*
Mrs. Daisy W. Myles, *Home Economics*

Marie N. Platte, *Physical Education*
Mrs. Romaine F. Scott-Robinson, *Core*
Mrs. Doris S. Sewell, *English, Core*
Rozelle S. Silvey, *Manual Arts*
Wilhelmina E. Smith, *Mathematics*
John E. Swanson, *Industrial Arts*
Mable D. Thomas, *Mathematics*
Mrs. Jennie M. Walburg, *Remedial Reading*
Mrs. Clarice M. Wilson, *Music, French*
Alberta J. Withers, *Social Studies*
Margaret N. Young, *Librarian, English*

courtesy Vivian Dorsey, Geraldine V. Barbour

LINCOLN HIGH SCHOOL
CLASS OF 1951

(Excerpts from 1951 Dedication, Courtesy of Margaret Foreman-Williams and Gladys Thomas-Nelson)

When the members of this class entered Lincoln High School in September 1950, they planned to graduate in June of 1951, and they realized that they would be the last senior class to

Barbara Hill

graduate from this institution, and this had historical significance.

Realizing the heavy responsibilities that lay ahead, they quickly chose the necessary leadership to accomplish each task.

Yearbook Staff
Editors
Clarence Johnson
Bernetta McDonald

Business Managers
Howard Claggett
Margaret Foreman
Mary Young

Art Editors
Dorothy Johnson
John Onley

Advertising Managers
Donald Crampton
Edith Jackson
Delores McAbee
LaVerne Posey

Literary Editors
Mollie Crawford
Gloria Davis
Frieda Frazier
Barbara Hill
Margaret King

Faculty Assistants
George B. Barrick
Alta M. Clarke
Mrs. Geraldine J. Elliby
Mable D. Thomas ('44)
Margaret N. Young

Besides publishing a yearbook, many of them found the time to participate in extra-curricular activities.

"In November 1950, the Student Council held its first big school-wide campaign for the election of officers." The electoral returns revealed "Edith Jackson as President, Marion Wood as Vice-President, and Mildred Onley as Secretary."

During the year, they sponsored four projects—"Christmas Exchange Post Office to boost the sale of Christmas seals, Sale of School Book Covers to boost school spirit, Courtesy Week and Clean-up Campaign."

NATIONAL HONOR SOCIETY

The National Honor Society sponsored an "essay and poetry contest as well as a spelling bee and a popularity contest-social, at which LaVerne Posey was crowned Miss Lincoln High School" this school year. This exclusive group also "donated a basket of food to a needy family in Rockville, sent congratulatory notes to students who made the honor roll, and awarded an honor roll plaque to Room 1 and Science Building I for having the largest number of students to make the honor roll the first and second advisories."

SCHOOL SAFETY TEAM

The Lincoln High School "safety patrol was commended for its fine record this year. Its primary purpose, in promoting safety to avoid accidents on the buses and on school property, was fulfilled. Under the able leadership of its captain, John Onley, the patrol force was of invaluable assistance to the administration in carrying out school policies." The safety patrol force was "composed of 43 members who came through in fine style during the fire and air raid drills."

To encourage the safety patrolmen to be diligent in the discharge of their duties, "Corporal Butler, of the Montgomery County Police Department, made provisions for all patrolmen to take a trip to Washington, D.C., to visit the FBI (Federal Bureau of Investigation) building in November 1950."

"On May 15, 1951, they participated in a parade in Washington that consisted of patrolmen from all over the United States. Also in May, the patrolmen were invited to attend a baseball game at Griffith Stadium in Washington and a picnic in Longview, Maryland."

The safety team had a successful year because "the teachers and the students patiently worked with them."

N.H.A.

"The New Homemakers of America was an organization that consisted of 27 students who majored in the academic, general, vocational, and commercial courses.

The colors of the organization were blue and white, the flower was the red rose, and the motto was 'Better Homes for a Better America.'"

The organization had an agenda which included a variety of activities during the school year. The first chapter meeting was in September, at which they decided to meet twice monthly and to pay 15 cents in dues monthly.

In October, they had a Halloween dance and attended the regional meeting at the Robert Moten High School in Westminister, Maryland.

In December, they gave away two food baskets to needy families, had a Christmas party, and exchanged Christmas greetings with other chapters.

In February, they sent a box of first-aid supplies to the home economics classes of the College of West Africa in Monrovia, Liberia.

In March, they invited 10 new members to join their club.

In May, they gave an assembly program and had a picnic. Plans were also made to invite all the regional NHA Clubs—Cumberland, Frederick, Hagerstown, and Westminister—to Carver High School in the fall of 1951.

N.F.A.

The New Farmers of America "afforded its members an excellent opportunity to develop a type of leadership which was very essential for the modern successful farmer. This leadership ability was developed through chapter contests, judging, public speaking, and training received from the work in the club. These N.F.A. activities were designed to supplement training opportunities for boys who were planning to live in rural communities."

PHYSICAL EDUCATION

"Last fall, Lincoln High School was admitted to the South Atlantic High School Athletic Conference. The Tri-State Conference was composed of schools from Maryland, Virginia, and West Virginia."

The boys competed in basketball, baseball, and track. John A. Harvey coached baseball and basketball, whereas William Gordon (a new teacher) and Rozelle S. Silvey coached track.

Bessie M. Hill (Lincoln High School Class of 1942) coached the girls basketball and track teams. The girls basketball team made their presence felt when they "won runner-up honors at the annual basketball tournament. In addition, Kathleen Colmes and Catherine Taylor were named on the All-Tournament Team."

Kathleen Lane, a new teacher, coached volleyball.

The Lincoln Junior-Senior High

School physical education teachers included William Gordon (junior high), John A. Harvey (senior high), Bessie M. Hill (senior high), Kathleen Lane (junior high), and Rozelle S. Silvey (senior high). They taught "agility stunts, basketball, softball, sprintball, strength-balance, touch football, track and field, tumbling, and volleyball in the physical education classes."

BASKETBALL TEAM ROSTERS

BOYS
Thomas Brown
James Butler
William Butler
Leroy Carroll
Clifford Claggett
Howard Claggett
Howard Coleman
Johnny Coleman
Barge Davis
Welford Gaither
Paul Hawkins
Eugene King
Bernard Lee
Richard Prather
David Smith
Berlin Thomas
Robert Wise

GIRLS
Mary Albert
Rachel Bowie
Lucille Brown
Kathleen Colmes
Mollie Crawford
Alma Frazier

Ella Johnson
Margaret Johnson
Margaret King
Carrie Riggs
Catherine Taylor
Thelma Thomas
Evelyn Thompson
Gertrude Webster

LINCOLN HIGH SCHOOL BAND

Generous monetary gifts from "the Board of Education, the PTA (Parent Teacher Association), and contributors to the Band Drive enabled the school to purchase 21 new instruments."

The school band "participated on several programs which included a PTA concert, an assembly program, and the PTA's Annual Spring Program."

They planned "to have a concert band, a dance band, and a marching band" in the near future.

LINCOLN HIGH SCHOOL NEWSPAPER

The members of the senior high school newspaper staff met in the fall of 1950 for organizational purposes.

Newspaper Staff

Editor-in-Chief
Sadie Pumphrey

Co-Editor
John Olney

Art Editors
Raymond Baker
Dorothy Johnson
Gertrude Webster

Copy Editors
LaVerne Posey
James Turner

Manager
Ella Pumphrey

Secretary
Dorothy Johnson

Later, the Eaglette staff members gave a Sadie Hawkins Dance on Friday, November 10, 1950. The auditorium was turned over to the Dogpatch Dwellers who danced to the tunes of Billy Campbell's band.

During the school year, "the staff successfully issued their news eight times" and hoped to do greater work in their newspaper the following year.

MUSIC

The school strove to offer a musical program that would "meet the needs and interests of the students as well as serve the community."

Several vocal groups were organized—a Girls Glee Club, a Girls Sextet, and a mixed choral group. Besides performing at various school functions, "these groups were also popular participants in community activities."

The climax of the year's performances was "an operetta, 'Cinderella's Slipper,' which featured some of the school's best talent."

MATHEMATICS

Since in prior years, "Americans had become 'training conscious,' a mastery of at least basic skills was considered very essential" in the 1950's. "Accordingly, the Mathematics Department stressed a knowledge of the fundamentals of mathematics and the ability to apply that knowledge to the solution of practical everyday problems."

On the junior high level, "arithmetic was offered to eighth graders, and algebra, plane geometry, business arithmetic, review of mathematics, and trigonometry were offered in senior high school."

COMMERCIAL

Inasmuch as all individuals are "part of a great business world which touches every activity of their lives," it is imperative that the educational needs and wants of young people be satisfied.

"In the school's business department, the students were introduced, either through experience or through a study of the purposes of modern business, to the business services offered in their area," and they were taught "the proper use of these services."

HOME ECONOMICS

"Home economics was required of all junior high school students. The subject matter was general in scope, so that if no additional work in this field was elected in the senior high school, the individual would have received some of the basic elements necessary for homemaking and home and family living. This program was conducted in two to three one hour fifty-five-minute periods per week.

Home economics was an elective on the senior high school level with two courses offered—general home economics and homemaking. The general course was offered in three to five one-hour periods per week to non-vocational pupils who elected it. These students completed two home projects per year.

"The Home Economics Department also assisted with the supervision of the cafeteria, sponsored the school NHA Chapter, and assisted with social functions sponsored by the school and the PTA."

SHOP

"The purpose of the general shop was to give the students a chance to work with hand tools in six areas—ceramics, electricity, metal, plastics, power motors, and wood—and to get relevant and essential background in a phase which might interest them as a life's work."

ENGLISH

"In peace and in war, a democracy needs citizens with skill in listening, reading, thinking, the forceful expression of ideas and evaluating what has been learned."

"Likewise, it is believed that literature should arouse and maintain appreciation, interest, and enjoyment of the materials and should encourage exploration in broader areas of literature."

"The curriculum provided for broad areas of development, which included opportunities for individual differences, for teacher-pupil planning, for testing evaluation in all areas of study."

AGRICULTURE

Interested boys participated in "a diversified program of work, so that they might have the opportunity to develop an appreciation for rural life and to gain more information about the occupations in the different phases of agriculture. In order to gain some of the working skills and techniques for success, each boy had a home project."

THE NIGHT BEFORE FINALS
—The Yearbook Staff

'Twas the night before finals and
all through the house,
The only creatures stirring were me
and a mouse.
The mouse kept scurrying around
my chair
As I sat cramming, too weary to
care.
The clock on my dresser struck a
solemn two,
But I still had hours of studying to
do.
The extent of my knowledge was
pitifully thin
Against that French I could not
win.
And there was algebra and English
and chemistry,
And music and problems of democracy.
I knew my teachers were snug in
their beds,
While visions of parallelograms
danced through my head.
My eyes grew weary, my head
dropped low;
It was at that point that I must
have dozed.
But who should my troubled
dreams invade?
All of the teachers of the high
school grades!
They were making up question-
naires, much to my sorrow,
That were guaranteed to trip us
tomorrow.
Miss Clarke told Mr. Stith, confi-
dentially,
Of the tests she had made in
psychology.
"This is the one for my senior class;
You can bet your life that the
rascals won't pass."
Miss Withers was busily filling
page ten,
With history blanks. How ...? Why
...? Who ...? When ...?
While Mrs. Evans cleared her
throat,
She reached for her pen. Two hours
she wrote
Who was Shakespeare? What did
he do?
Who killed Macbeth? Was he a
knight, too?
What is a verb? Who was Scott?
Write a drama with a complex plot.
I heard in the distance, the failure
bell toll;
But Mr. Silvey kept right on calling
his roll.
Now Hawkins and Helms, and
Johnson and Lee,
Your projects are not finished, your
grade is "E".

Mrs. Brown and Mrs. Wilson
devised a plan
For adding a year to our school
span.
If we passed in chemistry by luck,
not skill,
Mrs. Wilson in French our chances
would kill.
And vice versa, if in French we
passed,
Mrs. Brown would stop us in
chemistry class.
Mr. Roberson didn't have to coop-
erate,
His physics had already spelled
our fate.
With her problems Miss Thomas
was satisfied;
Einstein couldn't solve them if he
tried.
Mrs. Elliby and Miss Young were
adding their share
With tests that would surely gray
our hair.
Mr. Moore had a meeting with all
the rest,
He was scolding them about their
easy tests.
"Miss Hill, Mr. Holsey, and Mrs.
Myles,
Mr. Genies, Mr. Harvey - I under-
stand; I'm surprised.
Your tests are too easy - something
must be done.
"Our motto this year is 'Fail Every-
one.'"
Let's take a few minutes and add
to each test

Questions you know our students
can't guess.
With a nod and a smile he left the
room,
But the words he had spoken had
sealed our doom.
I awoke the next morning as the
clock struck eight;
My mother was calling, "You're
going to be late!"
My work was unfinished, my
lessons unlearned
What sort of average could I hope
to earn?
Well, I failed my exams as you can
guess,
And to Mom and Dad I had to
confess.
All three of us had a good hard cry,
Oh when will I graduate from
Lincoln High?

After pursuing their various academic
programs for 10 months and passing
their challenging final examinations,
62 seniors were ready to march to a
different beat, this time to the cadence
of "War March of the Priests" and
"Pomp and Circumstance" because it
was graduation time.

GRADUATING EXERCISES
Lincoln High School
Monday, June 18, 1951

Class Motto
"We Learn not for School,
But for Life."

Class Colors
Blue & White

Class Flower
Red Rose

Valedictorian
Lillian Smallwood

Salutatorian
Edith Jackson

GRADUATES
Alma Allen
George Worthington Awkard
Lorraine Rebecca Bell
Alice Rebecca Bishop
Martha Arlean Brown
Doris Gaynelle Claggett
Howard Thomas Claggett
Howard Wallace Coleman, Jr.
Cora Rebecca Cooke
Elaine Virginia Copeland
*Donald Clinton Crampton
*Mollie Mathew Crawford
Gloria Eloise Davis
John Willis Ellis
*Margaret LaVerne Foreman
Freida Mae Frazier
Daniel Willard Genies
Kenneth Eugene Green
*Melvin Ulysses Hallman
Charles Sylvester Harper
Herbert Hawkins
Paul Hawkins
Leo Helms
*Barbara Joan Hill

Sterling Clifton Holland
*Edith Louise Jackson
*Clarence Henry Johnson
Eleanor Elizabeth Johnson
Margaret Elizabeth Johnson
Eleanor Elizabeth Kelly
Margaret Marie King
Mollie Marie Lambert
Ann Virginia Lee
Phyllis Elizabeth Love
Bernice Savannah Lyles
Bertha Mae Marbley
Rhudell Curtis McAbee
Betty Lou Virginia McDonald
Burnetta Elizabeth McDonald
Betty Eleanor McKelvin
Joseph McKinney
*Mildred Elizabeth Onley
Annie Marie Palmer
Julius Cyril Parrott, Jr.
Lois Jean Prather
Elizabeth Adelaide Richards
*Katie Janet Ricketts
Carrie Catherine Riggs
Peggy Ann Simpson
Ruby Ann Slaughter
*Lillian Mae Smallwood
Delois Rosa Thomas
*Gladys Isabelle Thomas
Raymond Alfred Thomas
Robert Thomas
Thelma Louise Thomas
Evelyn Louise Thompson
Paul William Thompson
Carroll Maurice Washington
Geraldine Viola Waters

Robert Eugene Wise
Ulysses Grant Zeigler

Member of National Honor Society

Graduating Exercises
Theme
"Education for Survival"

Processional

Flag Salute
National Anthem

Invocation
Reverend John R. Brooks, Pastor,
Sharp Street Methodist Church,
Sandy Spring, Maryland

Choral Selection
"The Halls of Ivy"
(Russell and Knight)
The Girls Glee Club

Dramatization
Senior Class

Introduction
Edith Jackson
"We See Our Problem, Realize the
Consequences, And Offer Our
Challenge"

Conclusion
Lillian Smallwood

Choral Selection
"This Is My Country"
(Al Jacobs)

The Girls' Glee Club

Presentation of Diplomas
Willie W. Barrow, Member,
Montgomery County
Board of Education

Greetings from the Junior College
Mrs. Carolyn Johnson Awkard
Lincoln High School Class of 1942

Scholarship Awards

Selections
The High School Band
"In a Canoe Waltz"
(Forest L. Buchtel)

Poem
(Forest L. Buchtel)

Benediction
Reverend C. E. Smallwood, Pastor,
John Wesley Methodist Church,
Clarksburg, Maryland

*L to R: Marjorie Smith, Roland Hall,
Ruby Slaughter*

Recessional

(The audience is requested to remain seated until after the recessional.)

FACULTY

Dr. Parlett L. Moore, *Principal*
Mrs. Genevieve S. Brown,
Vice-Principal
*George B. Barrick , *Art*
*Mrs. Louise S. Carpenter, *Music*
Alta M. Clarke, *Counselor,*
Psychology
Mrs. Edna R. Evans, *English*
Mrs. Geraldine J. Elliby, *Business*
Maurice C. Genies, *Shop*
John A. Harvey, *Physical Education*
Director
Bessie M. Hill (Class of 1942),
Physical Education
Bernard E. Holsey (Class of 1939),
Agriculture
Mrs. Daisy W. Myles, *Home*
Economics

William C. Robertson, *Biology,*
Physics, Mathematics
Rozelle S.Silvey, *Shop*
Herbert J. Stith, *Band, Music*
Mable D. Thomas (Class of 1944),
Mathematics, Business
Mrs. Clarice M. Wilson, *French,*
English
Alberta J. Withers *Social Studies*
Margaret N. Young, *Librarian,*
English

* Part-time in Senior High School

Edward U. Taylor, *Supervisor of*
Colored Schools
Maxwell E. Burdette , *Supervisor of*
High Schools
Dr. Edwin W. Broome,
Superintendent of Montgomery
County Schools

courtesy Margaret Foreman-Williams,
Gladys Thomas-Nelson

CARVER HIGH SCHOOL CLASS OF 1952

The Class of 1952 entered Lincoln Junior-Senior High School in 1947. "They bore the humiliation of their freshman title bravely. They were determined to show the world that they too were important and were ready to accept their share of the school's laurels. They proved it by walking off with field meet medals."

"As tenth graders, they were caught in a web of intra- and extra-curricular activities, and they were confident in themselves. They participated in the activities of the athletic teams, Dance Club, Dramatics Club, National Honor Society, and Tri-Hi-Y."

By the time their junior year rolled around, they discovered that their list of extra-curricular activities had grown and had become more challenging. "The big event of that year was the Junior-Senior Prom, and Edith Jackson reigned as queen over that grand festivity."

When Carver High opened its doors in September 1951, the eager Class of 1952 entered with renewed enthusiasm, energies soaring, and excitement mounting. These high spirits were due partly to relocating to a new senior high school, the first senior class to enjoy this privilege, and mostly because they were seniors. With the dawn of their senior year came lots of obligations—class leaders, a yearbook, extracurricular activities, graduating exercises.

On the basketball court, Catherine Taylor drew a lot of attention with her crowd-pleasing performances of 30-plus points per game. At the end of the season playoffs were held in Piedmont, West Virginia, where teams from the Tri-State Athletic District (Maryland, Virginia, West Virginia) competed for the championship. The Carver Girls team had a heartbreaking loss in the championship game by a mere two points, according to Coach Bessie M. Hill and player Catherine Taylor.

Many of the seniors were active participants in various extracurricular activities—Assembly Committee, Athletic Committee, basketball team, Choral Club, Cosmetology, Dance Club, Dramatic Club, Finance Committee, Future Teachers of America, Hi-Y, National Honor Society, New Farmers of America, Newspaper Staff, Safety Patrol, Student Council, Tri-Hi-Y.

They dedicated their yearbook, the 1952 *Carver Eagle*, "to Mrs. Genevieve S. Brown, their outstanding vice-principal who retired that year."

From the standpoint of popularity, "Delores McAbee and William Talley were King and Queen and were crowned Miss & Mr. Carver High School, at the Annual National Honor Society Social."

Now that they were noble seniors, they had to march to a drum with a different beat. They had to proceed at a stepped-up tempo, because of a more intensified program of activities than they had followed during their junior year. Their major concern was to master their academic studies, and 75 graduating seniors later marched to "War March of the Priests" and "Pomp and Circumstance" in a procession to receive their academic diplomas and certificates on Monday, June 16, 1952.

It is worthy of note that a member of this class, Helen James, composed the Carver High School Alma Mater, which underwent some minor changes in later years.

Junior Class Officers

President
Sadie Pumphrey

Vice-President
Virginia Boston

Secretary
Delores McAbee

Assistant Secretary
Lucille Brown

Treasurers
Arleen Smith
James Turner

Senior Class Officers

President
Marion Wood

Vice-President
Lucille Brown

Secretary
Gertrude Webster

Assistant Secretary
Delores McAbee

Treasurer
Douglas Johnson

Sergeants-at-Arms
Oscar Bagley
Wesley Walker

Yearbook Staff

Editor
Dorothy Johnson

Co-Editor
Delores McAbee

Advertising Manager
Lucille Brown

Business Manager
Alma Frazier

Secretary
Mary Albert

Typist
Virginia Boston

Senior Superlatives

Best Public Speakers
William Talley & Marion Wood

Top Scholars
Helen James & John Onley

Best Songbirds
Lucille Brown & Floyd Wims

Best Athletes
David Smith & Catherine Taylor

Best Artists
Raymond Baker &
Dorothy Johnson

Best Leaders
John Onley & Sadie Pumphrey

Best Disposition
Roberta Hallman & Henry Tibbs

Best Smile
Leroy Dove &
Lorraine Washington

Best Service
Florence Coffield,
Pauline Graham &
Dennis Owens

Most Popular
Barge Davis & Sadie Pumphrey

Tallest
Mary Albert &
Wellington Crutchfield

Most Likely to Succeed
Raymond Baker & Iola Stemley

CARVER HIGH SCHOOL ALMA MATER

Hail to thee, oh Carver High
'Tis of thee we'll ever sing
For we love our alma mater
And for thee our praises ring.
To thy ideals we'll be true
Whether life brings joy or tear
To thee we'll ever bring our laurels
We'll ever serve thee, Carver dear.
- Helen James, Class of 1952

Class Motto
"Not at the Top, But Climbing."

Class Colors
Blue & White

Class Flower
Red Rose

Valedictorian
John Onley

Salutatorian
Helen James

GRADUATES

^Ernestine C. Adams
Nathaniel Winfield Addison

245

Phyllis Alfreda Addison
Mary Alice Albert
*Oscar L. Bagley
Raymond Leroy Baker
Wesley Leroy Beckwith
Rhudell Thelma Bell
*Florence Virginia Boston
Helen Lucille Brown
Claude Nathan Byrd
*Florence Mildred Coffield
**Elsie Mae Colmes
Gordon Stanley Crawford
^Wellington Nathaniel Crutchfield
Margaret Anne Davenport
Barge Davis
^Lorraine A. Davis
Kenneth Paul Fred Dimmie
Leroy Roland Dove
Clarice Amanda Doye
Golden Driver, III
Alma Theresa Frazier
Shirley Anne Frazier
Paul Louis Gassaway
Margaret Glenn
*Ethel Pauline Graham
*Florence Hackney
*Evelyn Corrine Hallman
*Evelyn Roberta Hallman
Ernest Linwood Hill
Charles Eguster Hoes
Nadine Thelma Howard
Freddie Isreal
**Helen Elizabeth T. Jackson
*Helen Bernice James
Adrian Johnson
Alverta Louise Johnson
Dorothy Virginia Johnson
Douglas Lorenzo Johnson

Joann Bernice King
James Everett Lewis
Katherine Jane Lomax
Merle Eugene Lyles
Hazel Jeanette Marbley
Delores Almeda McAbee
Paul Leon McKinney
*John Henry Onley
Dorothy Jane Orem
Dennis Owens, Jr.
Richard Albert Parrott
Catherine LaVerne Posey
June M. Prilliman
Sadie Louise Pumphrey
Juanita Marion Riggs
Albert Russell Sewell
Joseph Thomas Simpson
Arline Frances Smith
David Smith, Jr.
Lelia H. Smith
Earl Conrad Starke
*Iolamary Priscilla Stemley
William Thomas Talley
Catherine Taylor
Frederick Alfred Templeman
**Evelyn Mae Thomas
James Louis Thomas
William Wesley Thomas
Henry Tibbs
Sadie Myrtene Turner
Wesley Carold Walker
Loraine Marie Washington
Georgie Gertrude Webster
Floyd Norman Wims
*Marion Annabelle Wood

*Member of National Honor Society
**High School Extension
^Candidate for Certificate

FACULTY

Dr. Parlett L. Moore, *Principal*
Mrs. Genevieve S. Brown,
Vice-Principal
(Retired in February)
George B. Barrick
Alta M. Clarke
Mrs. Edna R. Evans
Maurice C. Genies
John A. Harvey
Bernard E. Holsey
John A. Jones
Mrs. Daisy Myles
Bessie M. Hill
Rozelle S. Silvey
Herbert J. Stith, Jr.
Calvin C. Rubens
Mable D. Thomas
Mrs. Blanche T. Vessels
Mrs. Ruby E. Washington
Mrs. Clarice Wilson
Alberta J. Withers
Lorenzo A. Woodward
Margaret N. Young

Maxwell E. Burdette, *High School
Supervisor*
Dr. Edwin W. Broome,
Superintendent

GRADUATION PROGRAM

Processional
"Priests'
March" from *Athalia*
(Mendelssohn)

Flag Salute

National Anthem
Audience

Invocation
Reverend Walter E.Williams,
Pastor, Jerusalem Methodist
Church, Rockville, Maryland

Choral Selection
"Stout Hearted Men"
(Romberg)

Salutatory
Helen James

Band Selection
"Blue Danube Waltz"
(Strauss)

Valedictory
John Onley

Choral Selection
"Halls of Ivy"
(Russell)

Address to Graduates
Dr. Irene C. Hypps, Associate
Superintendent of Schools, Division 2, Washington, D.C.

Band Selection
"Syncopated Clock"
(Anderson)

Presentation of Diplomas
Mrs. Durward V. Sandifer, Member, Montgomery County Board of
Education

Band Selection
"Thespian Overture"
(Frangkiser)

Benediction
Reverend Joseph Stemley,
Pastor, Emory Memorial
Methodist Church,
Emory Grove, Maryland

Recessional
"Pomp and Circumstance"
(Elgar)
*courtesy Edith Hill-Owens, Florence
Coffield, Delores McAbee*

CARVER HIGH SCHOOL CLASS OF 1953

The Class of 1953 was the second largest class (71) to graduate from Carver High School and the fifth largest class to graduate from Rockville High School, Lincoln High School, or Carver High School.

ANNUAL GRADUATING EXERCISES
Lincoln High School
Wednesday, June 17, 1953

Class Motto
"Wisdom is Knowledge and Knowledge is Power."

Class Colors
Blue & White

Class Flower
Red Rose

Valedictorian
Percival T. Ricketts

Salutatorian
Henrietta Katherine Jordan

GRADUATES

Kenneth Awkward
*Helen Bacon
Mary Bishop
*Phyllis Borders
Kathryn Boston
Thelma Brown

James Butler
William Butler
Leroy Carroll
Clifford Claggett
Horace Claggett
Annie Coleman
Harriett Coleman
Evelyn Coleman
Kathleen Colmes
Earl Contee
Clarence Crampton
Julian Daniels
Florice Davis
June Dorsey
Melissa Driver
Elizabeth Foreman
Leroy Foreman
Roland Foreman
Francis Frazier
Rhoda Frazier
Alphonzo Freeman
Barbara Gaither
Doris Gaither
*Welford Gaither
^Mildred Garland
*Mattie Garrett
Shirley Gray
Gladys Greene
Leroy Hackey
Louis Helms
*Lillian Henderson
Lillian Hill
Willis Hill
Harold Hopkins
Constance Hopps
Richard Howard
Agnes Jackson

249

Eleanor Johnson
*Ella Johnson
*Roland Johnson
*Henrietta Jordan
William Kelly
Dorothy King
Eugene King
Bernard Lee
*Shirley Mayes
Frederick Edward McAbee
Shirley McKinney
Barbara Morrison
Leroy Offord, Jr.
Lawrence Offutt
Delores Penry
Clayton Powell

Rosie Powell
Richard Prather
Margaret Randolph
*Percival Ricketts
*Sadie Mae Ross
Sylvia Shelton
*Edith Smith
Howard Smith, Jr.
Barbara Talley
Upton Talley
James Thompson
Madeline Catherine Zeigler

*Member of National Honor Society
^Candidate for Certificate

courtesy Helen Bacon

CARVER HIGH SCHOOL CLASS OF 1954

The Class of 1954 was the third high school class to graduate from new Carver High School. From a historical standpoint, this class can be considered significant.

There was a revival of interest in dramatics after the stage curtains were installed, and several one-act plays were presented to the students and the community with outstanding performance by the casts.

The Carver band attained such a degree of excellence in its performance that it was invited to participate in two statewide band programs and to present a number of concerts throughout Montgomery County and nearby areas, including Coppin State Teachers College and Morgan State College of Baltimore.

The school served as host to the Tri-State Athletic Union's Basketball Tournament this year, thereby providing for the community another type of recreational-social experience."

Once they reached the senior high level, their active participation in the various extracurricular activities made the years pass by swiftly, and before they knew it, their senior year was upon them with all of its challenges and history. This class was the second class to have 75 graduates and thereby, along with the Class of 1952, set a record for having the largest number of high school graduates from any of the three historically black high schools.

Class Motto
"We Choose Our Way."

Class Colors
Blue & White

Class Flower
Red Carnation

Valedictorian
Thelma M. Moore

Salutatorian
Shirley J. Holston

GRADUATING EXERCISES

George Washington Carver High School, Thursday, June 17, 1954
7:00 P.M.

CLASS ROLL
Doris R. Adams
Dorothea Velvia Bell
Bernice Elizabeth Bennett
Spencer Everette Boston
Barbara Elaine Braxton
Mary D. Brown
William O. Burriss
Charles Roosevelt Byrd
Wilma Frances Byrd
Joseph Theodore Carter
**Norine Elizabeth Chase

Clarence Wilbur Claggett
Donald A. Clarke
Douglass Ellis Clarke
George Cooper
Melvin Cooper
Lawrence Copeland
Warren Gordon Crutchfield
Eugene Daniel
Estelle Louise Dawes
Alfred M. DeGraff
Shirley Estelle Dorsey
Edgar Eugene Dove
Melvin Driver, Jr.
Marie DeLoris Frazier
Stansbury Frazier
Hazel Melvinia Gray
*Rose Althea Genies
Nancy Jane Glenn
Florence Marina Graham
David Lloyd Harriday
Blanche Romaine Harris
Shirley Elaine Harris
Sherman A. Harrison, Jr.
Alice Christine Hawkins
Erma Lucille Hawkins
*Jacquelyn Lorraine Hawkins
*Kermit Roosevelt Hawkins, Jr.
Vernell Elizabeth Hebron
Charles Edward Hill
Marjorie Hoes
*Shirley Jean Holston
Stanley Jackson
Betty Louise Johnson
Leroy Alvin Johnson
Kenneth Johnson
Leandrew Jordan
Clara Brice Kenner
Lillian King

Robert King
Shirley Rosalie Kinslow
Norman Francis Lancaster
Jerrylee Ernestine Lefeged
*Joyce Juanita Love
Clara Louise Lyles
*Richard Thomas Lyles
Lawrence Madison
Sylvia Marbley
*Thelma Marie Moore
Richard W. Murray, Jr.
**Nathan Orem
Julia Anne Payne
Laurell R. Phillips
*Harlean Constance Prather
**Bruce Sewell
Samuel Sewell
Mary Louise Simms
Alice Golden Simpson
Marva Joanne Stewart
Mildred Elizabeth Thomas
Celestine Virginia Walker
Ruize Waters
Lena Elnora Williams
Geraldine Marie Withers
Sterling Zeigler

*Member of National Honor Society
**Candidate for Certificate

Graduating Exercises

Processional
"War March of the Priests"
From *Athalia*
(Mendelssohn)

Flag Salute

Invocation
Reverend C. E. Smallwood, Pastor,

Mt. Zion Methodist Church, Silver
Spring, Maryland

Choral Selection
"This Is My Country"
(Waring)

Dramatization
"Preparation, The Gateway to
Success"
(Senior Class)

Band Selection
"Skater's Waltz"
(Waldteufel)

Presentation of Diplomas
Willard G. McGraw, Vice-President,
Montgomery County Board of
Education

Band Selection
"Gypsy Festival Overture" (Hayes)

Greetings from the Junior College
Betty Talley,
Lincoln High School Class of 1949

Awards

Choral Selection
"Finlandia"
(Sibelius)

Benediction
Reverend T. G. Barrington, Pastor,
Emory Grove Methodist Church,
Emory Grove,
Maryland

Recessional
"Pomp and Circumstance"
(Elgar)

Scholarship Awards
Morgan State College
$200.00 - Thelma M. Moore

*Montgomery County Board of
Education*
$150.00 - Harlean C. Prather
(Carver Junior College)

*Grand United Order of Odd
Fellows Lodge No. 6430
Sandy Spring, Maryland*
$150.00 - Estelle T. Dawes (Carver
Junior College)

*Montgomery County Teachers
Association*
$150.00 - Kermit R. Hawkins, Jr.
(Carver Junior College)

Carver National Honor Society
$50.00 - Shirley J. Holston

*Parent-Teacher Council of
Montgomery County*
$50.00 - Shirley J. Holston

*Women's Auxiliary Central
District Association of Baptist
Convention
Baltimore, Maryland*
$50.00 - Leandrew Jordan

*Zorah Chapter No. 36,
Eastern Star
Rockville, Maryland*
$25.00 - Lorraine Hawkins

Dr. Parlett L. Moore, *Principal*
Dr. Forbes H. Norris,
Superintendent

253

Class Song
(Tune: "September Songs")

It's been a long, long way
From the first to the eleventh grade
But the days grow short, when you
reach the twelfth grade.
It's been a long, long way
To meet commencement night,
But the days are short if it's in your
heart.

We shall say farewell to the best of
schools
Dear Carver High, we'll miss you
so.
Farewell dear Carver, we're sorry
to leave you,
But it is clear that we can't stay.

*courtesy Margaret Foreman-Williams, Gladys
Thomas-Nelson, Florence M. Graham*

Carver High School Graduates, Class of 1954

CARVER HIGH SCHOOL CLASS OF 1955

On the first day of school in September 1954, the members of this class entered the portals of Carver High School with faces of joy and of sadness. Some were joyful because they were eager to be challenged with curricular and extracurricular activities, as well as to be with their classmates, schoolmates, and teachers on a daily basis, while others may have been sad since they had to depart from their enjoyable, carefree summer vacation. Whether they wanted to be there or not, they did start their senior year in style.

They chose as their officers "Ethelreda Harrison (President), Rose Marie Dorsey (Vice-President), Marylah Clark (Secretary), Blanche Hall (Assistant Secretary), and Wesley Prather (Treasurer)." These officers operated under the skillful leadership of Miss Mable D. Thomas and Miss Clarice Wilson.

The Annual Staff was composed of "Ethelreda Harrison (Editor), Robert Hill (Associate Editor), Wesley Prather (Business Manager), Geraldine Addison, Georgeana Barbour, Emma Beckwith, Marylah Clark, Alma Daye, Rose Marie Dorsey, Christine Dove, Blanche Hall, Ida Harris, Ella Hawkins, Virginia Henderson, Annette Jones, Roberta Lyles, Shirley Owens, Glenda Taylor, Bernice Thompson, Ruth Wa-

ters, and Frances Wims (Staff Members). Mrs. Jessie Snowden was their adviser."

The senior class dedicated their annual to "Miss Mable D. Thomas and Miss Clarice Wilson, their faithful and tolerant senior advisers, who gave many hours of their time to help cultivate senior dignity and to extend guidance." These teachers were chosen to be the recipients of this honor because they "were inspiring, helpful, and willing to lend their never-tiring aid."

The seniors were well-represented as officers and members of the various student organizations.

"Marylah Clark was president of the Commercial Club, and Virginia Henderson was the secretary.

Odelia Dove was captain of the girls' basketball team.

Osce Francis was vice-president of the NFA (New Farmers of America).

Robert Hill was a member of the Assembly Committee.

Joseph Holston was president of the NFA.

Harold Howard was president of the Student Council, captain of the Patrol Force, president of the National Honor Society, president of the Hi-Y, president of Assembly Committee, and member of the track team and Debating Club.

John R. Moore, Jr., and Harry Smith were members of the Hi-Y.

Annnabelle Moten was president of the NHA (New Homemakers of America) and president of Dramatics Club; Glenda Taylor was vice-president of the NHA; and Shirley R. Hebron and Phyllis Prather were members.

Wesley Prather was vice-president of the Student Council.

Ethel Shelton was president of the Dance Club, and Blanche Hall was the vice-president.

Alvin Thomas was co-captain of the football team."

Still others were actively involved in the band and Choral Club.

In the spring, there were "10 young ladies who vied for top honors for the May Day festivities. In the end, Marylah Clark was crowned May Queen on May Day."

Then, the most memorable event in their high school career—GRADUATION—took place on Wednesday, June 8, 1955, at 7 P.M. There were 67 seniors who marched to "War March of the Priests" and "Pomp and Circumstance."

Class Motto
"There Will Always Be Frontiers to Conquer."

Class Colors
Blue & White

Class Flower
Red Rose
Valedictorian

Harold W. Howard

Salutatorian
Rose Marie Dorsey

CLASS ROLL

Frances Adams
Geraldine Irene Addison
Emma Elizabeth Beckwith
Adville A. Bell
Frances Lee Bell
Mildred A. Brown
Marylah Barbara Clark
Pauline Virginia Coleman
Milford Cooper
Geraldine C. Cross
James Wesley Davis
Peggy Ann Davis
Walter Leroy Dimes
*Rose Marie Dorsey
Christine Othelia Dove
Chain Odelia Dove
William Randolph Dove
Ralph Eugene Driver
Richard Eugene Dyson
Osce Francis
Blanche Louisa Hall
Ethelreda Harrison
Ella Louise Hawkins
Shirley Rebecca Hebron
Ralph Montgomery Helms
Audrey Henderson
Virginia Elizabeth Henderson
Joseph Howard Holston
*Harold Winthrop Howard
Mary Madeline Hungerford
Henry Richard Jackson
Idaway Jackson

Byron Leon Jones
**Shirley Jean Johnson
Paul King
Clifton Dowayne Lee
Joseph I. Marshall
Mary Frances Marshall
Shirley Delores Matthews
Ethel McElroy
John R. Moore, Jr.
Annabell Virginia Moten
Doris Mae Moten
Shirley Ann Owens
Ronald E. Parrott
Phillis Annette Prather
Wesley Prather
Benjamin Randolph
Willia Ann Selby
Ethel M. Shelton
Charles S. Smith
Harry Robert Smith
Robert Stewart
Betty Anne Stevenson
Cyrus Glenn Taylor
Glenda Irene Taylor
Alvin Glen Thomas
**Richard Charles Thomas
Bernice Marie Thompson
Leonard V. Tibbs
Dallas Eugene Waters
Janice Glendora Williams
Michael Edward Williams
Earl Alexander Wims, Jr.
Frances R. Wims
Gasery Eugene Wims
DeWitt Marbley, Jr.

*Member of National Honor Society
**Candidate for Certificate
Dr. Parlett L. Moore, *Principal*

Graduating Exercises

Processional
"Priests' March"
from *Athalia*
(Mendelssohn)

Flag Salute

Invocation
Reverend C. E. Smallwood,
Pastor, Mt. Zion Methodist Church,
Silver Spring, Maryland

Solo
"Goodbye"
(Fosti)
Dallas Waters

Dramatization
"Seniors at the Bar"
(Class)

Choral Selection
"Halls of Ivy"
(Russell and Knight)

Presentation of Diplomas
Lathrop Smith, Member,
Montgomery County
Board of Education

Band Selection
"Ambition Overture"
(Bennett)

Greetings from the Junior College
Gerald Hitch

Awards

Band Selection
"Norma's Dream"
(Bennett)

Benediction
Reverend Walter Williams, Pastor,
Jerusalem Methodist Church,
Rockville, Maryland
Recessional
"Pomp and Circumstance"
(Elgar)

SCHOLARSHIP AWARDS

Morgan State College
$300 - Harold Howard
$250 - Rose Marie Dorsey

*Parent-Teacher Council of
Montgomery County*
$50 - Harold Howard

Board of Education
$150 - Michael Williams
(Carver Junior College)

Montgomery County Teachers Association
$150 - Virginia Henderson (Carver
Junior College)

*Woman's Auxiliary Central
District Association of Baptist Convention
Baltimore, Maryland*
$50 - Sidney Smith

Carver National Honor Society
$50 - Rose Marie Dorsey

*Zorah Chapter No. 36
Eastern Star
Rockville, Maryland*
$25 - Frances Wims

courtesy Harold W. Howard

CARVER HIGH SCHOOL CLASS OF 1956

The Class of 1956 was the only class that graduated from Carver High School that had the same number of graduates (56) as the last two digits in the year of graduation. It was the second class to have this unusual characteristic; the first was the Lincoln High School Class of 1948 with 48 graduates. Eight of the graduates—Georgeana Barbour, Alma Daye, Joseline Holston, Annette Jones, Ernest Kyle, Ida Prather, Robert Thornton, and Joyce Turner—went to institutions of higher learning to increase their knowledge and to become more competitive in the job market.

CARVER HIGH ANNUAL GRADUATION EXERCISES

Class Motto
"Enter to Learn,
Go Forth to Serve."

Class Colors
Blue & Pink

Class Flower
Red Rose

Valedictorian
Annette Jones

Salutatorian
Alma Daye

CLASS ROLL

Alice Dorothy Adams
*Georgeana Beatrice Barbour
Cecil E. Brooks
**Melvin Carter
Catherine Mollie Christian
Christine Clarke
Charles Henry Copeland
Mary Marie Copeland
Gertrude Elaine Crutchfield
*Rodney Tyrone Davis
*Alma Rebecca Daye
Barbara Anne DeGraff
Donald Edward Dorsey
Alene LaVerne Dove
Julia Hayes Fields
James Foreman, Jr.
Alda Mary Frazier
*Jean Frazier
Leonard Roger Frazier
*Ula Bernice Gray
*Vauda Diana Greene
Ida Mae Harris
Gladys Marie Hawkins
*Shirley Estelle Hawkins
Carol Henrietta Henderson
Robert C. Hill
*Joseline Holston
Otis Hope
Merle Elaine Hopkins
Violet Isreal
*Margaret Earl Jackson
Junius Lee Johnson
*Annette Ethonia Jones
*Ernest Earl Kyle, Jr.
Roberta Idella Lyles
Winifred Marbley
Lester James Nelson

Kenneth Owens
Carolyn Renee Prather
Ida Prather
Willistine Prather
Katherine Beatrice Randolph
Donald James Reid
Alice Marie Ross
Clyde Shelton
Josephine Alemita Smith
Marie Alice Stewart
*Ruby Gertrude Taylor
*Ruth Geraldine Taylor
*Robert Herbert Thornton
Regina Aletta Tracy
*Joyce Patricia Turner
Elizabeth Lee Tyler
Mildred Aurellia Warren
Ruth Ann Waters
Esther Olivia Watkins
*Member of the National Honor Society
**Candidate for a Certificate

Joseph Hallman, Ida Mae Prather, Jean Frazier, Irving Prather

GRADUATION PROGRAM

Academic Procession

Invocation
Reverend S. Peyton Manning, Pastor, Brooke Grove Methodist Church, Laytonsville, Maryland

Welcome
Harlean C. Prather, Carver Junior College

Trilogy
"Significant Changes in Contemporary Life"
Robert Thornton

"The Role of Education in a Changing Society"
Alma Daye

"A Human Relations Approach to Changes in the New Era"
Vauda Greene

Epilogue
Annette Jones

Choral Club
"Sanctus"
(Gounod)

Address
Dr. Donald E. Deyo Dean, Montgomery Junior College, Takoma Park, Maryland

Band
"Triumphant Overture"
(Mesang)

Presentation of Candidates for Degrees
& Diplomas
Dean Parlett L. Moore

Conferring of Degrees &
Presentation of Diploas
Mrs. Helen G. Scharf, President,
Montgomery County
Board of Education

Band
"A Peacock's Fancy"
(Osterling)

Benediction
Reverend William E. Bishop,
Pastor, Hughes Memorial
Church, Washington, D.C.

Recessional

SCHOLARSHIP AWARDS

Trustees Scholarships to Morgan State
College, Baltimore, Maryland
$200.00 - Georgeana Barbour
$300.00 - Annette Jones

Financial Aid Grants to Morgan State
College, Baltimore, Maryland
$200.00 - Georgeana Barbour
$200.00 - Vauda Greene
$192.00 - Joseline Holston

Montgomery County Education
Association Scholarship to Maryland
State Teachers College,
Bowie, Maryland
$200.00 - Alma Daye

Carver Chapter of National Honor
Society
$25.00 - Ernest Kyle

Carver High Future Teachers of America:
Annette Jones, Ida Mae Prather, Joyce
Turner, Roberta Lyles, Georgeana Barbour,
Alma Daye

Board of Education Scholarship to
Montgomery Junior College, Takoma
Park, Maryland
$185.00 - Robert Thornton
(Full Tuition)

FACULTY

Dr. Parlett L. Moore, *Principal*
Mable D. Thomas, *Vice-Principal*
Mrs. Bessie O. Barnes
Mrs. A. J. Cunningham
Rupert Curry
Mrs. Sylvia W. Davenport, *Secretary*
Miles R. Frazier
Raleigh Fuqua
Maurice C. Genies
Mildred Griffin
Bessie M. Hill
Bernard E. Holsey
John A. Jones
Mrs. Joan T. Kelly
Mrs. Alta C. Meeks
Mrs. Naomi Millender
Mrs. Daisy W. Myles
Calvin C. Rubens

Mrs. Rosa D. Shelton
Rozelle S. Silvey
Mrs. Jessie Snowden
Herbert J. Stith, Jr.

Mrs. Anna G. Venable
Mrs. Ruby E. Washington
Alma West

courtesy Alma Daye

CARVER HIGH SCHOOL CLASS OF 1957

Out of a class of 164 ninth graders at Lincoln Junior High School in June 1954, "only 143 of them enrolled as tenth graders at Carver High School in September 1954." They enjoyed the modern facilities at Carver High School immensely. During this school year, "Eleanor Harris won the oratorical contest with her oration entitled 'I Speak for Democracy.'"

At the beginning of the exciting school year 1955-1956, they learned "that many of their fellow classmates had left to attend integrated schools" that were closer to their homes. The "93 juniors elected Ida Genies as president and Michael Isreal as vice-president" to provide them with the necessary leadership. Their biggest task was "planning to give the seniors a prom."

Athletically speaking, "Reginald Coleman, Alexander Harriday, Dewey Isreal, Michael Isreal, Douglas Kane, Donald Payne, and Preston Ramey were the star football players," and "Henry Jenkins was captain of the boys basketball team."

Academic studies, planning for the senior prom, and sports were not the only things that the juniors were capable of doing, for "many of them participated in the 'Extravaganza' of the year and an operetta entitled 'In Gay Havana,'" which indicates that they were well-rounded.

In September 1956, they started "the most momentous year of all with 68 classmates and a new principal, Silas B. Craft. Their senior class sponsors were Mrs. Jessie Snowden and Mrs. Anna Venable."

"The graduating Class of 1957 dedicated the Carver Eagle to Dr. Parlett L. Moore, who was deeply concerned with the progress of the school, faculty, students, and community during his long stay in Montgomery County. Because of his guidance and encouragement," they admitted that they would be "better able to make adjustments in this complex society."

During this very significant year, "Brenda Waters was elected president of the Student Council; Doris Daniels was elected editor of the yearbook; and Laura Frazier won a trophy for soliciting the greatest number of yearbook patrons."

The members chosen as class officers were "James Prather (President),Doris Daniels (Vice President), Doris Howard (Secretary), Reginald Coleman (Assistant Secretary), Mary Alice Jackson (Treasurer), and Donald Payne (Sergeant-at-Arms)."

Along the line of popularity, "Leona Jenkins reigned as Homecoming Queen and Miss Cinderella."

They acknowledged that their "high school career had been very eventful and enjoyable, that they had accomplished a great deal during those precious years, and that these memories will remain forever in their hearts."

GRADUATING EXERCISES

Wednesday, June 12, 1957, 7 P.M.

Valedictorian
Doris Daniels

Salutatorian
Brenda Waters

CLASS ROLL

Lillian Louise Baker
George Edward Boswell
Ruth Mae Brooks
Louie Earl Brown
Shirley Mae Brown
Susie Lee Etta Brown
Paul Edward Carroll
Reginald Eugene Coleman
Charles Howard Copeland, Jr.
Gilbert Eugene Crutchfield
*Doris Shirley Daniels
Phyllis Arlene Davis
Bernice Allene Day
Shirley Drexell
Bernice Marie Elliott
Mary Anne Ellison
Thelma Estelle Foreman
Laura Jane Frazier
*Ida Mae Genies
James Horace Genus
Esther Mae Hallman

Dorothy Louise Hammond
Alexander Harriday
Eleanor Frances Harris
Doris Minerva Howard
Dewey Isreal, Jr.
Frances Jackson
Mary Alice Jackson
James Henry Jenkins, Jr.
Dorothy Lavenia Hebron
Leona E. Jenkins
Naomi Loretta Johnson
Gladys Ann Joppy
Douglas Lee Kane
John Theodore Lancaster, Jr.
Gillette Mitchell Lee, Jr.
Ruth Elizabeth Lefeged
John Samuel Moten, Jr.
Donald E. Payne
Thomas Cornelius Plummer, Jr.
Leslie Vinson Plummer
James Donald Prather
Preston Delaney Ramey
Dorothy Ann Randolph
Sterling Maxwell Ricketts
Denver Harrison Saunders, Jr.
Marjorie Sharpe
Annie Mae Small
Elmore H. Stewart
George Windsor Swales
Charles Edward Thomas
Yvonne Elizabeth Thompson
Hattie Tibbs
**Emma Twyman
**Genevieve Twyman
Rose Inez Walker
*Brenda Vicilla Waters
Elaine Lottie Weedon
Forest Warden Wilson, Jr.

*Member, National Honor Society
**Candidate for Certificate

Graduating Exercises

Processional

Invocation
Reverend Thomas E. Brooks,
Pastor, Sharp Street Methodist
Church, Sandy Spring, Maryland

Music
"Jesus, Priceless Treasure"
(Bach)
The Carver Choir

Prologue
Brenda Waters

Trilogy
"Each Moment is Golden and
None to Waste"
George Washington Carver

"In Every Era - Golden Moments"
Lillian Baker

"For Contemporary
Opportunities-Readiness"
Ida Genies

"Then Why Not for Every
Man-Fulfillment?"
Eleanor Harris

Epilogue
Doris Daniels

Music
"At Worship"
(Towle)

Senior Chorus

Remarks
Dr. Forbes H. Norris,
Superintendent, Montgomery
County Schools

Presentation of Senior Class
Mr. Silas E. Craft, Principal,
Carver High School

Presentation of Diplomas
Mrs. Harold H. Kramer, Member,
Montgomery County
Board of Education

Music
"Sunset Star Overture"
(Frangkiser)
The Carver High School Band

Benediction
Reverend Thomas E. Brooks

Recessional

Scholarships and Awards
*Trustee Scholarship to Morgan State
College, Baltimore, Maryland*
$150 - Doris Daniels

*Board of Education Scholarship to
Montgomery Junior College, Takoma
Park, Maryland*
$185 - Brenda Waters
(Full Tuition)

*Lincoln-Carver Parent-Teacher
Association Scholarship*
$50 - Doris Daniels
$50 - Brenda Waters

Citizenship Awards
(Daughters of American-Revolution,
Chevy Chase Chapter)
Denver Saunders & Brenda Waters

Josten's Awards
Citizenship - George Swales
Journalism - Eleanor Harris
All-Around Student - Ida Genies
Oratory - Eleanor Harris
Student Council - Brenda Waters

FACULTY
Silas E. Craft, *Principal*
Mable D. Thomas, *Vice-Principal*
Mrs. Alta C. Meeks, *Counselor*
Mrs. Bessie B. Barnes, *American History, World History, POD*
Mrs. Anjarone Cunningham, *Algebra, Social Studies*
Rupert G. Curry, *Physical Education*
Miles Frazier, *Auto Mechanics*
Raleigh Fuqua, *Dry Cleaning & Tailoring*
Maurice C. Genies, *Driver Education*
Mildred Griffin, *History, Psychology, English*

Mrs. Joan T. Kelly, *Art*
Rufus Kelly, *General Science, Chemistry, Biology*
Mrs. Carrie B. Luck, *Physical Education*
Mrs. Doris Mosley, *Librarian*
Mrs. Daisy Myles, *Domestic Science*
Calvin C. Rubens, *Business Education*
Rozelle S. Silvey, *Vocational Carpentry*
Mrs. Jessie Snowden, *English*
Herbert Stith, *Music*
Mrs. Anna Venable, *French, English*
Mrs. Ruby E. Washington, *Algebra*
Alma West, *Cosmetology*

STAFF
D. Green, *Secretary*
Mrs. Gladys Claggett, *Head Dietitian*
Leslie Gaines, *Chief Engineer*
Mrs. Mabel A. Hill, *Assistant Head Dietitian*
N. Orem
D. Reed

courtesy Gloria Campbell-Jones, Mable D. Thomas, Yvonne Thompson Copeland

CARVER HIGH SCHOOL CLASS OF 1958

At the outset of their senior year, 61 graduating seniors elected Arthur Copeland to lead them in their final year at Carver High School. They recognized that their senior year would be a very challenging one; consequently, they chose a competent leader.

Another position that needed capable leadership was editor of the annual; Phyllis Waters was selected to shoulder this responsibility. The rest of the staff included William Hebron (assistant editor), Margaret Randolph and Pamela Gaunt (typists), Arthur Copeland, Gloria Horn, Richard King, Josephine McDonald, and Ethel Talley (staff members).

The seniors who helped to plan the 1958 *Eagle* were Charleen Briscoe, Gloria Campbell, Larry Davis, Dorothy Daye, William Hebron, James Houston, Eugene Martin, Josephine McDonald, Margaret Randolph, Phyllis Waters, and Ella Wims.

The class dedicated the 1958 *Eagle* to Mrs. Mabel A. Hill because of their love and admiration of "a wonderful person" who was "a devoted mother to her eight children," six of whom are Lincoln High School alumni and two graduates of Carver High School. They acknowledged that she was one of their "most distinguished citizens, always eager and willing to participate in school and community affairs." They also made known that Mrs. Hill was "a dependable friend and kindred soul in whom they could confide."

Charles Saunders, Student Council president for the school year 1957-1958, ably led this organization which had a membership of 20.

Besides being deeply involved in their academic studies, these seniors participated in a variety of extracurricular activities. Some were members of the Student Council, Patrol Force, and Charm Club; some participated on the baseball, basketball, football, and track teams.

On November 8, 1957, Barbara Davis reigned as Miss Homecoming and Jean Mason-Johnson (Class of 1946) reigned as Miss Alumna.

"On November 15, 1957, Dorothy Daye, Lorraine Hammond James Holston, Alice Jackson, Karlton Jackson, Ethel Talley, Delores Taylor, Evelyn Weedon, and Ella Wims participated in a senior-class recital."

"Josephine McDonald reigned as Miss Carver. Her senior attendants included Gloria Horn, Margaret Hungerford, Nettie Johnson, Rosetta Sewell, Delores Taylor, Priscilla Taylor, Alice Thornton, and Phyllis Waters. Senior class President Arthur Copeland saluted Miss Carver with a bouquet of the senior flowers; junior class President Hazel Dorsey greeted Miss Carver with white carnations."

One highlight of the May Day festivities was the crowning of "Gloria Campbell as May Queen. Senior Gloria Horn served as one of her attendants."

The seniors enjoyed their final Carver High School social event at the Junior-Senior Prom on May 50, 1958. Then, they prepared for the culminating activity—GRADUATION.

Senior Superlatives
Most Loyal
Floyd Cabell & Evelyn Weedon

Most Athletic
Gloria Campbell &
Franklin Wilson

Most Sincere
Arthur Copeland & Peggy Gray

Most Fickle
Lorraine Hammond &
William Thomas

Best Dancers
Pamela Gaunt & Ralph Patterson

Most Dependable
William Hebron & Ella Wims

Most Attractive
James Holston & Ethel Talley

Most Dramatic
Gloria Horn

Wittiest
Gloria Horn & Gerald Stewart

Most Ambitious
Karlton Jackson &

Margaret Randolph

Best All-Around Student
Cecil Prather

Quietest
James Pumphrey & Shirley Selby

Liveliest
Melvin Pumphrey &
Alice Thornton

Neatest
David Roberts & Priscilla Taylor

Most Talented
Thomas Ware & Phyllis Waters

GRADUATION DAY
Sunday, June 8, 1958, 7 P.M.

Valedictorian
Phyllis Waters

GRADUATES
Kathleen V. Albert
Elsie T. Bell
Marguerite V. Bennett
Charleen F. Briscoe
Doris J. Brown
Ruth F. Bryant
Alfredia Ella Byrd
Floyd W. Cabell
Gloria M. Campbell
Betty M. Chatman
Peggy A. Clarke
Shirley A. Clipper
Arthur Copeland
Edward L. Davis
Dorothy Daye

Carroll Gant
Pamela Gaunt
Peggy Gray
Lorraine Hammond
William Hammond
Audrey Hebron
William Hebron
Audrey Hoes
James Holston
William Hood
Gloria Horn
Willie Hughes
Margaret Hungerford
Alice Jackson
Karlton Jackson
John Johnson
Nettie Johnson
Richard King
Frederick Lancaster
Josephine McDonald
Kenneth Marbley
Ernest Martin
Eugene J. Martin
Ralph Patterson
Emilie Y. Plummer
Cecil T. Prather
James G. Pumphrey
Melvin N. Pumphrey
Margaret J. Randolph
David E. Roberts
Francis A. Robinson
Charles Saunders
Shirley V. Selby
Rosetta R. Sewell
Gerald Stewart
Ethel Talley
Delores Taylor

Priscilla Taylor
Leroy Thomas
William Thomas
Alice Thornton
Thomas Ware
Phyllis Waters
Evelyn Weedon
Franklin Wilson
Ella Wims

FACULTY

Silas E. Craft, *Principal*
Mable D. Thomas, *Vice-Principal*
Mrs. Alta C. Meeks, *Counselor*
Mrs. Bessie B. Barnes, *Psychology & Social Studies*
Mrs. Mamie Clarke, *Science*
Rupert G. Curry, *Physical Education*
Raleigh Fuqua, *Dry Cleaning & Tailoring*
Maurice C. Genies, *Driver Education & Industrial Arts*
Mrs. Julia Magwood-Harris, *Mathematics*
Mrs. Margaret Hill, *English & French*
Mrs. Joan T. Kelly, *Art*
Rufus Kelly, *Science*
Carrie B. Luck, *Physical Education*
Mrs. Naomi J. Millender, *Special Education*
Mrs. Daisy W. Myles, *Home Economics*
Calvin C. Rubens, *Business Education*
Rozelle S. Silvey,

Vocational Woodwork
Mrs. Jessie B. Snowden, *English*
Herbert J. Stith, *Music*
George B. Thomas, *Librarian*
Mrs. Anna G. Venable, *English &
French*
Alma West, *Cosmetology*
Lorenzo A. Woodward, *English &
Social Studies*

STAFF
Mrs. Gladys Claggett, *Dietitian*
Mrs. Mabel A. Hill, *Assistant
Dietitian*
Marylah B. Clark, *Secretary*

*courtesy Gloria Campbell-Jones, Phyllis
Waters*

CARVER HIGH, SCHOOL
CLASS OF 1959

When the Class of 1959 arrived at Carver High School as sophomores, in September 1956, Silas E. Craft was their principal, and Mable D. Thomas was their vice-principal. There were four areas of study—academic commercial, general, and vocational—in which 19 teachers taught. These curricula prepared the students for higher levels of learning, as well as for immediate employment.

Some of the hands-on courses were auto mechanics, commercial education, cosmetology, dry cleaning, vocational home arts, and vocational woodwork.

Some of the extra-curricular activities included band (which traveled throughout the state), baseball,

Home Economics Class—Sharing a meal cooked by students
Calvin Rubins, Mary S. Bruce, Daisy Myles, Shirley Hawkins, and an unidentified student

basketball, dramatics, football, student organizations, and track.

At the inception of their junior year, 1957-1958, they found that many of their fellow classmates had departed to attend integrated schools. However, this exodus from Carver High School to a formerly all-white school, that was in the vicinity of their homes, did little to dampen their spirits, for they had only one goal in mind—graduation from high school.

In September 1958, the number had decreased again, but the show had to proceed as planned, because this was their all-important year.

Seniors Mildred Drakeford, Constance Duvall, Edna Lefeged, Mary Talley, and Ethel Watkins were the Carver High School majorettes.

Lionel Owens was editor of the Newspaper Staff; other senior members of the staff included Mary Anthony, Doris Dove, Doris Jackson, and Geraldine Watkins.

Doris Dove was president of the Student Council and Lionel Owens was the other senior member.

Mary Bruce, Mildred Drakeford, Constance Duvall, Cecile Y. Hackey, Shirley A. Hawkins, Thelma Taylor, Blanche Thompson, and George Watkins were members of the Business Club.

Mary Anthony, Doris Dove, Shirley A. Hawkins, Gertrude Hebron, Ann Powell, Rosin Selby,

Etta Taylor, and Ethel Watkins were members of the Charm Club.

The lone senior member of the New Homemakers of America was Peggy Hebron.

"Raymond Cabell, Margaret Johnson, and Blanche Thompson were members of the Patrol Force.

Wendell Talley was the only senior member of the Dramatic Club.

Patrick Morris was the captain of the varsity basketball team. Charles Lyles and Maurice Randolph were the other senior members of the team.

Probably the heaviest responsibility that the seniors undertook was the production of the 1959 *Eagle*. Mary S. Bruce was editor; Lionel Owens was assistant editor; Mildred Drakeford, Constance Duvall, and Cecile Hackey were typists; and Allen Bell, Ronald Claggett, Gwendora Hebron, and Thelma Taylor were members.

Carver High 1959 Yearbook Staff Seated: Gwendora Hebron, Cecile Hackey, Mary S. Bruce, Mildred Drakeford, Constance Duvall Standing: Anna G. Venable, Lionel Owens, Thelma Taylor, Ronald Claggett, Allen Bell

Valedictorian
Mary Bruce

Salutatorian
Theodore T. Kelly

GRADUATES

Paul Eugene Addison
Mary Elizabeth Anthony
Allen Webster Bell
Howard M. Bell
Howard S. Braxton
Mary Sandra Bruce[1]
Raymond Edward Cabell
*James N. Chase
Ronald E. Claggett
Clarence William Curtis
Allen Alexander Dove
Doris Beatrice Dove
Mildred Anita Drakeford

Senior Class Officers
President
Doris B. Dove

Vice-President
Theodore T. Kelly

Recording Secretary
Mildred A. Drakeford

Corresponding Secretary
Edna Lefeged

Treasurer
Lionel E. Owens

Constance Faith Duvall
*Ernest H. Green
Cecile Yvonne Hackey
Emory Holland Hackey
Barbara Mae Hall
Myrtle Rebecca Hall
Frances Georgia Hawkins
Shirley Ann Hawkins
Shirley Maxine Hawkins
Gwendora Lucille Hebron
Peggy Bernice Hebron
Doris E. Jackson
Rudolph Samuel Jackson
William W. Jackson
Gloria Odelle Johnson
Joann Johnson

Margaret Ann Johnson
Lawrence M. Kelly
Louis Wade Kelly
Theodore Thomas Kelly[2]
Albert W . King
Harold Andrew King
Charles John Lyles
Nedra Bernice Lynch
Theodore Franklin Moten
Leroy T. Murray
Patrick Charles Norris
Lionel Everson Owens
Ann C. Powell
Maurice A. Randolph
Rose Mae Selby
Joseph Warren Stevens

Carver High School Graduates, Class of 1959

Eugene H. Stewart
Mary A. Talley
Robert Wendell Talley
Etta Lucille Taylor
Thelma Ernestine Taylor
Blanche Louise Thompson
*Mary Beatrice Turner
George James Waters
Ethel Mae Watkins
Geraldine Elizabeth Watkins

ALMA MATER
Hail to thee! Our dear Ole Carver;
'Tis of thee we sing.
For we love thy noble spirit;
Let thy praises ring.

Carver High! Carver High!
Banners white and blue
We will give our faith and honor
To thy ideals true.

SCHOLARSHIPS
*Board of Education Scholarship to
Montgomery Junior College*
$150.00 - Doris Dove

FACULTY
Silas B. Craft, *Principal*
Mable D. Thomas, *Vice-Principal*
Mrs. Alta C. Meeks, *Counselor*
Mrs. Thelma Burke, *Nurse*
Mrs. Mamie Clarke , *Science*
Rupert G. Curry, *Physical Education*
Miles Frazier, *Auto Mechanics*
Mrs. Alberta Withers French,
Psychology & Social Studies

Raleigh Fuqua, *Dry Cleaning*
Maurice C. Genies, *Driver
Education & Industrial Arts*
Mrs. Edithe B. Gordon, *Special
Education*
Mrs. Julia Magwood-Harris,
Mathematics
Mrs. Margaret Hill, *Psychology,
English, Geography & History*
Bernard Holsey, *Mathematics*
Rufus G. Kelly, *Science*
Mrs. Carrie B. Luck, *Physical
Education*
Mrs. Naomi Millender, *Special
Education*
Mrs. Daisy Myles, *Home Arts*
Calvin C. Rubens, *Business
Education*
Rozelle S. Silvey, *Vocational
Woodwork*
Kenneth Stewart, *Civics & English*
Herbert J. Stith, *Music*
George B. Thomas, *Librarian*
Mrs. Anna G. Venable, *English*
Mrs. Jennie Walburg, *History &
English*
Eddie B. Washington, *Art*
Mrs. Ruby E. Washington, *English*
Alma West, *Cosmetology*

[1] *highest scholastic average*
[2] *second highest scholastic average*
* *candidate for certificate*

*courtesy Gloria-Campbell Jones and
Mary Bruce*

CARVER HIGH SCHOOL CLASS OF 1960

In September 1959, the distinguished Class of 1960 walked the halls of Carver High School with mixed feelings. They were happy that they were seniors soon to graduate and sad because their alma mater would no longer exist as an institution of learning where they could visit old friends and teachers in the future. Carver High would become the headquarters for the Montgomery County Board of Education. They had the distinction of being the last class to graduate from Carver High School prior to the integration of Montgomery County public schools in September 1960, and they vowed to be ever mindful to uphold its ideals and traditions.

During this all-important year, organization was important. They elected Wilbur Adams (President), Barbara Albert (Vice-President), Edna Lefeged (Recording Secretary), Geraldine Payton (Corresponding Secretary), Peggy Prather (Treasurer), and Richard Johnson (Sergeant-at-Arms) to direct their senior activities.

The responsibility of composing the last edition of the Carver High School *Eagle* was delegated to "Geraldine Payton (Editor), Marvina Furlow (Assistant Editor), Charles Campbell (Business Manager); Barbara Albert, Alice Hill, Mary Mason, and Edna Smith (Typists); Wilbur Adams, Ernest Cooper, Marcus Dorsey, Peggy Prather, Oliver Tyler, and Carroll Tynes (members) under the sponsorship of Mrs. Anna Venable."

The 1960 *Eagle* Staff dedicated this edition of the Carver High yearbook to "Mrs. Alta C. Meeks since she possessed a generous portion of common sense, a skillful hand, and a keen perspective of their problems." They felt that they "would not be as well-prepared to assume their responsibilities without having had her unfailing guidance."

The members of this class were active in the various school organizations, and they participated in many school-related activities. They enjoyed the sponsorship of the experienced Carver High School faculty members who equipped them with knowledge and training to take the next step in their young lives.

After completing the required number of credits prescribed by the Maryland State Department of Education, 53 graduating seniors marched in an academic procession to receive their awards, certificates, diplomas, and scholarships on Friday, June 17, 1960. Following this memorable event, the Class of 1960 became alumni of Carver High School.

Senior Superlatives
Most Ambitious
Geraldine Dayton & Oliver Tyler

Best All-Around
Maude Hawkins, Joyce Holston &
Henry Neal

Most Athletic
Wilbur Adams & Eleanor Bowie

Most Dependable
Dorothy Hamilton, Maryann
Jackson, Vernon Jackson &
Hazel Williams

Best Dressed
James Lancaster & Peggy Prather

Best Of Friends
Joyce Holston & Maryann Jackson,
Patricia Clipper & Doris
Stevenson

Liveliest
Barbara Albert & Robert Prather

Most Mannerly
Joseph Prather, Edna Smith &
Joseph Thompson

Quietest
Joseph Kyle & Alfred Presbury

Most Sincere
Edna Lefeged, Richard Thomas &
Charles Williams

Most Talented

Charles Campbell, Geraldine
Dayton, Delores Prather, Edna
Smith & Carroll Tynes

Most Talkative
Ernest Cooper, Alice Hill,
Delores Prather & Howell Prather

GRADUATING EXERCISES

Valedictorian
Marcus Dorsey

Salutatorian
Joseph E. Thompson

CLASS ROLL
Barbara Jean Albert
Wilbur Allen Adams, Jr.
Helen Romaine Byrd
Charles B. Campbell
Ernest B. Cooper
Patricia Ann Clipper
William H. Copeland
Marcus Dorsey[1]
Josephine LaVerne Driver
Marvina Virgie Furlow
Alphonso G. Gray
Clarence Greenlee
Emma Mae Hackey
William O. Hackey, Jr.
Dorothy A. Hamilton
Maude Ionia Hawkins
Alice Louise Hill
Joyce Noel Holston
John Edward Jackson
Linwood Sylvester Jackson
Maryann Catherine Jackson

Vernon Roy Jackson
*William Jackson
Mary Elizabeth Jenkins
Ernest G. Johnson
Richard Allen Johnson
Robert Allen Johnson
Joseph Edward Kyle
Edna L. Lefeged
James Talten Lancaster, Jr.
Mary Frances Mason
Brenda LaFaye Monroe
Henry W. Neal
Letha Geraldine Payton
Delores Virginia Prather
Herbert R. Prather
Howell Prather, Jr.
Joseph Prather
Peggy Maxine Prather
Robert Eugene Prather
Alfred Eugene Presbury
Charlotte Romaine Pumphrey
Edna Mae Smith
Doris Louise Stevenson
James Howard Taylor
Richard William Thomas, Jr.
Joseph Edward Thompson
Oliver Eugene Tyler, Jr.
William Alexander Tyler
Carroll Robert Tynes
Charles Robert Williams
Hazel Estelle Williams
David Harold Young

[1] *valedictorian*
[2] *salutatorian*
Candidate for Certificate

ALMA MATER

Hail to thee! our dear old Carver
'Tis of thee we sing
For we love thy noble spirit;
Let thy praises ring

Carver High! Carver High!
Banners white and blue
We will give our faith and honor
To thy ideals true.

Graduating Exercises
Processional

Invocation
Reverend James Prather, Pastor,
Popular Grove Baptist Church,
Quince Orchard, Maryland

Band Selection
"Our Waltz"
(Herfurth)

Greetings
Wilbur Adams

Choral Selection
"Halls of Ivy"
(Russell and Knight)

Presentation of Speaker
Mr. Silas E. Craft, Principal, Carver
High School

Address
Mr. Paul E. Huffington, Assistant
Director, Division of Instruction,
State Department of Education

Band Selection

"Sunset Star Overture"
(Frangkiser)

Presentation of Senior Class
Mr. Craft

Presentation of Diplomas
Mrs. Harold H. Kramer, Member,
Montgomery County
Board of Education

Presentation of Awards
Mr. Leslie I. Gaines, President, PTA
Mrs. Wilhelmina Funderbunk,
Counselor

Farewell
Marcus Dorsey, Valedictorian

Music
"After Graduation Day"
(Geraldine Payton)

Alma Mater
The Audience

Benediction
Reverend Prather

Recessional

SCHOLARSHIPS AND AWARDS

All-Around Student
Wilbur Adams

Student Council
Joyce Holston

Leadership
Geraldine Payton

Citizenship
Dorothy Hamilton
Ernest Johnson
Joseph Prather
Peggy Prather
Edna Smith
Richard Thomas

Service
Maude Hawkins
Joseph Kyle
Hazel Williams

Music
Emma Hackey
Oliver Tyler

Athletics
Wilbur Adams

PTA
Hazel Williams

Scholarships to Montgomery Junior College
Board of Education
Marcus Dorsey

Student Council
Hazel Williams

FACULTY

Silas E. Craft, *Principal*
Mable D. Thomas, *Vice-Principal*
Mrs. Wilhelmina S. Funderburk,
Counselor
Mrs. Thelma Burke, *Nurse*
Mrs. Mamie Clark, *Science,
Mathematics, Geography*

Rupert G. Curry, *Physical Education*
Miles R. Frazier, *Auto Mechanics*
Mrs. Alberta W. French, *History,*
Psychology
Raleigh Fuqua, *Dry Cleaning*
Maurice C. Genies, *Industrial Arts,*
Driver Education
Mrs. Margaret Hill, *English,*
Psychology, Geography
Rufus Kelly, *Science*
Mrs. Mazie Lassiter, *Librarian*
Mrs. Carrie B. Luck, *Mathematics*
Mrs. Naomi J. Millender, *English,*
History
Mrs. Daisy W. Myles, *Home*
Economics
Rozelle S. Silvey, *Vocational*
Woodwork
Kenneth Stewart, *Civics, English*
Herbert J. Stith, Jr., *Music*

George B. Thomas, *Business*
Education
Mrs. Anna G. Venable, *English*
Mrs. Jennie Walburg, *English,*
History
Eddie Washington, *Art*
Mrs. Ruby Washington, *English,*
Mathematics
Alma West, *Cosmetology*
Mrs. Emma Wright, *Physical*
Education

STAFF
Mrs. Gladys Claggett, *Dietitian*
Marylah Clark, *Secretary*
Mrs. Louise Davis, *Secretary*
Mrs. E. Hill, *Dietitian*
Mrs. Mabel A. Hill, *Dietitian*

courtesy Marcus Dorsey,
Oliver E. Tyler

ABOUT THE AUTHOR

Warrick S. Hill was born in Baltimore, Maryland in 1926. He was educated in the then-Montgomery County dual public school system, where he graduated from Spencerville Elementary School and Lincoln High School in Rockville as class salutatorian. He earned a Bachelor of Science degree in mathematics at Morgan State College (now Morgan State University) in Baltimore and a Master of Arts degree at George Washington University, where he was inducted into the Phi Delta Kappa Honor Fraternity for Educators. He has done post-graduate studies at Catholic University, Columbia University in New York, and the University of Maryland.

During his 38-year teaching career (12 in Calvert County and 26 in Montgomery County), he served as a high-school mathematics teacher, mathematics department chair, assistant principal, and chair and co-chair of the Montgomery County Superintendent's Committee on Mathematics. He found teaching to be an enjoyable challenge and a very rewarding profession.

Warrick was an award-winning teacher in three Maryland high schools (W. Sampson Brooks in Prince Frederick, Robert E. Peary in Rockville, and Immaculata College in Rockville). During his tenure, he garnered many honors and accolades from his students, high school and college officials.

In addition, Warrick served his country as an instructor of non-military subjects and an administrative assistant in the United States Army (Pennsylvania, Virginia, Japan, and South Korea) during the Korean War.

Warrick married the former Christine C. Carter, and they have three adult sons and six grandchildren and two great-granchildren He enjoys spending quality time with his wife, communicating with his family and friends, traveling, sports, reading, performing his church responsibilities, and working on his lawn.

INDEX

Pratt, Sylvester, 167
Presbury, Alfred Eugene, 276, 277
Prilliman, June M., 246
Prince George's County Public Schools, 31–32
Procton, Annie L., 109, 112, 152, 156, 167, 168, 169, 172, 173, 176, 177, 178, 180, 181, 186, 187
Pugh, Estella Jean, 140, 146
Pumphrey, Bernice, 167
Pumphrey, Charlotte Romaine, 277
Pumphrey, Gladys, 167
Pumphrey, James G., 268, 269
Pumphrey, Mary Anna, 215
Pumphrey, Melvin N., 268, 269
Pumphrey, Sadie Louise, 235, 244, 245, 246

Q

Quiller, Jack M., 152, 154, 155

R

Raby, Violet. *See* Isreal, Violet
Ramey, Margaretta Elizabeth, 146
Ramey, McAdoo, 149, 150
Ramey, Preston Delaney, 263, 264
Ramey, Thelma, 189, 190
Randolph, Annie, 167
Randolph, Benjamin, 257
Randolph, Dorothy Ann, 264
Randolph, Florence, 167
Randolph, Katherine Beatrice, 260
Randolph, Margaret J., 250, 267, 268, 269
Randolph, Maurice A., 272, 273
Reid, Donald James, 260
Rhodes, Annie L.. *See* Procton, Annie L.
Rhodes, Dorothy M., 109, 152, 157, 167, 168, 169, 171, 172, 173, 176, 177, 178, 179, 181, 182, 186
Rhodes, Hazel Elizabeth, 189, 196, 199
Rhoe, Caleb, 58, 70, 127, 134, 137, 138
Richards, Elizabeth Adelaide, 240
Ricketts, Katie Janet, 240
Ricketts, Percival T., 249, 250
Ricketts, Sterling Maxwell, 264
Ricketts, Wilbur Allen, 167, 171, 173, 176, 177

Ricks, Bernice E., 167, 176, 177, 178, 180, 181, 182, 186, 188
Ricks, Dallas, 167
Ridgley, Alma A.. *See* King, Alma A.
Ridgley, James Ellsworth, 201, 203
Ridgley, Norman Briscoe, 71, 81, 152, 153, 154
Ridgley, William Henry Morice, 153, 155, 163
Riggs, Blanche Louise, 153, 154
Riggs, Carrie Catherine, 235, 240
Riggs, Edith, 218, 220, 221, 224
Riggs, James Edward, 140, 143
Riggs, Juanita Marion, 246
Riggs, Oliver, 213, 224
Roberson, William C., 242
Roberts, David E., 268, 269
Robey, Mary, 149
Robinson, Catherine Louise, 167, 177, 186
Robinson, Francis A., 269
Robinson, James T., 74, 75, 153, 157, 158, 190
Robinson, Lucille Elizabeth, 143
Rosenwald Fund, 28, 32, 35–36, 40
Ross, Alice Marie, 260
Ross, James Daniel, Jr., 230
Ross, Robert Leonard, 165, 167, 177
Ross, Sadie Mae, 250
Rubens, Calvin C., 86, 247, 269, 274
Russell, Elenora Marie, 230
Ryan, Maso Palmer, 70, 74, 148, 150, 158

S

Sandifer, Durward V., 225, 247
Saunders, Charles, 267, 269
Saunders, Denver Harrison, Jr., 264, 266
Scharf, Helen G., 261
School Acts of 1868, 1870, and 1872, 21, 26–27
Scott, Grace, 218, 219, 224
Scott, Lucy V., 45
Scott, Paul Freedman, 122, 123
Scott, Robert Augustus, 212, 215
Scott, Romaine F., 224, 231
Segregation, 61, 79, 81, 87–88, 91–95, 98, 102, 110–112

298